THE MOSLEM WORLD OF TO-DAY

THE MOSLEM WORLD OF TO-DAY

EDITED, WITH A FOREWORD AND CLOSING CHAPTER

By

JOHN R. MOTT

Chairman, International Missionary Council

GYAN

Published by

Gyan Publishing House
5, Ansari Road
Daryaganj, New Delhi-110002
Phone: 011-47034999, 9811692060
E-mail: books@gyanbooks.com

Distribution Network
gyanbooks.com
India, USA, Canada, UK, Australia, France

ISBN : 978-81-212-6372-6 (PB)
First Published, 1925

2nd Impression 2022

Printed at: Gyan Press, Delhi.

THE MOSLEM WORLD OF TO-DAY
Author: JOHN R. MOTT

THE MOSLEM WORLD OF TO-DAY

EDITED, WITH A FOREWORD AND CLOSING CHAPTER,

BY

JOHN R. MOTT

CHAIRMAN, INTERNATIONAL MISSIONARY COUNCIL

FOREWORD

THE Moslem world of to-day is markedly different from that of yesterday. The social and religious system of Islam, for centuries the most rigid, exclusive, resistant, and, as some would say, the most intolerant of all, has during the first quarter of the present century, and notably during the last decade, been undergoing stupendous and well-nigh unbelievable changes. Almost every Moslem land—in Africa, in Western, Central, and Southern Asia, and in the East Indies—is ablaze with new national and social aspirations and ambitions. Throughout these vast regions the traveller in these days is vividly conscious of the thrill of a new life. On every hand he finds an earnest struggle to achieve a political organization of a more democratic and constitutional form. This is often coupled, however, with pronounced hostility to Western governments. The most remarkable event of all has been the abolition of the Caliphate. The effect of this startling development has been like dropping from its place the keystone of an arch, for true it is that the Caliphate has been the binding centre of the extensive and imposing arch of Pan-Islamism. This weakening of the sense of solidarity and moral unity of the Moslem peoples will be felt increasingly. In profound and far-reaching significance it may be likened to the break-up of the Holy Roman Empire. Almost as wonderful has been the social upheaval, the most impressive evidence of which is the elevation in so many Moslem countries of the status of women.

The renaissance of Arabic culture, the rapid multiplication of periodicals and of book and pamphlet literature, the great increase in the numbers of Moslem youth in schools and colleges of Western learning, and the rising and surging tide of new thought, all bear witness to a notable intellectual awakening. The new search for truth and the ferment of dynamic and even of revolutionary ideas are exerting a great emancipating, liberalizing, and transforming influence. The larger political and intellectual freedom leads inevitably to greater religious freedom. Reactionary conservatism, inertia, and intolerance are giving way to the spirit of scientific inquiry. Moslem teachers and writers reveal that they have a growing realization of the weaknesses of Islam as a religion to meet the social, national, and international demands of the modern age or to satisfy the searching questions of the mind and the deeper longings of the heart. They seem to be aware of the disintegrating processes within and the dangerous impacts from without. With increasing numbers of Moslems the old complacency has given way to a genuine solicitude and to a hopeful spirit of reform. A re-evaluation of Islam as a religion is taking place, and Moslem thinkers are seeking to restate both their offensive and their defensive apologetic.

A Moslem world undergoing such varied, such extensive, such profound, and such momentous changes is of supreme interest and concern to all Christendom. As a matter of fact, the attention of Christians is to-day riveted on Islam as at no time since the Moslem invasion of Europe. And well it may be. The position, trends, and purposes of a religion of over 230,000,000 adherents necessarily have large meaning to the Christian religion, with its world mission and programme. The fact that possibly as many as seven out of every eight Moslems in the world are living under the flag of one or another Christian nation serves to accentuate their significance to all who bear the Christian name. The attitude and welfare of the followers of Islam have a vital bearing on the international and interracial relations of mankind, and, therefore, on the peace of the world. Now that the world has found itself as one body, it can no longer be a subject of indifference to any part of the world, and most certainly not to any Christian people, what conditions obtain and what the tendencies, ideals, and ambitions are in any other part. Such vital and burning issues as we see now absorbing the Moslem peoples present a challenge and an opportunity to the Christian faith. The threatened and impending disintegration of Islam calls for an adequate substitute. Only Christ and His programme can meet the need. The new generation in whose hands rests the destiny of all the Moslem lands—a generation which has so recently come under the spell of the modern age, and whose brain and heart are beginning to surge with new thought and social passion—make an irresistible appeal to Christians everywhere to present in their message, in their lives, and in their relationships, a winning and convincing apologetic.

This matter of the attitude of Christians and of Christian nations toward Islam and its adherents is most vital and pressing. What the attitude of Christians is to be will determine that of Islam to Christendom. Great is the need of Christianizing the impact of the so-called Christian nations upon the Moslem world. It is to be feared that much of the diplomacy, the territorial designs, the administrative policy, and the commercial activities of Christian Powers have been and still are non-Christian as judged by their effects. The spread of Western materialism and of the corrupt influences of modern civilization, unless the adequate counteracting and transforming energies of vital Christianity are more largely brought to bear, will result in making the last state of Moslem lands worse than the first.

There is need, likewise, on the part of the Christian movement, as it comes to the Moslem world, of exercising larger toleration. Happily the modern approach of Christian missionaries to Moslems is a much more positive, constructive, fraternal, and co-operative one than generally obtained in earlier days. Only as the programme of Christianity is based upon a sympathetic understanding of the Moslems (and upon unselfish co-operative service with them) is there any prospect of winning them, but along that pathway there is infinite hope. With such intimate and helpful contacts, and with such an atmosphere of faith as this attitude and practice will afford, there must be presented the message of the living Christ and His redemptive Gospel. In this way only will there be broken the spell of fear, fatalism, and despair which rests upon multitudes of Moslems, and will there be imparted to their lives the superhuman faith, freedom, and hope which only He communicates to men.

The twenty-three papers which constitute this volume of composite authorship present with real comprehension and living interest many of the more important aspects of the Moslem world of to-day and describe the causes underlying the tremendous changes which have taken place in Islam in recent years. They show convincingly why this situation is one of urgent interest and concern to all Christendom. With penetration and sympathy they reveal the attitude which should characterize Christian nations and Christian Churches, as well as individual Christian workers. The authors of the various papers have been in intimate and vital contact with Islam, most of them for a long period of years. Their interest has not been merely academic but one of heart concern as well. They have prepared their contributions without collaboration with one another. The aim in the volume has not been to present a complete and symmetrical treatment of all aspects of Islam, nor to treat all Moslem lands, but rather to present a composite view of those phases of the subject which to-day are of most living interest and which most need to be lifted into prominence.

The editor has made no attempt to unify the points of view of various authors. Because of this fact it is somewhat remarkable to find such a consensus among so large a group of writers of widely differing background, experience, and outlook. In order to bring the volume within the desired limits, and to avoid certain repetition, it has been necessary to abridge a few of the papers. It need hardly be added that each writer is responsible for the views set forth in his paper.

We have been unable to provide references for all quotations because of inability to reach certain of the writers within the time limit set for publication. Moreover, it has been impossible to be entirely consistent in transliterating Arabic and other oriental terms. General usage has been followed rather than scholastic precision attempted. Particular recognition is given to Henry H. King and Charles H. Fahs for their painstaking collaboration in the processes of editing and proof-reading. We are also under obligation to Professor J. C. Archer of Yale University, Professor R. S. McClenahan of the American University at Cairo, and Professor W. G. Shellabear of the Hartford Seminary Foundation for bringing their expert knowledge to bear in the review of the various manuscripts and for many invaluable suggestions. Thanks are also due to the editors of *The International Review of Missions* for permission to use in amended form the materials of the last chapter.

JOHN R. MOTT.

CONTENTS

THE IMPACT AND INFLUENCE OF WESTERN CIVILIZATION ON THE ISLAMIC WORLD

BY THE REV.

JAMES L. BARTON, D.D., LL.D.,

Senior Foreign Secretary, American Board of Commissioners for Foreign Missions

CHAPTER I

THE IMPACT AND INFLUENCE OF WESTERN CIVILIZATION ON THE ISLAMIC WORLD

ISLAM, in its doctrine, its traditions, and its practices, has been declared to be stereotyped beyond possibility of change. Principal Fairbairn,[1] Sir William Muir,[2] Lord Cromer,[3] William Gifford Palgrave,[4] Lord Houghton,[5] and Stanley Lane-Poole, as well as others, have taken the ground that Islam is inflexible, unprogressive, incapable of adapting itself to new conditions, stationary. Palgrave says: "It justly repudiates all change, all development," and Lord Houghton adds: "Whatever savours of vitality is by that alone convicted of heresy and defection."

If this is true, then we should expect little influence on the Islamic world from contacts with Western civilization. While theoretically Islam may not change in form or in practice, the fact remains that marked modifications have taken place, especially within this generation, and many others are indicated. Most of the divisions in Islam are evidence of internal change both in beliefs and in practices.

[1] *Contemporary Review*, 1881, p. 806.
[2] *Annals of the Early Caliphate*, London, 1883, p. 459.
[3] *Modern Egypt*, New York, 1908, vol. 2, p. 202.
[4] *Narration of a Year's Journey through Central and Eastern Arabia*, London, 1865, vol. 1, p. 372.
[5] Quoted by Samuel Graham Wilson, *Modern Movements Among Moslems*, New York, 1916, p. 12.

We shall consider, first, what are the impacts between Islam and the Western world; and, secondly, what influences upon Islam are resulting from these impacts.

Since Islam ceased to expand by conquest, Moslems have remained largely aloof from the rest of mankind. Also in the world of art, literature, education, science, commerce, and civilization they have seemed to occupy spheres by themselves. They generally occupy areas not attractive to the ordinary traveller and commercial agent. Moslems have not sought outside contacts, and have offered little inducement for the approach of other peoples. It is only within this generation that the Islamic world has experienced the shock of external impacts. These have come about through a variety of sources and of changed conditions.

In the first place, Mohammedan countries have been invaded by Western tourists and travellers in increasing numbers and for various purposes. At the same time, many Moslems have found their way into Western lands. This intervisitation has been facilitated by newly constructed railroads, steamship lines, and automobile routes. Railroads in India, Turkey, Persia, Syria, Egypt, North Africa, and even in Arabia are comparatively recent. Public automobiles are in regular service in North Africa, Arabia, India, Persia, and in many other Moslem countries. The Moslem world has begun to travel, and Moslem lands are being invaded by travellers, concessionnaires, and commercial agents from the outside.

The minds of the Moslem youth have been awakened from the lethargy of centuries, furthermore, by the impact of Western learning. Modern education has entered most Moslem countries. Up-to-date colleges and universities have been established in many of the great Moslem centres. Mohammedan youth were slow to avail themselves of the advantages these institutions offered. Taking note, however, of the advantages gained by non-Moslem students through Western learning, Moslem youth have begun to seek these advantages for themselves. In increasing numbers Moslem men have sought education abroad in most of the great centres of learning in Europe and America. The attendance of Moslem students in mission schools and in modern institutions in Moslem lands has greatly increased since 1920. Western schools in Turkey and Persia are overcrowded, and are turning away Moslem students who are almost demanding admission. Among Moslems in India school attendance has risen from 3 per cent. thirty years ago to 15 per cent. at the present time. Mohammedans of the East Indies, and, in fact, of nearly all Moslem lands, are seeking modern education.

A third means of contact with non-Moslem lands has been an increased knowledge of Western languages. Modern events have demonstrated to the Islamic world that Arabic and native vernaculars alone are inadequate to meet the demands of the present age. While they may regard Arabic as a sacred language, Moslems are discovering that it is not the language of world commerce or of that learning which permits profitable contact with the West. European languages have necessarily found a place in the more advanced modern Islamic schools, while from the first these languages have constituted an important part in the curricula of all Western schools in Moslem countries. English, French, and German have commanded the largest places.

With the acquisition of a Western language there inevitably follow a desire and a demand for literature in that language. This influence, constantly upon the increase, is arousing new ambitions and is implanting in the minds of this Moslem generation ideas out of harmony with tradition. Eighteen sets of the *Encyclopædia Britannica* were sold in two years to Arab customers by a single book-shop in Iraq. New ideas which have no place in the old Islamic scheme of the universe are coming in like a flood.

The effect of the war has been revolutionary and startling. Moslems of many countries were involved, and upon different sides in the conflict. The Arab and the Turk, the Turk and the Indian Moslem, fought each other. In nearly all of the national armies there were Moslem contingents. The call for a *jihad* had failed, and Moslem was arrayed against Moslem in deadly combat. Nationalism came to the front and religion receded. The war took Moslems into lands strange to them and among peoples hitherto unknown. Old seclusions were forcibly broken up. Moslems of many races were thrown into a whirlpool of nations.

The spectacle of Christian arrayed against Christian revealed the lack of solidarity in the Christian world and destroyed in the minds of many Moslem leaders that fear of and respect for the Christian domination of Moslem races. The Indian Moslems caught new visions of independence. The Arabs dreamed of a new Arab kingdom. Egypt determined to throw off a foreign yoke. North Africa entertained a hope of autonomous self-government. Persia adopted a constitution. Turkey achieved a new measure of independence. The Mohammedan world awoke from the war with ideals of democracy as opposed to the old conception of theocracy.

Among the influences and results of the impact of Western life upon the Islamic world, the first to be considered is the multiplication of contacts which have forced intelligent and observing Moslems to note the differences between the two civilizations. This has led to sharp discussions as to the merits and demerits of the two. The place of women among the nations of the East is a matter of comment. The low state of education in Moslem countries, and especially among women, has been interpreted as one of the chief causes for the backward state of Islamic civilization. It is only within the last few years that the Persians have begun to realize the vast superiority of Occidental education. In Arabia there is a growing conviction that Islam is not up-to-date, that the powerful nations in the West have won their place in the world through education and through better social laws. The educated Moslems of all countries are beginning to see the economic and social values in modern philosophic and scientific principles and in Western social and economic truths. The pull is towards those ideals prevalent among Christian nations and away from traditional Islam.

S. Khuda Bukhsh, an Indian Moslem and an Oxford graduate, contrasts many of the customs of Islam with those of Christian nations to the detriment of the former. The present Turkish Government has gone to the extreme limit in officially adopting national, economic, and social laws and regulations which for centuries have been regarded as contrary to the teachings of Islam. The abrogation of the Caliphate and the expulsion of the Caliph was a radical and startling step taken in order to prevent interference in the modernization of Turkey by an unprogressive religious hierarchy.

Eshref Edib Bey made the following statement in St. Sophia in Constantinople to a vast Turkish audience:

"In an epoch when all the inhabitants of the earth are advancing into new realms of science, in a period when all cities and all nations are going through an evolution toward a final ideal, let us escape from this laziness which has caught us in its grasp. Let us free our lives from this dark veil of ignorance." [1]

When intelligent Moslems began to appreciate the deficiencies in their own systems they began to agitate for better education among their own peoples. This movement for better schools has already gained great momentum in Persia, Turkey, Arabia, Egypt, North Africa, and Malaysia. Moslems in India are establishing colleges like the Moslem colleges at Aligarh, Vaniyambadi, Peshawar, Hyderabad, and Lahore. Even the Amir of Afghanistan, in his earnestness to spread education, has instituted travelling schools for nomadic tribes. French, Italian, and German professors and doctors have been imported to conduct the more important of the national schools. *Christian Literature in Moslem Lands* reports that " there is a striking post-war desire for education, and there are crowded schools everywhere. Ability to read is everywhere coveted."

Social changes are no less revolutionary. This fact is most apparent in the new freedom for women and in the agitation over plural marriages, hitherto assumed to be one of the constant features of Islam. An educated Indian Moslem recently spoke of the hideous deformity of Moslem society, and of the vice and immorality, the selfishness, self-seeking, and hypocrisy which are corrupting it throughout the world.

A prominent Turkish lawyer in Constantinople who recently printed a series of six articles in one of the leading Turkish papers of that city upon the subject of marriage and divorce, says:

[1] Reported to the writer by a missionary of the American Board.

"The younger men revolt against the Moslem custom, and declare that such things ought not to be allowed in the twentieth century. These younger men look upon Moslem polygamy and divorce as a curious antique."[1]

The author advocates the promulgation of a law forbidding the marriage of more than one wife. He also declares that Turkish women are demanding the registration and publication of marriages, "a custom adopted everywhere in the world." This forceful article called out but little protest. The founder of the sect in the Punjab, India, known as "the people of the Koran," says that he considers polygamy as bad as fornication. A National Assembly of Albanians recently held at Tirana declared that their fundamental principles of independence include the prohibition of polygamy and the abolition of the wearing of the yashmak used by women to cover their faces. In Turkey and in Persia the use of the veil by women is rapidly becoming obsolete.

This sweeping social change affecting the place of women in society is greatly aided, in fact has its origin, in the new education that is reaching the women and girls as well as the men of all Moslem countries. The new and the old jostle one another throughout the Islamic world to-day in the spheres of education, social transformation, and religious discussions. The fathers for the most part cling to the old, while the younger generation have a genuine desire to lift the entire social, intellectual, and religious order to new levels.

A new spirit of mutual tolerance is also to be noted. There are yet many who believe that Mohammedans are universally bloodthirsty and cruel, and that it is impossible to have friendly relations with them. Within

[1] Translated for the writer from *Iqdam*, a Constantinople paper, by the Rev. Charles T. Riggs.

a single decade in Western schools and universities, in relations of host and guest, in conversations upon matters of morals and religion, in the formation of treaties as well as in the contacts of war, there has been created a new measure of mutual appreciation. Moslems have not hesitated to declare that there is much in Christianity that they admire and accept, while Christians have learned that the followers of Islam are not wholly barbaric. Familiarity and better acquaintance are producing an increasing measure of mutual respect.

A desire for democracy in place of theocracy is an outstanding example of change of ideal which has been carried into practical operation in Turkey. Within twenty years Turkey represented a government whose sovereign regarded himself, and was acclaimed by the people, to be the Shadow of God on earth. He claimed divine and absolute authority over his own people, and through his office as Caliph a large measure of authority over all Moslems. The Sultan has been deposed by his own subjects, the Caliphate abolished, and a constitutional democracy established which makes no claim for authority above that of the voice of the people. Turkey has separated Church and State.

Persia has adopted a constitution which gets its authority from the people. Egypt has set aside ecclesiastical law in civil affairs. If the common interpretation may be accepted, the fifth stripe in the new flag of democratic China gives to the Mohammedans of that country a status equivalent to that of a racial group. The government of Iraq under King Feisal does not claim divine sanction. More important than written constitutions and regulations is the constantly rising spirit of freedom that is spreading to all Moslem peoples. Nationalism is a vital force among Moslems to-day, setting aside divine fiat law and substituting laws that spring from the will of the people.

Within a century there has never been a time more propitious for a general Moslem uprising than the period immediately preceding the Great War. Throughout his reign the Caliph, Abdul Hamid II of Turkey, assiduously cultivated Moslem unity. His emissaries penetrated the great Moslem centres preaching the strength and solidarity of that religion which was destined by Allah to become the one supreme, dominant religion of the world, and the Caliph of Islam, the one triumphant ruler. Contacts and alliances with European nations aided in furthering the design. Mecca and Medina were used as centres from which to propagate among all Moslem peoples the gospel of unity and ultimate victory.

The supreme moment came at the outbreak of the Great War, when the call went forth from the Caliph to all the faithful to rise and strike for Moslem liberty. The complete failure of the call for the *jihad* is a matter of history. There is far less possibility of a coalition of the Moslem peoples of the world now than there was at that time. Pan-Islamism has become impossible. Turkey has lost her peculiar relationship to the Moslem world by the abolition of the Caliphate and the expulsion of the Caliph. Arabia is hopelessly divided; Egypt claims fellowship with no other Moslem country; Persia is under a constitution; India seeks self-government at home, but contemplates no alliance with outside countries; the Moros are content under American rule; the Moslems in the Dutch East Indies have a rising spirit of self-determination; and Russian Moslems are held by the Soviet régime. There appears to be no chance whatever for a new spirit of Pan-Islamism to get a foothold in any Mohammedan country.

Even though Pan-Islamism is no longer practicable, religious leaders in the Turkish Grand National Assembly have attempted to secure the passage of laws for the protection of the faith and for the punishment of the religiously careless. Lord Ronaldshay, in his *India, a Bird's-Eye View*,[1] says:

"The views which the Mohammedan deputation [of the All-India Moslem League] placed before the Viceroy in 1906 were those of a community acutely conscious of the fact that it differed fundamentally in its religious, social, and ethical ideals from the majority of the inhabitants of the land in which it dwelt; and further, that, faced with a movement in the direction of the democratic constitutionalism of the West, it was in danger of losing that which it desired above all things to maintain, namely, the individuality which it derived from its participation in the world of Islam."

This awakening to new perils constitutes a real Islamic achievement. It brings a unity in action as well as unity in spirit and resistance, binding together races and different nationalities. It presents a new and formidable barrier to an approach that would further disintegrate Islam. In the attempt to save itself from the disastrous results of the higher criticism of its sacred books and ancient traditions, a new barrier is erected against other religions.

Soon after the Chinese Republic was formed, the more enlightened and energetic among the men in the Moslem communities in various parts of China began banding themselves together into societies in order to stir up and promote a new enthusiasm for their faith. In Mesopotamia the old and the new jostle one another with confusing and startling contrasts. Modern innova-

[1] Page 239.

tions like the motor-car, aeroplanes, moving pictures, Western intoxicants, a great increase in periodical publications, are more and more becoming a part of the daily life of the Arab and fire him with a new vision of another golden age. The religious leaders are aroused by this unprecedented awakening of the Arab youth which shows a corresponding apathy toward religious ideas and practices. The religious forces are arousing themselves to stay the rising tide of unbelief.

A prominent Indian Moslem, Mr. Jafar Ali Khan, recently said:

> "The combined attacks of Christian Europe against the integrity of Islam and the covert and overt designs of Western Powers against the remnant of Turkey have made too deep an impression upon the mind of Moslems to be easily effaced."

The defeat of the Turk united the loyal followers of the Prophet in India against the British and drove them to make with the Hindus a common cause against "their common enemy." With them the question was not so much religious as political. They defended their faith in order to present a united front in their resistance. They have belittled religious differences in order to strengthen the bands of resistance. Moslems everywhere are beginning to see in the flood of new literature and the multiplying modern Press a new agency for the solidification and unification of their co-religionists perhaps as powerful as the Mecca pilgrimage. In Syria and Egypt, as well as in other Moslem countries, there is a general effort to produce a new religious literature that will reconcile modern science and ancient Islam. To this one phase of modern thought the intelligent world of Islam is devoting its best energies. The Wahhabi movement in Arabia and the Ahmadiya movement in India are but results of this attempt to meet new conditions.

A reinterpretation of Islam in terms of modern science has become necessary if the new generation of enlightened men and women are to be held true to the faith. None see this more clearly than do the intelligent Moslem leaders who view with uneasiness the spread of Western learning in all Moslem countries and among both sexes, attended by a loss of religious zeal. A writer in China says :

"The impact of modern thought is producing results which tend to cause a breaking away from orthodox Chinese Mohammedanism. This is due in part at least to a feeling that Islam is unable to meet the demands of modern life. Attempts are being made to meet these demands."

Stewart Crawford of Beirût writes :

"The methods of Western higher criticism are being adopted by some of the younger scholars in Islam, who are attempting a new exposition of the literature and the tendencies of their religion. The orthodox leaders are disturbed by this new freedom in the use of the sacred book. But they are unable to check the tendency of modern education to create new forms of religious activity and of personal piety in the Moslem world."

S. Khuda Bukhsh says :

"Mohammedans are free to adopt whatever is good in any civilization. All religions are alike in their governing principles. There is nothing in the teachings of Mohammed which conflicts with or militates against modern civilization. Modern Islam, with its hierarchy of priesthood, gross fanaticism, appalling ignorance, and superstitious practices, is a discredit to the Islam of the Prophet."

Therefore he calls for reforms, intellectual, social, and religious, and refers to the present as "the dawning era."

Modernism in Islam is an attempt to bring the thought and the life of Moslem peoples into harmony with the present age and to reconcile Oriental learning and tradition with the new literature, new ideas, and modern science. The modernist preaches a gospel of free inquiry, of a tolerant spirit, and of a higher morality. The reformers in Egypt, in public addresses and in writings of all kinds, are advocating under the watchword "Back to the Koran," or "Back to Mohammed," a break with the great body of tradition. Some of these devotees of modern interpretation are inclined to idealize Mohammed. They all, however, appear to agree in the purpose to break with antiquated customs and laws and to bring Islam into harmony with Western thought. One of the modern methods of the reformers is to introduce textual criticism. This method is demonstrated in the publication of the Woking Koran, with parallel Arabic and English texts and in a binding like that of an Oxford Bible.

The contention for liberty of thought, of interpretation, and of action, with the spirit of independence increasing as modern education and the spread of modern literature become more general, opens a fresh door of approach to the Moslem world and provides a common ground for a new Christian approach. Wherever the idea prevails that it is not a sin to discuss philosophy and religion, a formidable barrier is removed. Wherever the right to doubt the authority of ancient traditions is conceded, discussion and inquiry will inevitably follow.

Dr. Zwemer tells us that "in the city of Meshed, once as exclusive as Mecca itself and still the glory of the Shia world, there is complete liberty. Moslem newspapers criticize the Moslem ecclesiastics." Dr. Robert E. Speer reports that a Moslem editor told him that there was no hope for Persia until the power of Islam is shattered. There seems to be a widely expressed opinion in Persia that the spirit of constitutional government and that of Islam are forever incompatible. This same idea prevails in Turkey; the conservatives declare that constitutional government has destroyed the power of Islam, the liberals that it has given liberty to Moslems to think and act according to the dictates of their consciences. The Press in Turkey is free to discuss religion and life as it has never been before. In the treaty between Great Britain and the King of Iraq, signed in 1922, there are articles giving religious liberty, freedom of conscience, and the free exercise of all forms of public worship. Dr. Zwemer reports that extensive correspondence with missionaries in many Moslem mission fields brings out the general expression of a hope that they are facing the dawn of a new day of liberty.

In Malaysia the hitherto unruffled waters are being stirred and the symptoms of awakening life appear. Western education, eagerness for scientific enlightenment, thirst for modern intellectual equipment, are the tokens of the new day. The Ahmadiya movement has absorbed some of the principles of Christianity, especially upon the side of ethics. It is a sign of progress in the direction of intellectual emancipation. An educated Turk recently said to a missionary:

"Of all the forms of liberty, that of the liberty of conscience is the most essential and the most sacred. A man who is not free to choose and to declare his belief loses hold of his own soul. The purposes of education and instruction ought to be to prepare the individual to be self-reliant and not to depend upon society. It ought to develop and strengthen character more than intelligence." [1]

The Rev. J. Tackle, of India, writes:

" The spiritual revolt against a cold formalism, rationalism, and traditionalism, in the Islam that preaches a lonely, inaccessible, unfeeling deity, is spreading everywhere."

Dr. Speer reports that there is in Persia a manifest dissatisfaction with Islam among the thinking people. There is talk among the intelligent part of starting a Protestant movement in Islam. The desire for social reforms, now so general throughout the world of Islam, presents a common ground for arousing a new interest in the larger spiritual needs of society and the race.

Gottfried Simon writes:

" I have noticed discontent with the teachings of Islam among those Moslems who have come into contact with Christianity, and also among Malay pilgrims, who, on returning from Mecca, cast away their turbans and give strong utterance to their indignation at the practices of Mohammedanism."

The Sultan of Sulu, the Mohammedan religious leader of all the Moros, not only patronizes the schools among his people but sent his daughter to the United States for further studies after she had completed the course taught in local schools. The Moslem Albanians have practically broken with Islam by the prohibition of polygamy, the exposure of the faces of their women, the abolition of ceremonial ablution, prostration, and genuflections in prayer. In Egypt there is a growing feeling of national unity between Moslems and Christians which

[1] Reported to the writer by the Rev. Dr. William N. Chambers, of Adana.

is now assuming more the appearance of permanence than heretofore.

Islam of a generation ago is passing into new forms. Religious, social, and intellectual revolutions are in progress in the Islamic world. This movement is more general and more fundamental than any similar religious movement since the Reformation. It seems to be but at the beginning. Awakened intellects will not brook fanatical dictation. Blind tradition cannot stay the rising tide of reason as applied to religion. Moslem States are falling into line with the world sentiment in favour of intellectual and religious freedom. Propagation of Islam by force is no longer advocated. A free Press is regarded everywhere the sign and guaranty of personal freedom. Modern education is accepted among Moslems of every country. In its train follow an awakened Press and re-evaluation of Islam as a religion to meet the needs of a people and a State.

THE RENAISSANCE IN THE MOSLEM NEAR EAST

BY

DR. JULIUS RICHTER,

Professor of Missions, University of Berlin

CHAPTER II

THE RENAISSANCE IN THE MOSLEM NEAR EAST

THE Near East has an area almost as great as the United States and about half as many inhabitants. Yet its population is much more diverse than even that of the United States. Even leaving aside the Oriental Churches, there are the Egyptians and the Arabs, the different Syrian aboriginal tribes like the Druzes and the Nusairis, the Turks and the Kurds, the many Persian tribes and the Afghans ; almost all of them with different languages, traditions, and outlook. Yet in spite of all differences there has seemed to be a curious homogeneity of the higher life. It was the world of Islam with Mecca as its heart, Cairo as its head, and Constantinople as its hands.

The situation has been changed considerably during the last twenty-five years by that world-wide movement outside of the old Christian countries which we describe as the world renaissance. We remember that wonderful century from 1450 to 1550 in the history of Europe. For seven centuries Western Europe, apart from the greater part of the Balkans and of Russia, had been an isolated peninsula shut off from the rest of the world by a cordon of Moslem countries, reaching from Spain and Morocco in the West across North Africa and Asia Minor to the White Sea. And this seclusion had been so absolute that even the name of the prophet Mohammed and all but the haziest tradition concerning India and China had been lost.

It is true, Europe had built up in this isolation a remarkable civilization, a beautiful architecture with wonderful cathedrals, astounding systems of theology and philosophy, and a good deal of beautiful poetry. But the material which they worked upon was always more or less the same. They were like children who, with the same small wooden blocks, one day build a house, the next day a church, the third day a castle. So their systems in one generation were realistic, in the second nominalistic, in the third sceptic. But there was no wide enlargement of their scope and outlook.

Then from the midst of the fifteenth century the scene changed rapidly. Venetian and Florentine traders advanced into the Near East; Christopher Columbus discovered America; Vasco da Gama found the sea route to India. New worlds and wide realms of knowledge dawned upon that generation. The art of book printing, the compass, gun powder, and numerous other inventions followed. The great civilizations of Greece and Rome rose out of their graves with their wonderful poets, philosophers, historians, sculptors, and architects. An unheard-of mass of new material of knowledge and learning really flooded Western Europe like a rising tide. The astounding fact was that in connexion with this new spiritual flood a great number of first-rate men arose, indeed a larger number of brilliant geniuses than have lived contemporaneously in Europe in any other age: painters like Raffael Sanzio and Leonardo da Vinci, sculptors like Michelangelo, poets like Dante, Petrarch, and Boccaccio, politicians like Machiavelli, religious reformers like Savonarola, learned men like Erasmus and Reuchlin, and many others. It was the famous *cinquecento*, the high-water mark of literary Europe.

Yet altogether there were interesting and instructive differences among the countries in which the humanitarian Renaissance was centring. Half of Europe in the same century experienced that deep religious revival movement of the Protestant Reformation. These nations were rejuvenated in the deepest springs of their national life. They became the advancing nations of Western and Northern Europe, Holland with its wonderful expansion, Great Britain with its world-wide colonial empire, Sweden almost suddenly emerging out of its northern remoteness under Gustavus Adolphus, Germany with its wonderful spiritual development of philosophy by Leibnitz, Immanuel Kant, Schelling, and Hegel, of poetry, by Lessing, Schiller, and Goethe, of music, by Haydn, Mozart, Beethoven, and Richard Wagner, almost all of them grown on the ground of the German Reformation. On the other hand, those nations which rejected and crushed the Protestant revival movement, like Italy, Spain, and Portugal, were spiritually and morally and soon, also, politically crippled. The wonderful flower of their springtime did not yield fruit because it lacked the spiritual vitality of the Protestant Reformation.

The application of this marked historical parallelism is interesting with regard to every Asiatic country. It is particularly striking in the Moslem Near East. It is a well-known fact that those countries have cultivated a reactionary conservatism and an intolerant fanaticism. Al Azhar University at Cairo and other similar centres of Arabic learning have maintained a mediæval scholasticism of an extreme character. And the whole life of the Moslem population has been regulated by the supposedly divine law of the *Sharia* and by an enormous mass of senseless superstition. And as in a stuffy house with closed windows and barred doors, the political and religious leaders were quite reluctant to let in the fresh breeze of the modern life. One needs only to remember the reign of Abdul Hamid in Turkey, hardly two decades ago.

Now the situation has totally changed since the beginning of this century. Every country has opened its doors, however reluctantly, to the modern world life of Europe and America, and, by reason of the fact that the Near East lies just before the doors of Europe, the rising tide is the more irresistibly flooding country after country and district after district. The more highly educated classes who, particularly in Paris, but later in London and Berlin too, have come under the influence of modern civilization, in their wholesale admiration of everything European and modern have fallen into agnosticism and scepticism. Many families of the middle class are trying to get the best out of the changed conditions, and order their members to learn each at least one of the world languages, to be prepared for all chances. And behind them all there are the blind and fanatical leaders of the old Moslem régime, the *ulama* and *mufti* and *kadi*, who feel the sources of their influence and of their income slipping away, and the broad masses of the ignorant lower classes, farmers and craftsmen, who in their conservatism resent all innovations and are the easy prey of the reactionary agitation of their religious leaders.

Again, this transformation of the Moslem Near East presents very different aspects in the different countries. In some, like Persia, there is a curious divergence between an extremely fanatical and imperious priestly class and broad masses of modernist people who welcome the foreigner, and even the missionary and his gospel, with open arms. In others, like Egypt, which have become high-roads of world traffic and of globe-trotters, the European and modernist influence is permeating all classes and districts. In others, again, like Turkey, a despotic dictatorship is attempting brutally to crush all non-Turkish influences and concerns as well as the old-Turkish reaction, maintaining its reckless autocracy in the face of almost equal opposition from modernism and from reaction. In a country like Afghanistan the modern light has been longest and most definitely shut out and a change only now seems slowly to appear.

Of course all this transformation of the Moslem Near East is deeply influencing the Protestant missionary movement. It is opening new doors and pointing to new opportunities. Yet it seems not to be in the matter of accessibility that the central problem of Christian missions lies. It is a far larger question looming in the background. Will there be, parallel to the humanitarian Renaissance, a strong, deep religious revival movement which can do for the Islamic countries what the Protestant movement did for Western and Northern Europe?

It is hardly possible that such a religious revolution and rejuvenation will come out of Islam itself. Whoever has watched its sterility, its petrification and disintegration during the last half-millennium, particularly since the Turkish sultans became dominant in the Near East, will not doubt that its spiritual vitality is spent. What there is left of really or of seemingly vital forces is insignificant and insufficient for so great a task. It is one of the tragic events of modern history that the Caliphate has been given up by the Turks of their own free will. The Caliph was at no time a spiritual head like the Prophet or the Pope.

Yet if it was one of the main purposes of Mohammed's mission to win the recognition of Allah as the legitimate sovereign of the universe and to subject all nations to his absolute divine law, the function of the Caliph was after all the central religio-political office in the Moslem community. Its bearer represented the claim to universal rule. The idealism and the fanatical hope of one-eighth of the human race has centred for a millennium round this curious idea, which has now been abandoned. The Turks have expelled the last Caliph from their country; he is living as an exile somewhere in Europe. The spurious attempts of other Moslem rulers to adopt the title and claim of the Caliph have been futile.

It has sometimes been alleged that the Moslem dervish orders retained that vitality from which a spiritual restoration of Islam might develop. Yet he who has studied the Senussi movement in Italian Tripoli or the Ikhwān movement in Central Arabia sees almost no chance in that direction.

Yet in the time of the Reformation, too, the inspiration of the religious revival in most countries came from outside, from Wittenberg and Geneva. Will it in our age come from Christendom? The really central question is: Has a missionary Protestantism vital power and spiritual energy enough to flood the spiritual deserts of modern Islam with the rising tide of a spiritual revival which will lead to a religious reformation and transformation? That such an evolution is possible can hardly be doubted. Islam and Christianity are near enough one to the other to be deeply influenced by each other. Half of their spiritual heritage they have in common. And the spiritual development of Islam in the first few formative centuries from Mohammed to al-Ghazālī was largely under the influence of Hellenized Christianity or Christian Hellenism.

Here we are confronted with a crucial question: Has modern Christianity a convincing and comprehensive gospel which is able not only to command the full and unreserved allegiance of the Moslem, but also to yield the vitalizing and transforming power of a spiritual reformation? Evidently a reduced Christianity of the First Article, just claiming Jesus as a saintly prophet of the fatherhood of God and of the brotherhood of man, has not this power. It can only purge Islam of some real or apparent excrescences and effect a deepening of some of its issues. It would mean no change of religion. It would simply attempt to bring about a similar reduction in Islam as it has attempted in Christianity. The impotence of an intellectualized and impoverished Christian message in its reaction upon Islam is its final sentence. An eloquent declaration that the unbroken resistance of Islam is no reflection upon the vitality of Christian missions scarcely hides this awkward fact from the standpoint of the superficial onlooker. And all undertakings of Christian philanthropy and of social helpfulness are no real and effective substitute for a poor and ineffective message.

So Moslem missions become the very *Hic Rhodus, hic salta* of modern Protestantism in its missionary function. We remember how, in quite similar circumstances, St. Paul in his letter to the Galatians developed his fundamental conception of Christianity against the shallow Jewish monotheism of his day. Is not modern Islam, crystallized in a bulky system of theology, in many lines somewhat similar to the old Judaism of the scribes and of the Talmud? Will it, then, not be a wise plan to consider very carefully the apologetics and polemics of St. Paul to see clearly our issue and its possibilities? The apostle is quite definite in his assertion that it is not any actions of our own that bring about the righteousness of God, but the divine love revealed in the reconciliation through Jesus Christ. It is on this objective fact of salvation through God's love and mercy that he puts the whole emphasis.

Yet, to be quite clear about the difficulty and perplexity of our task, is it not helpful for us to realize that, after all, Christian missions among the Jews failed in the first two centuries, and Jewish missions have never recovered from that fundamental failure? And evidently our chances with regard to the Moslems in our generation are not greater, or even so great. Yes, we have the same renaissance in contemporary Islam which Judaism experienced in the first century in its vital touch with the Hellenistic civilizations. And men like the Jewish philosopher Philo show how far that renaissance went and how deeply it modified the narrow Jewish conception. Yet, besides Apollos, we know of scarcely one Alexandrian Jew for whom this Hellenistic renaissance became a bridge into the Christian faith. What convincing proof have we that the effect will be more lasting and more favourable in Islam at present? And our missions are burdened with the wrong political traditions of the so-called Christian Powers.

It is true, we ourselves are convinced that the decay and downfall of political Islam and of the Ottoman Empire was the unavoidable consequence of inner deterioration; yet we can understand how the overwhelming majority of the Moslems may see in it the treacherous machination of a supercilious policy—not the saving knife of the amputating physician, but the reckless avarice of insatiable Powers preying on the poor "Sick Man of the Bosphorus." It is this traditional hatred of the European Powers, coupled with a deep-seated suspicion of their motives, that renders all missionary approach in Islam so difficult. And the widespread lack of confidence on the part of the Christians, the fruit of more than a thousand years of failures and defeats in their relations with Moslems, enhances this difficulty in our own camp.

Has the Protestantism of our time vitality and spiritual energy enough to start a thoroughgoing religious revival, a reformation which in this case really would mean a transformation in the Islamic countries of the Near East? Only then would the renaissance mean the same, and bring the same beneficent results, as in the *cinquecento* of Europe.

THE CALIPHATE YESTERDAY, TO-DAY, AND TO-MORROW

BY

D. S. MARGOLIOUTH, D.Litt., F.B.A.,

Laudian Professor of Arabic, Oxford University

CHAPTER III

THE CALIPHATE, YESTERDAY, TO-DAY, AND TO-MORROW

At the time when the Caliphate agitation was at its height one of its spokesmen in England asserted that, unless there were a Caliph who was an independent sovereign, the daily prayers of all Sunni Moslems would be invalid. This person was a Shii lawyer, and therefore of doubtful authority on this matter; and indeed the Sunni Lawbooks, which enumerate the conditions whereby prayer is rendered valid, do not seem to know of this condition. At the time when these lines are being written there is no longer a Caliph who is an independent sovereign; for, though the abolition of the Turkish Caliphate in March 1924 was immediately followed by the assumption of the office by the King of the Hejaz, who was then independent, this Caliph has since been driven from his realm, and, having abdicated his kingship, though not his Caliphate, can no longer give validity to Sunni orisons, if the condition mentioned be really required. The North African Caliph lost his independence in 1911; and it would appear that no other potentate of consequence holds the office. The conference summoned to meet in Cairo in March 1925 has been postponed for a year; should it, on convening, succeed in making an appointment, and should that appointment obtain recognition among Sunni communities, the fact will

4

be that for many months the Islamic world will have remained without an independent Caliph. This has not happened since the death of the Prophet; many a dynasty which claimed the Caliphate has fallen; but hitherto there has always been another ready to take over the torch.

The question of the Caliphate is rendered obscure by certain assumptions, which, unless they are scrutinized, are apt to mislead. The word *khalīfa* means "substitution," or "substitute." In pre-Islamic Arabic it is used for "viceroy"; when the Prophet left his capital for raids, pilgrimage, or for some other purpose, he would appoint a "substitute" to discharge his duties during his absence. When he had departed on his last journey, a substitute was required. Such a substitute should, of course, have been a prophet; but his followers made no claim to be the recipients of revelations, and no credence was given in official circles to those persons who took the opportunity to urge their claims to prophetic gifts. The substitute could then discharge only the sort of duties which were executed by those who had acted as the Prophet's substitutes during his lifetime. They could administer; but they could not legislate.

A man's natural substitute is his son; the hereditary principle was even more widely recognized in the East than in the West. Had Mohammed left a son, his right to the succession would probably have been at least for the time unquestioned; but his sons died in infancy. He had, however, allied various influential persons to himself, either by giving them his daughters, or by himself marrying theirs; and from the relations thus obtained his first five followers were chosen. The first two were fathers-in-law; the second two, sons-in-law;

the fifth a brother-in-law. The "substitute" was in each of these cases a member of the Prophet's family; the last of this series founded a dynasty. Although it is strictly correct to say that with this dynasty the hereditary principle became established in Islam, yet the fact should not be ignored that its founder's predecessors were all of them allied by marriage to the Prophet.

The reign of the first of these was very short; the second, third, and fourth met with violent deaths; the precedents for getting rid of an obnoxious Caliph by violent means were thus established at the commencement of Islamic history. The causes of the insurrection wherein the third Caliph fell are obscure; if the clue of *cui bono?* (who was the gainer?) be followed, suspicion must rest on Ali, the Prophet's cousin and son-in-law, whose adherents, the Shia, to this day look upon his three predecessors as impious usurpers. But that murder led to a war of succession, since the Prophet's favourite wife, whose father had been the first Caliph, had a grudge against Ali, and was determined that he should never sit safely on that throne; she lent her influence to another cousin of the Prophet, who presently fell in battle, but whose son after some years set himself for a time on the Prophet's throne; while a brother-in-law of the Prophet, who was related to the third Caliph, and claimed to be his natural avenger, found in the Koran a text which justified him in assuming the sovereignty, and, being a man of consummate ability, founded, as has been seen, an hereditary dynasty. Since the commencement of the first War of Succession, just a quarter of a century after the Prophet's death, there has been no unity in Islam.

The word *khalīfa*, then, if taken literally as substitute for the Prophet, but limited to administrative functions, implies that the Moslem community remained somewhat as he left it: an Arab nation, ruled from Medina. But in fact, after his death it spread by rapid conquest over large portions of Asia, Africa, and Europe; and the difficulty of communication, together with the sentiment of nationality, rendered these provinces far harder to retain than to conquer. Moreover, it was not forgotten that the founder of Islam had organized an army and raised himself to a throne in the character of religious reformer; this furnished a precedent which able and ambitious men could follow. Numerous persons in this capacity took the title Substitute for the Prophet; several, finding it easier to advocate the claims of someone else rather than their own, founded kingdoms and placed supposed heirs of the Prophet on the throne.

Now all these Caliphs were legitimate in the opinion of their adherents. Sometimes those adherents were few in number; in several cases, as in those of the South Arabian and in some of the African dynasties, the territory over which they ruled was neither extensive nor thickly peopled; but the title which was won by the sword was defended by argument. One who is a member of the Moslem community may well hold that one dynasty was legitimate and another usurping; but those who are outside the community have no criterion whereby they can thus distinguish them. In modern Europe, owing to the popularity of *The Arabian Nights*, the word Caliphate naturally suggests Baghdad; but the Abbasid dynasty, with that city as capital for nearly the whole of its duration, was at no time in control of the whole Moslem community; the family which they had displaced founded a dynasty in Spain and North Africa, and presently felt strong enough to resume the title of Caliph, and ere long yet another Caliphate was established in

Egypt. It is an accident that the fame of these Caliphates has found little echo in modern Europe. The rulers whom they produced were, in the opinion of large masses of men, "substitutes" for the Prophet.

When an Arab made himself master of an Arabic-speaking population, he usually took the title of Caliph; for to decline it would imply that he considered himself dependent on, or at least inferior to, some potentate who held it. The simultaneous existence of three Cæsars in Europe was due to similar considerations. But when a foreigner made himself master of an Arabic-speaking population, there was an incongruity in his assuming the title of Substitute for the Prophet; hence another plan was followed. Some member of the legitimate family was left in possession of the title, whereas the real power was in the hands of the usurper. The date A.H. 324 (A.D. 936) is of capital importance in Islamic history, since in that year a Turkish officer, one Ibn Raiq, for the first time made such an arrangement with the Abbasid Caliph. For more than two centuries this system prevailed in Baghdad, and it was afterwards in a somewhat excessive form continued in Egypt.

In Baghdad, where the Abbasid family represented the founders of the city, the Caliph was revered by the population, and, though the foreign usurpers thought little of deposing and blinding a Caliph who gave trouble, they found it worth their while ordinarily to keep on good terms with the Caliph, and were eager to ally themselves by marriage with the imperial family. The Caliphs, therefore, under these usurpers enjoyed considerable influence, and exercised it in judicial and religious affairs; in consequence, they were able ultimately to shake off the yoke and for a time assume independence. The case was different in Cairo, which had been founded by another branch of the Prophet's family, and where, in consequence, there was no tradition of loyalty to the Abbasid dynasty. When, therefore, the able though unscrupulous Sultan Baibars accepted the claim of a supposed representative of the Abbasids, and received investiture from him, on condition that all the functions of sovereignty were delegated to himself, the sacrifice which he made to the sentiment of legitimacy was small; for the suzerain whom he appointed was entirely dependent on himself, and had no natural following in the country. If, as a foreigner, he could not be Caliph in an Arabic-speaking country, he by this expedient secured himself against dependence on any other Caliph. And these Egyptian Abbasids were allowed no interference with any branch of public affairs.

When a foreigner was sovereign of a foreign (non-Arab) Moslem population he had not to reckon with the sentiment that has been mentioned, and could, if he thought fit, assume the title Substitute for the Prophet. This happened both in Turkey and in India. Other titles were more familiar in these countries, just as in England, though the King has the title "Defender of the Faith," it is rarely used. Only the Ottoman Sultan or the Moghul Emperor was Caliph not because he had inherited the office from a relation of the Prophet, but because he was a Moslem king.

The question therefore, Who is the legitimate Caliph of the Moslems? has about the same amount of meaning as the question, Who is the legitimate king of the Christians? Neither of these communities constitutes a political or even a religious unit; both are divided into nations and into sects. The nations will have their political and the sects their religious heads.

Yet there is one feature of the Islamic system which

involves unity, and that is the Pilgrimage. Every Moslem ought at least once in his life to make a pilgrimage to Mecca; and reverence to the Prophet requires as well a visit to Medina, where his grave is. This is not feasible unless these Sanctuaries and their approaches are in the hands of a Moslem power; it must be the business of some such authority to secure to the Moslems the chance of discharging this obligation. Hence the power that is in possession of the Sanctuaries occupies a peculiar position in the Moslem world; and sovereigns who were not in possession of these Sanctuaries have hesitated to take the title Caliph in consequence. Normally, it may be said, they have been in the possession of the most powerful Moslem government of the time; and so, when the Caliphate of Egypt had come to an end, and a century later that of Baghdad also terminated owing to the Mongol conquest, the Sherif of Mecca of the time applied to the Moslem sovereign whom he supposed to be the best qualified from the point of view of power to take over the obligation. When the two Caliphates of importance were the Ottoman and the Moghul, the latter proposed that each of them should have possession of a Sanctuary.

Although, then, the Ottoman Sultan could claim the title Caliph on the principle that has been explained, he first became *de facto* Caliph when he entered into possession of the Sanctuaries; and with the loss of them his title lapsed, inasmuch as the Moslem community no longer depended on him for the possibility of discharging their duty of pilgrimage. At the time when the Ottoman president abolished the office, which he could do only for Turkey, there was good reason for thinking that this question of the pilgrimage would soon become a practical one; and the danger which this astute man foresaw has materialized. The Sanctuary of Mecca has passed out of the possession of the King of the Hejaz into that of the Wahhabi ruler, whose attitude towards pilgrims cannot be certainly foreseen; correspondents of the newspapers assure us that this ruler, so far from interfering with the pilgrims, will encourage their arrival, if only for financial reasons; but the ruler's fanatical followers may have something to say in this matter, and they may well impose such conditions on pilgrims as may make them unwilling to visit the Sanctuary so long as the Wahhabi régime prevails. Moreover, while these lines are being written, Jidda, the port of Mecca, is still in the hands of the new King of the Hejaz, and serious difficulty would be occasioned to pilgrims by the port and the Sanctuary being occupied by mutually hostile Powers. Possibly the ex-King of the Hejaz still clings to his title Caliph because he hopes he may be able to restore the situation. Certainly any real Caliph would be compelled to clear it up. For the Sanctuary of Islam ought not to be in the hands of a sect which, in proportion to the others, is exceedingly small and notoriously fanatical in its attitude towards those others.

When this difficulty is pointed out to Moslems, they reply that the duty of pilgrimage is in the Koran made conditional on ability; if the pilgrimage became impossible owing to the occupation of the Sanctuary by a Power that did not permit it, then the obligation would lapse. This view is clearly sound; but therewith the sole factor which maintains unity in Islam would also disappear, for it was by separating the religious from the political capital that the founder of Islam secured for his system the ability to outlast the constantly increasing divisions and the rise and fall of dynasties. The fall of a Caliphate could not affect this; the possession of the religious capital by a fanatical sect would seriously impair it.

There would seem, at the moment, to be two proposals before the Moslem peoples: one, that representatives should meet in Mecca to determine the future of the Sanctuaries; another, that such should meet in Cairo to settle the question of the Caliphate. It is difficult to suppose that the former of these congresses could do more than register the wishes of the Wahhabi Sultan; he has on his side the logic of the "stricken field," which few if any Oriental potentates have ever declined to emphasize. The persons who attend such a congress will certainly be unaccompanied by forces which would enable them to resist legislation of which they disapprove, and it is unlikely that those whom they represent would be in a position to back them up. It is asserted that the Wahhabis, on their entry into the Sacred City, proceeded to perform a series of acts which would certainly move the indignation of the bulk of the Moslem world; the "Station of Abraham" itself with difficulty (according to this report) escaped being broken up. The business of the foreign representatives will, then, at best be to communicate to those who despatch them the conditions on which the Wahhabi conqueror intends in future to permit the pilgrimage. Those conditions may be acceptable to the Moslem community, or they may be otherwise.

The Cairene project admits of far greater liberty of expression of opinion, for it is improbable that free speech will be suppressed. On the other hand, though the sheikhs of Al Azhar might well be consulted on points of religious law, it is not clear how either they or the delegates whom they invite could have any executive power. They themselves, in their manifesto asserted that the Ottoman Caliph had forfeited his rights owing to his proved inability to defend himself. In order to be consistent, they will have to confine their choice to a powerful prince. To select the Wahhabi Sultan would be equivalent to identifying Islam with Wahhabism: but the difficulties of choosing any other Moslem potentate would seem to be enormous. If the functions of their Caliph were to be purely passive, that is, to be mentioned in public prayer—he would certainly not be mentioned on the coins of any but his own State, —it is improbable that the ruler of one Moslem State would allow this to be done in his dominions for the ruler of another State; and it is improbable that any one of these personages would grasp at such a distinction. If, however, the Caliph is to have duties as well as rights, the recovery of the Sanctuary from Wahhabi hands would be the first which would be incumbent on him. It is exceedingly improbable that the sheikhs will find any prince who is willing to undertake this.

Moreover, the appointment of a Caliph by sheikhs and delegates is an innovation. Historical appointments of Caliphs were appointments of sovereigns, heads of governments; and these could naturally be made only by those who were actively engaged in public affairs and had personal acquaintance with the possible candidates. The ship of State could not be left for a moment without someone at the helm; and, where there was no actual law of succession, the court intrigue was the natural and probably the best method of securing a helmsman when the emergency arose. There is now no State requiring a helmsman; the Moslem world has dispensed with a Caliph for a considerable period, and it would be difficult to show that any Moslem had suffered, at any rate to any extent which the existence of a Caliph would have prevented. This fact was conceded by the sheikhs when they decided to postpone their congress. So far as a Caliph has any administrative duties, each Moslem State has its Caliph, or government, already. It is not conceivable that the choice made by sheikhs and delegates will affect this matter even in the slightest degree.

If, however, the Caliph to be appointed is to be merely an ultimate authority on religious questions, his character will be very different from that of former holders of the title. If we take Harun al-Rashid as the type of a Caliph—and his is the name most familiarly associated with that title—it is quite certain that he, at any rate, ostensibly subordinated his judgment to those who had made a profounder study of the law than himself. Having caught his son in the commission of a capital offence, he would have executed judgment, but held his hand when a jurist explained to him that he could not act on his personal knowledge, but only on the attestation of others. Certainly, among those who took the title of Caliph, there were persons who were themselves religious reformers; the title was taken, in most of these cases, after sovereignty had been won, and not in virtue of their claim to purify religion. The interpreter of the law is rather the Mufti, or the Sheikh al-Islam. Qualified jurists usually are tenacious of the right to dispute the rulings of the government Mufti, as the famous Mufti, Mohammed ʿAbdu of Egypt, experienced. Would the jurists resign this right in favour of a Caliph? And would the orthodox schools, which have lasted for eleven centuries, agree to amalgamate?

Forecasts that are based on general considerations are at times rendered false by the sagacity of statesmen; such persons can find outlets where those who have neither the experience nor the astuteness see only a blank wall. Hitherto, however, those students of Islamic history who declared the Caliphate agitation to be factitious and frivolous have been shown by the event to be right. It remains to be seen whether the future has any surprise for them.

THE INSTITUTION OF THE CALIPHATE AND THE SPIRIT OF THE AGE

ANONYMOUS

CHAPTER IV

THE INSTITUTION OF THE CALIPHATE AND THE SPIRIT OF THE AGE

THE word Caliph, in Arabic *khalīfa*, means successor, and it describes the person holding this office as the Successor of the Prophet Mohammed. As prophet, Mohammed had no successor: his prophetic office came to an end with his death. The Caliph succeeds only to the rule and authority wielded by the Prophet.

The Moslem Caliphate has existed in different centres successively for 1,292 years, and there have been times when several rulers in different countries have claimed the Caliphate, as, for example, in Baghdad, in Spain, and in Egypt.

The Caliphate has been held by different successive dynasties (in Mecca, 632–660; in Damascus, 660–750; in Baghdad, 750–1258; in Egypt, 1258–1517; in Constantinople, the Ottoman Caliphate, 1517–1924). There was also a Fatimid Caliphate in Egypt and North Africa, 908–1171.

The Republic of Turkey put an end to the reign of the Ottoman Sultans by a resolution adopted by the Grand National Assembly, November 1, 1922, and it discarded the name Ottoman in favour of the name Turkish. That resolution declared that "by the law of fundamental organization, the Turkish Nation having transferred its sovereign power to the moral personality of the Grand National Assembly, the Sultanate ended for all time on March 16, 1920," when the Republic was declared. A few days after the adoption of this resolution, on November 18, 1922, Abdul Mejid Effendi, the heir-presumptive, was chosen Caliph by the Grand National Assembly without any definition of his powers. Thus the Turkish Republic put an end to the Ottoman Sultanate, but continued the Caliphate as a purely spiritual office devoid of temporal power.

Historically, however, the Caliph has been a political functionary rather than a religious one. He has possessed no spiritual functions which are not possessed by all Moslems; so it was only a question of time how soon the Turks would perceive that there was no reason for the continued existence of the Caliphate.

The next step was taken by the Grand National Assembly in the beginning of March 1924, when it abolished the Caliphate also and expelled Abdul Mejid and all the members of the royal family from Turkey.

Abdul Mejid was the thirty-eighth Ottoman Caliph and the ninety-fourth in the line of succession from the death of Mohammed in 632 to 1924, not counting rival claimants to the office, of whom there have been as many as eight at one time (in the eleventh century).

The Ottoman Dynasty held the Caliphate from about 1517 down to the year 1924. The beginning of the Ottoman Caliphate is generally attributed to Sultan Salim, who is said to have taken it over from the Abbasid Caliph in Egypt in 1517; but there is much vagueness in the accounts of this event, and the Ottoman Sultans often regarded themselves as appointed by God to the Caliphate in accordance with two texts of the Koran, 38 : 25, " and we have made thee a caliph on the earth," and 6 : 165, " He hath made you caliphs on the earth."

The question now arises whether it is the Caliphate, considered as an office pertaining to the whole world of Islam, which has come to an end, or only the Turkish Caliphate, which will be succeeded by that of some other dynasty, as has been the case so often in the history of Islam. In order to form any opinion on this question we must understand the causes which led the Turks to repudiate the Caliphate, and the effects which this repudiation has produced among Moslems.

In the minds of the Turks religion and nationalism have been held as synonymous terms—an apostate from Islam was looked upon as a traitor to his nation. At the present time there is a strong tendency towards a purely secular nationalism divorced from religion. The Grand National Assembly is animated by a strong desire that Turkey should become a modern, progressive, homogeneous Moslem State. The abolition of the Caliphate is to be regarded as the result of this desire pushing them to a series of steps rather than as a policy deliberately conceived beforehand and consistently carried out. Every step taken led the way to the succeeding steps.

When the Assembly adopted a republican form of government they did not at once realize that this would lead them to abolish the Sultanate and the Caliphate, but they were carried along on the strong tide of the new nationalism. The creation of the Grand National Assembly invested with both legislative and executive functions robbed the Sultanate of its reason to exist, and the decree of the Assembly only registered what was already an accomplished fact. The Sultanate died when the Republic was born.

The Caliph then remained, it was said, as a purely spiritual leader,—the religious head. The Caliph, however, has never been a spiritual leader. He is no pope, and there is no place for a pope in Islam. It is difficult for Westerners to realize what a startling innovation the deposition of the Caliph was in Turkey. The Caliphs have not been theologians, nor have they proclaimed new doctrines or interpretations of the Sacred Law: the Caliphs themselves have been subject to the Sacred Law, as all other Moslems are, and the interpretation of that law pertained to the Ulama, or Scribes—the body of men learned in the law. When the temporal power was taken away from the Caliphs they were left without any adequate content for their office—an office without functions, for the Caliph is really a temporal sovereign and not a spiritual head.

Mawardi (quoted by Sir Thomas Arnold, *The Caliphate*, p. 72), defines the functions of the Caliph as follows: "the defence and maintenance of religion, the decision of legal disputes, the protection of the territory of Islam, the punishment of wrongdoers, the provision of troops for guarding the frontiers, the waging of war, *jihad* [or holy war], against those who refuse to accept Islam or to submit to Muslim rule, the collection and organization of taxes, the payment of salaries and the administration of public funds, the appointment of competent officials, and, lastly, personal attention to the details of government"—in a word, "the defence of religion and the administration of the State." Mawardi was writing in the eleventh century, but his distinguished contemporary, al-Beruni, recognized "that what was left in the hands of the Abbasid Caliph at that time was only a matter that concerned religion and dogmatic belief, since he was not capable of exercising any authority in the affairs of the world whatsoever."

That was the period of the degradation of the Caliphate,

and in 1924 the Caliph had again fallen into like degradation. The Caliph had no power, either political or spiritual; he had become a mere figurehead, whose chief functions were to receive visits and to attend the weekly ceremony of the Salamlik and of public prayer.

It was difficult to reconcile this empty existence with the dignity and authority which history and tradition have accorded to the Caliphs of Islam in the past. Abdul Mejid could not be satisfied with such a life, and many devout Moslems felt that such a position was not worthy of the religious head of the Islamic world. Notably the Agha Khan and Ameer Ali appealed to the Turkish Government to define clearly the powers and the authority of the Caliph and to give him a position commensurate with the traditions of his high office and of its relations with the world of Islam. Unfortunately, the Grand National Assembly saw in their intervention only collusion between these men abroad and certain parties in Constantinople, and they looked upon it as a covert attack upon the Republic. It seemed to them that the Caliphate could be exalted only at the expense of the Republic.

The bad feeling between Angora and Constantinople aggravated the difficulty. Turkey has virtually two capitals, the old one, Constantinople, enjoying a unique situation of unparallelled beauty on the European and Asiatic shores of the Bosphorus, a city abounding in historic associations, a centre of sea-borne commerce, and exposed to European influences; and the new capital, Angora, a small provincial town in Asia Minor, removed from foreign influences, in the midst of a peasant population, the terminus of a branch line of the Baghdad Railway, and having no adequate buildings in which to house the Government and its officials. The Caliph resided in the old capital, and the seat of government was in the new. If the Caliph had been transferred to Angora, where he would have been under the eye of the Government, he might have enjoyed a longer reign. Angora was exceedingly suspicious of Constantinople, looking upon it as a centre of foreign intrigues and only half-loyal to the Republic. Constantinople thought that a provincial town like Angora could not understand the problems of the metropolis or legislate wisely for its foreign trade.

The Angora men regarded the Caliph as the centre of intrigues hostile to the Republic and considered that the religious head of Islam was likely to be dangerous to the new State whenever it was weak. Abdul Mejid is an upright man, sincerely desirous of promoting the best interests of his people ; but the Assembly at Angora, looking at him from a distance, invested him with other traits of character, and became wholly estranged from the Caliphate which had lost its traditional hold upon them under the influences of the new nationalism.

The principal reasons which impelled them to abolish the Caliphate were :

1. *Economy.* They desired to get rid of the expense of supporting the former imperial family.

2. *Fear.* They feared that the members of this family would always be wedded to the old régime and would seek to restore it. They pointed to the plots and crimes which stain the history of the Ottoman Sultans, and they thought that whenever the Republic might be exposed to danger from without the members of the old dynasty would become an internal danger.

3. *Modernism.* They wanted to become a modern State which could take its place among the other nations on a basis of equality with them. To this end they believed that it was necessary to separate Church and

State. They proposed to do away with the *Sharia* (Sacred Law) and with the *medressés* (religious schools), to secularize education, and to remove the Department of Worship from the Cabinet.

These changes, so radical and so sweeping, startled the whole world; Turkey, and with her Islam, seemed to be breaking with the past and starting on new careers.

At first it caused a great deal of excitement in the Moslem world, which was taken quite by surprise at this sudden measure. Protests were made in different countries, notably in Syria and Palestine and in India, where the Moslems looked upon the abolition of the Caliphate as an attack upon the religion of Islam made by an ungodly government. In Egypt the first excitement seems to be giving place to acquiescence in the action of the Turkish Republic on the ground that it is a matter which concerns Turkey alone. This seems to carry with it the implication that the Caliphate of the Ottoman Sultans was merely a Turkish Caliphate, and not one legitimate and valid for all the world of Islam; but it has been generally held that the Caliph, as successor to the Prophet, was in some sense the religious head of the whole Moslem world. It remains to be seen whether that world will allow the Caliphate to lapse or whether it will revive the office in some new form. A meeting of the Ulama held in Cairo called for a Moslem congress to be held in 1925 to consider the question of the Caliphate; but the convening of that congress has been postponed for a year.

In Turkey itself the abolition of the Caliphate caused astonishment and bewilderment to many devout Moslems and to the common people generally. The question was often asked, In whose name is the prayer to be offered in the mosques on Fridays in connexion with the sermon (*khutba*)? According to the best authorities the name of the reigning Caliph ought to be mentioned in the prayer. The National Assembly issued instructions that prayer should be offered for the prosperity and welfare of the Republic of Turkey. The religious feelings of the people suffered considerable shock. In the past the Turks have been held together by devotion to their ruler and to their religion; now it seemed to them that the very foundations had been cut away from under them. They missed the religious sanctions of their long-established traditions. The Angora men considered that the functions of the Caliph are now vested in the Grand National Assembly, which will discharge them through a Council of Public Worship; apparently there is a loss of religious authority in the process of change, which it will be difficult to restore.

The consternation caused to pious Moslems by the abolition of the Caliphate may be compared to that felt by their predecessors in Baghdad when Hulagu put the Caliph to death, as described by Sir Thomas Arnold in *The Caliphate*, pp. 81, 82[1]:

"It is difficult to estimate the bewilderment that Muslims felt when there was no longer a Caliph on whom the blessing of God could be invoked in the *khutbah*; such an event was without precedent throughout the previous history of Islam. Their suffering finds expression in the prayer offered in the great mosque of Baghdad on the Friday following the death of the Caliph: 'Praise be to God, who has caused exalted personages to perish, and has given over to destruction the inhabitants of this city. . . . O God, help us in our misery, the like of which Islam and its children have never witnessed; we are God's, and unto God do we return.'"

[1] Quoted from C. d'Ohsson, *Histoire des Mongols*, t. iii, pp. 251–4.

The Caliphate had lost much of its historic sanctity in 1924; still, its abolition gave a severe shock to devout Moslems, and many are still unreconciled to it.

Whatever view may be taken as to the importance of the Caliphate, it can hardly be denied that it did constitute a bond of moral unity among the Moslem peoples of the world, and its abolition tends to weaken that unity.

The Law of Sunnite Islam requires that there be a Caliph. The author of the *Sharhu'l Muwakif* says: "The appointment of an Imam [Caliph] is incumbent upon the united body of Muslims according to the orthodox law of the Sunnis." The religious feelings and the traditions of Moslems call for the appointment of a new Caliph for all Moslems.

A commission from India is said to be urging that Mustafa Kemal Pasha, the President of the Turkish Republic, assume the office of Caliph. The argument for this course is that the strongest Moslem ruler should be the Caliph. Except in Turkey, Persia, Afghanistan, Turkistan, and Arabia, the Moslems of the present age live under the rule of non-Moslem sovereigns. For them the possession of civil power is not possible.

On the other hand, not all Moslems have accepted the Ottoman rulers as Caliphs. The Shias do not accept the Caliphate of the Ottoman Sultans, or that of any living ruler.

"The Shiahs hold the twelfth and last historic Imam, the Mahdi Mahomed, born in the middle of the third century of the Moslem era, to be the Lord of the Age and the Salvation of God; that though invisible, he still lives and looks after the affairs of mankind, both spiritual and temporal. They allow the title of Caliph to no one save the Lord of the Age, and deny that he has appointed any deputy."[1]

So the Shias, numbering perhaps 15,000,000, must be taken out of a universal Moslem Caliphate. Some Moslems hold that the Caliphate really lasted only thirty years. One Tradition represents the Prophet as saying:

"The Caliphate after me will endure for thirty years; then will come the rule of a king."[2]

The Sherif of Morocco is reverenced by his subjects as Caliph, and there are claimants of this office in other countries also. Hence, any Caliph who may be appointed will not be universally recognized by all Moslems.

No Caliph who may be appointed can fulfil the historic functions of the Caliphate, such as the guardianship of the two sacred shrines of Mecca and Medina and the civil power over all Moslems.

The sovereignty of the Caliph is incompatible with constitutional government. Sell, in *The Faith of Islam*, published in Madras in 1880, wrote words which sound like prophecy at the present day. He says (p. 87):

"It is a fatal mistake in European politics and an evil for Turkey to recognize the Sultan as the legal Khalīfa of Islam, for, if he be such, Turkey can never take any steps forward to newness of political life."

In view of this comment, it is highly significant that, when Turkey awakened and desired to take a step towards newness of political life, she should have felt constrained to throw off both the Sultanate and the Caliphate.

[1] *The Times*, London, September 24, 1924, "Report of the Conference on Living Religions within the British Empire."

[2] Sir Thomas Arnold, *The Caliphate*, p. 107.

In a revised and enlarged third edition, published in 1907, Sell prefaces this comment by quoting from Cunningham's *Western Civilization* (vol. 2, p. 118):

"'The rule of the Caliphs was, in its ultimate basis, a theocracy; it would submit to no limitations, and the objects which it set before itself, in the conquest of the world to the Faith and the attainment of Paradise by fighting for it, gave no scope for a doctrine of the responsibility of civil rulers and of duty to the governed.'

"The Council of the Ulama in July, 1879, anent Khairu'd-dīn's proposed reform, which would have placed the Sultan in the position of a constitutional sovereign . . . declared [this] to be directly contrary to the law. 'The law of the Sheri does not authorize the Khalīfa to place beside him a power superior to his own. The Khalīfa ought to reign alone and govern as master. The *Vakils* [Ministers] should never possess any authority beyond that of representatives, always dependent and submissive.'"

Sell adds:

"This is one of the most important decisions of the jurists of Islam. . . . It proves as clearly as possible that, so long as the Sultan rules as Khalīfa, he must oppose any attempt to set up a constitutional government. There is absolutely no hope of real reform."

This was written over forty years ago, and it states clearly the fact that this institution of Islam—the Caliphate—is incompatible with the spirit of this age and with reform. No ruler can accept this office without either breaking away from the historic conception of the Caliphate or parting with all ideas of progress and reform.

Hence we come to the conclusion that the Caliphate has lost its place in Islam because it is incompatible with constitutional government and reform. At the same time, it is also true that, in losing the Caliphate, Islam has lost a certain sense of solidarity and moral unity, and this loss will make itself felt increasingly. The Caliphate lost its reason for existence, and yet its abolition takes from Islam a certain element of strength.

FERMENTS IN THE YOUTH OF ISLAM

BY

BASIL MATHEWS, M.A.,

Literature Secretary, World's Alliance of Young Men's Christian Associations

CHAPTER V

FERMENTS IN THE YOUTH OF ISLAM

WHILE watching a torrent of Egyptian youth from Al Azhar University racing and roaring along the streets of Cairo to demonstrate before Zaghloul Pasha, I wondered whether any generation has ever been swept from ancient footholds by such a tidal wave as is surging around and over the youth of the Moslem world to-day.

That almost untranslatable French phrase, *le choc des idées* (carrying the sense not only of shock but also of intellectual combat and of a cavalry-charge of fresh thought), conveys something of the force of the sweeping movement that is at this hour transforming the meaning of life among the new generation of all Islamic peoples. The fact that the waves break upon youth born and bred within the most rigid, resistant, and self-complete of the world's religious and social systems makes the turmoil all the more turbulent and dramatic.

If we examine somewhat closely the causes of the incident of that shouting procession of students (trivial as it was in itself), we shall be carried to the heart of many of the ideas that are changing life so radically for youth. We shall also see some of the concentric forces that are irresistibly driving those ideas home. Any thoroughgoing examination of those ideas and forces must seem inchoate and confused. For the whole movement of thought and feeling is as confused as it is profound.

The fury that carried those undergraduates of Al Azhar University along the streets was wrath against a Labour Prime Minister in England who had just declared his allegiance to the understanding between Britain and Egypt by which the former retained its control of the Sudan. The precise rights and wrongs of that political question do not touch us here. The fermenting idea, however, which surely is our concern, was a vehement nationalism issuing in an uncompromising and unqualified clamour for self-determination. The facts that this clamour by Egyptians for self-determination for the Sudanese (who had not asked for it) overleaped the banks of consistent nationalism and that the Egyptian Prime Minister sent the demonstrating students back to their studies of the Koran rather chastened, only serve to illustrate the occasionally dizzy and uncertain results of these whirling movements.

The Prime Minister, Zaghloul Pasha, was himself perhaps the most astounding product of *le choc des idées* that could be discovered in the post-war world. Within some hours of this student demonstration the writer had opportunity of unhurried talk with him. It took one's breath away to remember, first, that this man was the first Egyptian to rule in Egypt (the oldest home of civilization in the world) since the Persians overthrew the Pharaohs over forty centuries ago; that he was the first ruler whom the Egyptians ever elected by their own will to supreme power; and that he who now exercised this supreme rule had only a few months earlier been a rebel in exile from his own land. The concentration of nationalistic will and passion in Egypt that brought Zaghloul Pasha to power had in Egypt actually brought Moslem mulvis into Christian pulpits and Coptic priests into Moslem mosques, bridging the yawning religious chasm between Christianity and Islam in a way that would have been incredible a decade earlier. In a word, for the first time perhaps in Islamic history political union with infidels was stronger than Islamic exclusiveness.

Nationalism, then, with its practical policy of self-determination, is the outstanding primary idea fermenting in the mind of Moslem youth to-day. The idea of self-determination was the central architectonic principle of President Wilson's Fourteen Points and of the Allied war aims, and as such, it was shouted (to use Walt Whitman's phrase) "across the roof-tops of the world," in all the languages of Asia as well as of Europe. This fact is often forgotten when we hear the same principles come back under such war-cries as *Swaraj* (i.e. "India for the Indians") or "Egypt for the Egyptians." Certainly the West ought not to be surprised that nationalism everywhere in the Moslem world is the fiercest of the fermenting forces among youth. Whether you walk in Delhi or Angora, talk with young Baghdadi merchants, Arab camelmen, or Algerian senior schoolboys, listen to the young bloods of an Afghan fighting force or the newer journalists and poets of the Persian plateau, the voice and accent are different, but the idea is in essence one.

In the mind of Moslem youth the idea of the nation has irreparably torn into fragments the enormous, heavy tapestry of Pan-Islamism. Nothing parallel to this has happened in the mind of any generation of youth since the Reformation shattered the unity of the Holy Roman Empire. In the case of Islam, as in that of the Holy Roman Empire, a unity, semi-religious and semipolitical in nature, has been shattered by a vivid series of smaller, more intense national unities. These national unities are, as indeed they were in the case of the Holy Roman Empire, wholly political in character, yet they call out a passionate devotion essentially religious.

The shock that the action of young Turkish nationalists has inflicted on the older Moslem consciousness came home to the writer in an unforgettable scene in the home of the Sheikh of Nain. The writer had ridden across the Plain of Esdraelon from Nazareth on a quiet pilgrimage, following from place to place in the footsteps of Jesus Christ and attempting, in visualizing His life in those places, to find rest of spirit and mind from the almost torturing pressure of the terrific problems of the post-war world. There, on the slopes of Mount Moreh, lay the primitive homes of the people of Nain. At the top of the village was the sheikh's home.

Calling upon him, we found that the Sheikh of Endor had cantered across the corner of the plain to visit his friend. Surely, one felt, no problem of the great world of unrest could send even an eddy into this backwater of remote simplicity. But within a few minutes the two sheikhs, with an agitation and vehemence unusual in Arabs holding authority, were urging me to bring it about that the Prime Minister of Britain send to Mustafa Kemal at once an appeal and a reprimand, calling on him to cancel his horrible acts of destroying the Caliphate in Turkey and of exiling the ex-Caliph. "It is wicked, wicked," they reiterated. "He is a bad, bad man." If we can imagine a Mussolini in Italy abolishing the Papacy and exiling the Pope; and if we can conceive the horror and anger of, say, a devout Roman Catholic in South America at the act, we arrive at some parallel idea of the chasm that to-day lies between the old Arab and the new Turk generation responsible for abolishing the Caliphate.

Curiously enough, however, the same fire of nationalism and the same desire for self-determination were burning in the Sheikhs of Nain and Endor as in the young Turks, for they went on to urge upon me with equal vigour these questions: "When are the British going to give to the Arabs the self-government that they promised to them during the war?" and "Why do the British favour the new Jews from Europe in Palestine more than the Arabs who have been there for three thousand years?"

There we were, in that remote spot, with the problems of white domination, of Asiatic self-determination, and of race-antagonisms as between Asiatics (Arab *versus* Jew), breaking in upon us in wave after wave. As I looked round the faces of the dozen younger men who had assembled from the village for the talk, it was clear that for them these were the supremely absorbing issues that were fermenting in their minds. Many of them were certainly unable to read; but they were discussing issues identical with those that reverberate in the cloisters of Al Azhar University and appear in the leading articles of Moslem daily papers from Bengal to Morocco and from Thrace to Abyssinia.

That discussion at Nain leads us to another cause of the new ferment in the mind of young Islam. It is that the end of the war saw a great extension of white, and, in the technical sense, Christian authority over Moslem peoples, due largely to the carving of Syria, Palestine, Iraq, and Arabia out of the old Turkish Empire. This intensified a hundredfold the already critical debate of the Moslem mind as to Western civilization—the life of Christendom. The moral standards of Western life

—its diplomacy and commerce, its absorption in material prosperity and in the expansion of its own control over other peoples, above all its actions and motives during and after the war—are challenged and debated with a singularly sustained vehemence wherever the young Moslem is assembled with his friends. They see, for instance, in Western diplomacy, European and American, a far more intense interest in oil than in Armenians. They believe that all the acts of Western statesmanship are dictated by the desire for imperial expansion or for commercial gain, or for both.

Paradoxically enough, in odd contrast with their moral condemnation of Western Christendom (a condemnation, be it noted, of which the touchstone is the Christian standard and not the Moslem), we find a swiftly increasing appreciation and imitation of Western technical science applied to raising the standard of living. The sewing-machine and the telephone, the electric light and the automobile, the typewriter and the dictaphone, the rotary printing press, the street car, and the cinema, may seem to be mere mechanical adjustments affecting life in its externals. When, however, those forces push ever in upon a life that has been practically static for centuries they become means of distributing the leaven through the lump. The sewing-machine is everywhere to-day replacing the hand-sewing of four thousand years. The writer met a caravan of camels striding down that most ancient pass in the world, the Cilician Pass, and carrying in the footsteps of Alexander the Great, of Cicero, and of St. Paul sewing-machines to the mothers and daughters of Tarsus. This alone means that the minds of the girls are moved toward the West that produces these machines, and begin to work in new modes. Adolescent boys and girls, the latter with their mothers in the harem galleries, witness at the cinema pictures of Western romance in which men and women meet on an equal plane, and where women have the freedom of the wide world—a world in which the relations of the sexes are presented in terms of the choice of youth by youth on a plane of personal attachment and choice. Mary Pickford, Pola Negri, and Gloria Swanson, when appearing on the film before tens of thousands of women and girls in an environment of Moslem social conditions and among people of a relatively low standard of literacy, are likely to be more potent instruments of social revolution than a hundred books on the theory of the family. For the millions of young men who see these films also receive a fresh conception of womanhood in which higher and lower qualities are strangely blended.

The discussion thus stimulated in the mind of the younger generation is only one element in a fresh hunger for new ideas. All the forces acting upon the younger and more malleable minds, the shattering impact of the war, followed by this intense ferment of discussion on nationalism, self-determination, race conflicts, and Western civilization, have combined to stimulate a quite unprecedented inquisitiveness of mind in Moslem youth. If any single thing was true of the pre-war Moslem mind it was that it retained the strong, unbroken Islamic sense of self-adequacy—the feeling that Islam was able to say the last word on any issue. To-day that complacency is gone. Moslem youth is scanning the horizons for other truth. Literacy has increased; but reading has leaped forward in a still more startling way. In particular, the young effendi class—the more intelligent business and professional men and men of leisure—are absorbing great quantities of this reading.

An examination of the bookshops frequented by

Moslems in Beirût, Constantinople, Agra, and Cairo to-day as contrasted with, say, 1914, would reveal a perfectly amazing development.[1] The writer found in Beirût a score of bookshops in which a constant stream of French fiction, of translations into Arabic, of European and American literature, and of books written in Arabic on a basis of Western reading, was eagerly absorbed. Cairo has 217 printing presses from which the production averages one book, brochure, or pamphlet in Arabic each day of the year.

A considerable and increasing proportion of these books presents at either first- or second-hand a considerable amount of material of current Western applied science. The literature in many cases assumes the open-minded yet critical attitude of twentieth-century Western thought. Or it presents, through fiction, the pagan, superficial aspects of the structure of the social order of the life of Western Europe. Even the attacks on Christianity in this literature are less and less from a Moslem point of view and more from the point of view of the destructive type of higher criticism which (though already discredited by Western scholarship) is a useful tool in the hands of the modern Moslem critic of Christianity. What is only just beginning to be realized is that the very assumptions and methods on which that higher criticism is built are drastically destructive of the more rigid structure of Islam.

The widespread influence of these varied types of literature leads to an outlook that is not Islamic and is not Christian. It is difficult to sum up its characteristics in a generalization. But, as a whole, it may be described

[1] See, for the whole of this subject, *Christian Literature in Moslem Lands*, New York, 1923. An authoritative report based on thorough investigation.

as a careless, unsystematic agnosticism, cheerfully cynical in outlook on the world, with few enthusiasms save those accompanying the assertion of independence.

This should lead to the recognition of the fact that, to impregnate the mind of Moslem youth with secular Western ideas, to break down through Western commerce Moslem traditional habits of business, to replace peasant industries with a highly organized factory system, is not to move an inch nearer to Christianity. When at dawn the factory siren calling youth to the factory has drowned the voice of the *muezzin* calling to prayer, and when the factory chimney has replaced the minaret, we have not moved toward the Kingdom of God.

This increasingly secular point of view of the young Moslem shows itself in astonishing ways that nearly take away the breath of folk to whom the unity of the Islamic religion, with its own social and political order and the old idea of the brotherhood of Moslems of all races, have come to be axiomatic. The most striking development here, of course, is the view frankly taken by a considerable number of young Turks that the great historic mistake made by the Turkish people was in embracing Islam. Islam, they say, has kept them in a backwater for centuries, so far as secular progress is concerned. That, they feel, is largely the reason why, while Western civilization has leaped forward in wealth and power, Turkish strength has steadily diminished. So they tend to turn from Islamic to racial, political, and economic unity and independence for the hope of the future. The marvellous driving force that has inspired Mustafa Kemal, perhaps the one essential genius in the world's politics to-day, the young Turks who act with him, and the women, like his brilliant wife, who urge his policies forward, is the national conception sung by Mehmed Emin Bey:

> "I am a Turk;
> My language and race are great."

"My language and race," secular ideas, be it noted, and not "my religion," or "my social system."

This divorce of race from religion, indeed this elevation of race and nationality into a faith, this break between Turkey and the Pan-Islamic policy, and the leaning of the young Turk and the young Egyptian to Western ways of life and even to Western ways of achieving their own separation from Western governmental or financial domination, means the dawning of a new day.

It is not, as might conceivably be the case in the Islamic world, a new day simply for manhood. In other chapters of this book the life of its womanhood is set forth; and in some places, as will be seen, little that is new appears to be happening. When, however, Moslem ladies in automobiles join in with nationalist processions through the streets of Cairo and the women make speeches in the street at times when the procession is held up; and when in centres like Angora, Constantinople, and Cairo, Moslem women, inspired by a new ideal of family life familiar already in the West, are organized to work for a higher minimum age for marriage, equitable divorce laws, the abolition of polygamy, and reforms in the marriage laws, it is clear that a new day is beginning to dawn here also. The writer has before him a late Turkish newspaper in which the short story tells of the fight of a young Turk for the right to marry the girl of his own choice, one who loves him and whom he loves, against the fury of his father, a Turk of the old Moslem school, who insists on his marrying a wealthy girl under an arrangement made solely by the old man without reference to the son's wish or to the girl's own desire. This is typical of the new ferment regarding the relation of the sexes, and of the chasm between the older and the younger generations. It is also a symptom of the fact that in the Moslem world, as everywhere, the ferment of ideas is at once created by and reflected in the periodical press of the whole area. The immense expansion of newspaper publication in the Moslem world is one of the most significant features of this new ferment of ideas.

Young Islam is reading to-day well over 1,500 daily and weekly papers, of which just over 700 are in Arabic and as many as 350 are in Persian. The influence of these runs far beyond the literate population. If you go up the Nile Valley, for instance, among the fellaheen villages you will see in each village a reader who, with the youth as well as the older folk of the village around him listening eagerly, reads aloud from the Cairo paper the news and the comment of the day.

Cairo is, of course, both as the intellectual head of Islam and as the nerve-centre of forces playing between North Africa, Nearer Asia, and Europe, the place of greatest ferment. But an isolated city like Baghdad, cut off by desert from the play of the world's life, has a dozen newspapers and other periodicals that bring in the story of the movements of the earth.

Among these movements from outside, Bolshevism is the most active, but its successes have been sporadic and local. Through all this post-war period, all over the Moslem world, youth has been subject to the intermittent waves of Bolshevik influence. In the first years after the war a veritable tidal wave of Bolshevik propaganda poured across the Caucasus into the Arabic, the Persian, and the Afghan lands; into North India and the Dutch East Indies; down the Ægean and across Anatolia into Egypt and across North Africa. But after the first enthusiasms were exhausted, and youth had had time to compare promise with fulfilment and to assess the actual working of the machine as contrasted with the paper-scheme, a reaction set in.

The present reactions of young Islam to Bolshevism are significantly different in the various countries concerned. Oddly enough, the most vigorous effect of Bolshevik propaganda among youth in the Moslem world is in the Dutch East Indies. There the relatively primitive Moslems swing towards the most extreme phase of sovietization, that is, clan communism. This is natural, as it fits their tribal background far more easily than state communism in a national or racial sense.

In British India we find here and there fervid nuclei of Bolshevik feeling. But, in relation to the total mass of 70,000,000 Indian Moslems, the element is insignificant and shows little sign of growth in volume or influence.

The furious early advance of Bolshevism like a forest fire into Moslem Persia and on into Afghanistan burned itself out almost as swiftly as it ran. Disillusionment followed close upon the heels of enthusiasm. In Turkey the hard, bright flame of nationalism has replaced all other movements in the mind of youth. The liaison between Angora and Moscow is a diplomatic affair—having no relation to movements of the spirit.

This does not mean that Bolshevism has entirely ceased to work as a leaven in youth. It may even be that the Soviet idea of political working by occupational groups (which is as old as the silversmiths at Ephesus, led by Demetrius) may be severed absolutely from the Marxist class-war communism with which it is associated in Russia, and may be applied by the new generation to the working of political institutions in Asia and Egypt.

At this point we need to warn ourselves against a danger. The "sound and fury" of these violent tides of human youth may hide from our eyes quieter, yet deeper and, in the long run, often more powerful streams. For instance, a close observer who penetrates into the inner forces of the great centres of Moslem life to-day will find sturdy and effective young personalities about whom little is said and nothing written because they do nothing sensational. He will also discover personalities, many of them quite young men, who are quietly changing the outlook of the neighbourhood, in places remote from the vehement modern centres. Their influence modernizes without occidentalizing; it usually creates a more open and friendly attitude toward the non-Moslem world. It stands, as a rule, for a constructive and co-operative spirit.

In a considerable—even a predominant—number of cases of this kind that have come under the writer's own notice and that have been conveyed to him by correspondents and in conversation, it has proved that the power of those young men (and occasionally women) has come from the fact that they have been educated in one or other of the colleges and universities established from America or Britain, or from both—established not to make Western ideas dominant, but to train a new and a truly Oriental young leadership.

They are proof, on the one hand, against the "wild and whirling words" of the revolutionary, whether Bolshevik or anarchist, and, on the other hand, against the blind, arrogant reactionary.

The young man in question may be a dentist or a doctor, a journalist or a lawyer, a teacher or a servant of government. He has, however, in receiving his education for the position that he holds and the work that he does, received something else. He has absorbed —say at Robert College, Constantinople; the International College, Smyrna; St. Paul's College, Tarsus; the American University at Beirût; the English College at Jerusalem, or the American University at Cairo, or the College at Asyût—a spirit of good-will, a capacity for co-operation, a will to progress, a sense of equity and of straight-dealing—in a word, the team-spirit.

It may well be that, at the end of the day, we shall discover that the men who have in their lives this less explosive ferment, this leaven of human strength of character, this blend of progress with permanence, are the real constructive forces of the new world in Moslem lands.

The most recent communication that has come out of a very difficult part of the Moslem world from an experienced and authoritative source is unexpected evidence of the working of this type of leadership on the side of exploration in religious fellowship. The writer says:

> "Abundant evidence is at hand of the desire on the part of members of all faiths for tolerant and practical application of religious teachings to the common problems of every-day life, character, and social relationships."

In this connexion there has been formed in this centre a prayer-circle of the faiths, in which discussions were opened, for example, by a Greek Orthodox layman on "Purity"; by a Persian Moslem on "Religion and Business" (the interest compelling them to run to two sessions); by a Tartar Moslem on "Morality and Religion" (running to three sessions); by a Greek Orthodox layman on "Service," and by an Armenian Protestant on "Religion and Life."

It is, then, obvious to-day, wherever you touch the life of Islam, that a profound disintegration of the fibre of the old life is going on with a thoroughness and a speed that increases every day. Looking back over our argument, we see how this must be so. When we have discounted all the ineffective and evanescent papers, the play of the remaining thousand newspapers upon the life of young Islam, from Constantinople in the North to Khartoum in the South and from Morocco in the West to Bengal or Java in the East, is incessant and transforming. When it is viewed together with the steady and increasing flow of popular books, the incessant flicker of the cinema films in every city and town, the fresh movement of life due to the penetration of the cheap motor-car into areas where, a decade ago, the bullock- or horse-wagon was the way of transport, the new linking up of areas by which to-day the railway-train runs in a night across the desert from Egypt to Palestine and the motor-service dashes in less than twenty hours from Damascus to Baghdad on a route which the camel could barely traverse in a week, the total influence is seen to be enormous. In addition, we need to note that large numbers of Moslem young men now go every year from North Africa to earn their living in France. There are no precise figures available as to the number of Moslems in France. The magnitude of the invasion, however, can be assessed from the fact that of one of the most primitive of the tribes—the Kabyles—100,000 have migrated to France, attracted by wages four times higher than those paid in Algeria. It is said that 40,000 of this tribe (who are Berber in origin and whose forefathers were Christian before the Moslem conquest of

North Africa), are living in Paris, beside an unnumbered host of Arabs and Turks and other Moslems.

It is not for us to draw inferences in this chapter as to the attitude that should be taken by those outside the Moslem world who care, as so many of us do care intensely, for the future welfare of its peoples. What we may well note here, however, is that so widespread and so deep a ferment issuing in so manifold a transformation of outlook among Moslem youth calls for a complete revaluation and reconsideration of the attitude of Christendom to the peoples of Islam. Progress can come only through co-operation, and if the youths of Christendom and of the Moslem world, as well as those of Farther Asia, are to help each other, they must understand each other. To do that, they must put aside the accepted attitudes of past and even of present diplomacies. They must cease to think of the Moslem mind as closed against new ideas. Especially is it necessary that those who look out on the world attempting to see it with Christian eyes should revise radically the alinement of their thought both as to the resistant attitude of the peoples of the Islamic faith and as to the quality of the contacts which the civilization of peoples who call themselves by the name of Christ should have with those who have been born in this astonishing day of new possibility.

ISLAM AND THE RACE PROBLEM

BY

C. SNOUCK HURGRONJE, D.Sem.Litt.,

Professor, University of Leiden; Counsellor to the Dutch Ministry of the Colonies

CHAPTER VI

ISLAM AND THE RACE PROBLEM

THE map of the world, in its recently revised form, has suggested to many sharp-sighted politicians the question when and where the next war is to break out, and whether it may be possible to prevent a renewed effort to settle the political dissensions of mankind by a contest of brute force. Hardly anybody will consider such a violent solution as durable, but any other issue is despaired of by the masters of diagnosis. Among the innumerable obstacles to a peaceful settlement none seems to be considered so insurmountable as the race conflict. Even those who think it possible to arrive at a mutual understanding concerning questions raised by difference of religion, language, civilization, or nationality, describe the race problem as a chronic illness without remedy. The racial characteristics are the only ones a man cannot rid himself of from his birth until his death, and the increase of the population of our globe, together with the decrease of all distances, are unmistakable omens of an acute racial conflict in the immediate future.

The Science of Races is too young to supply us with a clear formulation of the problem. Anthropology, archæology, comparative linguistics, and ethnography contribute what they can to direct her steps, but her movement still lacks security. The criteria she uses are ever changing: there is not yet a map of races supported by the consensus of competent scholars. When treating race problems of a practical nature even specialists, for the sake of simplicity, recur to the popular colour criterion. Many of them hold out before us terrifying pictures of the dangers menacing the white man from yellow, brown, red, and black races—dangers so enormous and so acute that all other contrasts in the human world appear to be mere trifles in comparison with them.

The measures recommended by some talented writers in order to exorcise the approaching crisis are of a radical and violent type. Their starting-point is the absolute excellence of the white race, or at least of that part of it to which they themselves belong; so the preservation of that portion of mankind is to be secured even at the sacrifice of all the rest. We cannot help fancying that, if such a view of the question came to be adopted by the excellent race, a racial struggle would ensue, compared with which the recent war would be no more than a child's game. But, although we must absolutely reject all tactics of that sort as inhuman and impracticable, we fully agree with the authors alluded to in deeming the race problem even more baffling than that of the establishment of political harmony between the nations of Europe.

Under such circumstances one is inclined to search for illumination in history, for racial conflicts have demanded solution from time immemorial, and an inquiry into the attitude of such a large international community as that of Islam concerning the question cannot fail to teach us some lessons.

Now we must bear in mind that the proportion of the system of Islam to the preaching of Mohammed was that of the full-grown tree to the seed from which it sprang: its growth occupied about three centuries. The scribes who taught and wrote during that period in the central countries of Islam, Arabia, Egypt, Syria, Mesopotamia, and Persia, though formally only interpreters of the "revealed" law, actually performed legislative work. So deep was their conviction that they only enounced what Mohammed would have said if he had lived down to their time that they boldly attributed their conclusions to the Prophet by means of fictitious traditions. Whenever we want to know Mohammed's personal opinion, therefore, we should consult almost exclusively the Koran as containing his authentic oracles. The system of law, dogmatics, and mysticism which assumed to fix everlasting rules for the individual, family, economic, and political life of the Moslems, arrived at completion in its main features only in the tenth century of our era. This system always left much room for difference of opinion as to details. Besides that, there has always been a gulf between doctrine and life in Mohammedan society; but, nevertheless, the Moslems all over the world show a remarkable unity in most respects, and the importance of their unanimous acknowledgment of the all-embracing system as the ideal of their international community can hardly be overrated.

Mohammed did not intend to preach a new religion. As he conceived it, his religion was the only true one from Adam down to the Day of Resurrection, preached by all the apostles of God, his predecessors. Several times in the Koran [1] Allah is said to declare emphatically that He sent Mohammed to warn a people, to whom no warner had been sent before. Eleven times [2] the word "Arabic" occurs in the Koran: it is always to accentuate

[1] Koran: 28: 46; 32: 2; 34: 43; 36: 5.
[2] Koran: 12: 1; 13: 36–7; 16: 105; 20: 112; 26: 192–9; 39: 28–9; 41: 1–28, 44; 42: 5; 43: 1–3; 46: 11.

the fact that this revelation is given in clear Arabic, without tortuous wording, so as to cut off all ways of exculpation from the heathen Arabs, for whom it is destined. There is no contradiction between these explicit statements, that Mohammed, the Arabic prophet, is sent to the Arabs, and other verses of the Koran, which call Mohammed and his mission a blessing for "man," "mankind," or "the world." On the one hand, these words are not to be taken in their widest sense when used by a man who during all his life had to do with Arabs only and who left to his successors as an unachieved task the subjection of Arabia to his religion. On the other hand, the fact that he was charged with the conversion of Arabia did not diminish the more inclusive character of the religion revealed in his Koran, for his was but the Arabic edition of the Eternal Book of Allah, and, when Jews and Christians rejected his divine mission, then in his mind this could be attributed only to corruption of their sacred scriptures, which in their unaltered form could not but confirm what was revealed to him by the only God, whom all of them adored.*

The universalization of the Koran was the natural consequence of the attempt of the newly Islamized Arabs to conquer the world. The wonderful success of their raids was undoubtedly due to the powerful impulse given by Mohammed to the energy of the Arabs, united for the first time under his banner; but this effect was not foreseen by him, much less was it the execution of a plan projected by him.

In full accordance with the former revelations, adhered to by the "People of the Sacred Book" (Jews and Christians), the Koran teaches the descent of man from Adam and Eve (Hawwa), implying the equality of all men, notwithstanding the variety of characteristics of individuals or groups. The actual multiplicity of languages and colours is described in the Koran, next to the creation of heaven and earth, as one of the magnificent signs of Allah's wisdom,[1] without any attempt to explain its origin. The Prophet of Arabia had no reason to combat, from this point of view, the enmity prevailing between human races; his application of the principle of equality was directed against the tribal fanaticism which divided the Arabs amongst themselves. Mohammed did not succeed in eradicating the tribal feuds of the Arabs altogether, but he enforced the universal recognition of the principle of equality, and he united all those tribes, whose division seemed hopeless, in such a way that they were able to perform actions amazing to the whole world.

The pregnant expression of Mohammed's doctrine of the unity of mankind is found in a passage of the Koran[2] evidently directed against the mutual quarrelling, sarcasm, scorn, and disdain occurring in the community of Medina. The exhortation could therefore have in view only Arabs, including perhaps a few Jewish followers of Mohammed, African, Persian, or Greek slaves, and some foreigners who happened to be staying there.

"The faithful are brethren; therefore make peace between your brethren, and fear God. Haply ye may obtain mercy. O believers, let not men laugh men to scorn who haply may be better than themselves. . . . O men! We have created you from a male and a female, and divided you into groups [the Arab word *shu'ûb*, used here, may denote tribes, nations, races or any other division of men] and tribes, that ye might know [distinguish] one another. The noblest of you in the sight of God is the most God-fearing; verily God is knowing, cognizant."

[1] Koran: 30: 21.

[2] Koran: 49: 10–13.

The difference of men in outward appearance and qualities is explained here in a naïve, teleological way as serving to distinguish individuals and groups from each other. Piety is called the only criterion for the estimation of the value of man—his attitude, that is, towards God and towards his fellow-creatures.

This supreme criterion was maintained in the system of Islam. Thereon it based a division of mankind into three main groups, almost identical with the grouping of civilized, half-civilized, and savage men, current amongst ourselves. That the degree of civilization was made dependent on religion in the flourishing period of Islam (A.D. 650–1000) goes without saying; such was the prevailing opinion of the Middle Ages. The first class were the Moslems, who enjoy the full light of revelation; the second the People of the Scripture, like Jews and Christians, who, because of their rejecting the mission of Mohammed, walk in the dusk, and whom the Moslems may only by moral means try to raise to their own height; the third are the heathen, who are to be incorporated into human culture by persuasion or by force, and in the worst case to be made innocuous to the civilized world. The culture criterion was applied, even independently of religion, so as to adopt into the second class nations like the Parsis, who, although not having sacred books recognized by Mohammed, were assimilated to the People of the Scripture on account of their social development.

Moslem world-empire, extending in the eighth century from Morocco and Spain to the borders of China, having absorbed a great part of the ancient empires and still seeing large possibilities of extension, regarded in Southern and Eastern Europe as a constant menace, represented indeed in the early Middle Ages the acme of civilization.

At that time no more vanity was necessary for Islam to feel called upon to lead humanity to its destination than there is now for white men spontaneously to undertake such a mission.

As to the difference of races, the system not only stuck to the Koranic edict, but it accentuated its contents by fictitious sayings of Mohammed, in which not only Arabic tribes, but nations generally, are put on the same level. "The Arab does not excel the non-Arab, unless he is the more pious of the two," is one of these sayings, attributed to the Prophet.

It cannot surprise us that it proved necessary repeatedly to inculcate this principle, if we think of the amazing energy shown by the Arabs in the triumphal progress of Islam through the world. Once being united by religion and having come out of their sterile peninsula, those nomads proved able to govern the cultivated nations succumbing to their fresh vital force, to change the administration of the conquered States to such an extent as their interests as overlords required, and to induce millions to gather around their Prophet's banner.

The Arabic language did no less miraculous work than the Arabic armies. In almost all the central countries of Islam it entirely supplanted the vernacular; to this day foreigners are in the habit of calling Syrians, Mesopotamians, Egyptians, and North Africans by the name of Arabs. During the first century Islamizing a people meant Arabizing it. The wonderful language of the desert adapted itself with incredible suppleness as an instrument for treating the most intricate theological, jurisprudential, and philosophical problems, universal history, geography, ethnography, grammar, and poetry, with the utmost precision and grace.

Conversion to Islam in those days meant becoming an Arab. The new Moslems adopted Arabic names, they were annexed as "clients" to Arabic tribes, and they tried as soon as possible to pass for genuine Arabs. Moslem science and literature, indeed, owe more to non-Arabs than to Arabs. When we speak of the rich Arabic literature and of the prevalence of Arabic science in the Middle Ages, we mean the international Moslem science and culture which had Arabic for their means of expression. It was only Persian, and some time later Turkish, which succeeded in obtaining a place in the second rank behind Arabic, and even that only after swallowing a great part of the Arabic dictionary. Malays, Moslem Chinese, Indians, Persians, Turks, and Egyptians, all of them have accurately to recite the Arabic Koran at the beginning of their religious instruction; the divine service they have to perform five times daily is full of Arabic formulæ; on Fridays and on the two official yearly festivals they attend an Arabic sermon. Although fully authorized to pray in their mother-tongue, on formal occasions they prefer praying in Arabic. In the principal towns of all Islamic countries there are men of letters able to converse in Arabic with their colleagues at the other end of the world.

The language is only one of many manifestations of the uniformity of life and thought, shown by the Moslem league of nations. Their common attitude is by no means a copy of that of the Arabs at Mohammed's time, any more than the universal Arabic is identical with the language of the Koran and of the ancient poets; but all those expressions of human life show an Arabic stamp characteristic of the central countries of Islam during the three centuries of growth of the system. Two Moslems, from whatever countries, arrive at mutual understanding in every respect sooner than two members of any other international association.

The unrivalled success of the Islamized Arabs is a phenomenon too complex to be explained by one or two causes ; but one of the important factors was certainly Mohammed's strongly accentuated limitation of his message to the Arabs. As circumstances transformed that Arabic message into a universal one, Islam had already become so Arabic to the very marrow that non-Arabs had in some degree to change language and life to feel at home in it.

This historical development was not fitted to make Mohammed's principle of equality deeply penetrate the minds of the Arabs. The Moslem State of the first century has rightly been called the Arabian empire. The Arabic supremacy was felt by the subjected nations as a heavy oppression, particularly by those who had attained the highest degrees of culture before Islam. The artificial grafting of individuals, families, and even entire nations on the genealogical tree of the Arabs served as a palliative ; but its use was naturally limited, and not all converts were willing to be naturalized in such a way. At length they demanded acknowledgment of their equality or even of their superiority on account of their own merits. Most of the Arabs, in whom Islam had not even extinguished the pagan tribal particularism, were not at once ready to accept such demands. They poured out streams of ignominy on the heads of those barbarians who dared to take up places near or above them at Mohammed's table.

Reaction did not fail to appear, however. After the rise of the Abbasids (A.D. 750) Persians and Turks rose to the highest ranks. In the second and third centuries of Islam there flourished a rich literature of racial competition. The opponents of Arabic prerogatives, in their turn, were not content with equality: they proffered arguments from history, sacred and profane, to demonstrate the inferiority of the Arabic race. Almost all Islamized nations partook in this literary strife. The non-Arab protagonists took their starting-point from the verse of the Koran (49 : 13) wherein the division of mankind into *shu'ûb* is mentioned, and they applied this word specially to non-Arabian "races," and the other one to the "tribes" of Arabia. Therefore the non-Arabian race-fanatics acquired the name of *Shu-'ûbiyya*, "racists." The Arabians vehemently contradicted the arguments of the "barbarians." It is curious to see all the *finesse* of Arabic prose and poetry used on both sides in this sometimes amusing, in the bulk, distasteful, literature, and still more curious to observe that some of the literary "racists" are of pure Arabic descent, whereas some of the defenders of the Arabic prerogatives have no Arabic blood in their veins.

This literature of insult had its following, but this was not the people in general, and least of all the scribes. These honestly upheld the religious principle of equality, albeit with just recognition of the nobility of the Arabs, based on their merits for Islam. Thus the doctrine admitted of no caliphs except those from Mohammed's tribe, the Koraish; this rule was only the theory of what was practised for six centuries, down to the fall of the Abbasids. Then, in the opinion of many interpreters of the law, the marriage of an Arabic woman with a non-Arab, of a woman of Koraish with a non-Koraishite, of a female descendant of Mohammed with a man of another family, is deemed to be a *mésalliance*, to be permitted only for exceptional reasons. But even these modest rules of nobility have never acquired the consensus needed to give them dogmatic force. The opinions on the *connubium* prevailing in different countries were in a large measure dependent on social circumstances. Since the Ottoman dynasty had obtained actual supremacy in the sixteenth century, the scribes as well as the mass of the people gave up their opposition against Caliphs of non-Koraishite or even of non-Arab extraction. Pamphlets have been written by descendants of Mohammed to defend the Turkish Caliphate, arguing that the value of man is determined by merit, not by birth.

Practically in the Moslem world neither birth nor colour has prevented men from reaching the highest positions. Persians, Turks, Mongolians, Berbers, and Negroes have occupied the most important state offices and acquired the greatest fame in scholarship. Islam offered a chance to all races, and all of them have availed themselves of it in the measure of their talents. In the mosque of Mecca during the lecturing hours students and professors with all gradations of complexion: coal-black, green (as the Arabs call a somewhat brighter nuance), brown, yellow, and white, may be seen fraternally gathering, and the same variety is shown by the citizens of the Holy City, sometimes even by the members of one family. The old propensity to mutual scorn, combated in the "race-verse" of the Koran, has not yet entirely died out, but the principle of equality is respected in practice as well as in theory. Moslem newspapers, when discussing the actual policy of European States with regard to Oriental countries, often take a pride in stating that political injustice, as represented by mandates, protectorates, or colonies, where "natives" are practically enslaved by their oppressors on account of their colour and race, have never found support in Moslem doctrine nor a place in Moslem history.

The attempt of Islam to unite all mankind under one banner has not been successful. The religious belief which underlies this form of civilization was unacceptable to a vast number, and the legal system, destined to regulate the whole of human life by unchangeable rules, showed too clearly the traces of the place where and the time when it took its origin, to become the universal law. Besides this, the early division of the theocratic Caliphate into numberless despotic kingdoms, making war upon one another in spite of their Moslem doctrine, stood in the way of the continuation of the union. But the race-paragraph of the system of Islam contributed much to the initial success and redounds to the perpetual honour of this international community.

Mohammed did not claim originality for his religion, and Christianity, to which he so often referred, had already removed the difference between Greek and Jew, Barbarian and Scythian, bond and free.[1] But the league of nations founded on the basis of Mohammed's religion took the principle of equality of all human races so seriously as to put to shame other communities. White men's churches kept closed to coloured Christians, a missionary boycotted on account of his marrying a negro woman, and the habit of lynching, are often quoted by Moslems as instances of the backwardness of Christian society. The ideal of a league of human races has indeed been approached by the Moslem community more nearly than by any other.

[1] Colossians, 3: 11.

THE REACTION OF MOSLEM INDIA TO WESTERN ISLAM

BY THE REV.

MURRAY T. TITUS, B.L.,

District Superintendent, Methodist Episcopal Church, North India Conference, Moradabad District

CHAPTER VII

THE REACTION OF MOSLEM INDIA TO WESTERN ISLAM

MOSLEM India, numbering 68,735,233 [1] persons, forms the largest single group of Moslems in the world. Dr. Zwemer points out, " The province of Bengal has a larger Moslem population than all Arabia, Egypt, and Persia together. The number of Mohammedans in the Punjab alone is nearly as large as in Egypt." Not only is it the largest group in the world, but it is also probably the most mixed group—mixed as to racial origin and sects. Here are the Arab, Persian, Turanian, and Mongol all blended with the Indo-Aryan and Dravidian strains in a community which comprises most of the various shades of theological opinion found in the Moslem world. The Sunni, the Shii, the Wahhabi, the Ismaili, the modern Mu'tazili, and the heterodox Ahmadi are all here. But, in spite of these wide variations, there is present that element of cultural coherence, characteristic of the Moslem world as a whole, and an essential community of thought and point of view that on occasion is able to speak with authority through its various representative bodies, like the All-India Moslem League, the Central Khilafat Committee, and the All-India Educational Conference, and the *Jamiat-ul-Ulama-i-Hind.*

Without question Moslem India very keenly feels her

[1] Census of 1921.

burden of responsibility for the welfare of the world of Islam. Geographically she knows herself to be the centre of that world, and, because of her contact with the deep spiritual currents so natural to the life of India, she is second to none in her zeal for the Faith. As *The Muslim Herald*, Madras, puts it:

"Situated as India is between the Far Eastern Muslims and the Muslims of the Near East, holding easy intercourse with Arabia, Persia, and Egypt on the one hand, and the Far Eastern countries on the other, it is obviously the duty of Islamic India to take the lead in advancing Islamic learning."

It is with this same conviction of responsibility for the Faith that the Ahmadi missionary goes to the ends of the earth, and the Ali brothers urge the claims of the Caliphate.

Moslem India to-day, therefore, is sensitive to all that takes place in the whole Moslem world: trouble on the Iraq frontier over the possession of Mosul oil, Egyptian disappointment over the Sudan, the possibility of foreign intervention in the settlement of the Hejaz affairs, the triumph of the Riff armies, dissatisfaction of Palestinian Arabs with the Mandate, are all broadcast to the ends of India from day to day by the ever-growing Moslem vernacular and English press, with the result that even in the villages, to a large extent, Moslems are alive to what is happening to their brothers in various parts of the world, and are prepared to show their sympathy

The attitude of the Indian Moslem is frankly Pan-Islamic. Since the days of the well-known promoter of modern Pan-Islamism, Sultan Abdul Hamid II, India has ever shown a warm response to the extension of the power and prestige of the Caliphate over the Moslem nations of the world. Even during the Great War, when

Moslem Indians were fighting the armies of the Caliph, they were ever and anon seeking to justify their seemingly inconsistent action with the argument that, because they were helping the victorious Allies, they would be able on that account to help secure better peace terms for the Caliph and the Moslem world, as a reward for their loyalty. In fact, as soon as the war was over, the organization known as the Central Khilafat Committee, with headquarters in Bombay, was started, and large sums of money were secured to press for the restoration of Turkey to sovereignty, and to free Arabia, Syria, Palestine, and Mesopotamia from foreign control, all of which centred around the prime object of the preservation of the Caliphate. A delegation was sent to London and to the Peace Conference at Paris, an extensive propaganda was kept up in both India and England, and great was the disappointment at the terms given to Turkey by the ineffective Treaty of Sèvres. The deep interest of Indian Moslems in the preservation of the Caliphate is clearly summed up in a paragraph of an address presented by the Indian Khilafat Deputation to the Viceroy, Lord Chelmsford, at Delhi on January 19, 1920, which reads:

"The preservation of the Khilafat, as a temporal no less than a spiritual institution, is not so much a part of their [the Indian Moslems'] faith, as the very essence thereof; and no analogies from other creeds that tolerate the lacerating and devitalizing distinction between things spiritual and things temporal, between the Church and the State, can serve any purpose save that of clouding and befogging the clearest of issues. Temporal power is of the very essence of the institution of the Khilafat, and Mussulmans can never agree to any change in its character or to the dismemberment of its Empire." [1]

[1] *The Indian Khilafat Delegation Publications*, No. 1, p. 6.

But not only were the Sunni Moslems interested in the preservation of the Caliphate. When it became known that Turkey was herself making plans for the abolition of her connexion with it, two of the leading Shii Moslems of India, Sir Syed Ameer Ali and H.H. the Agha Khan, submitted their famous letters of protest to Turkey, and did all that could be done to show how seriously the religious feelings and prestige of the whole Moslem world would be injured by such a revolutionary step.

Then, of a sudden, came the message announcing the banishment of the Caliph and the abolition of the Turkish Caliphate. Reuter's message, however, could not be accepted as authentic by the distracted Moslem leaders. Cables were sent in feverish haste both to the banished Caliph and to Mustafa Kemal Pasha asking for authoritative information. With what distress and consternation the whole Moslem community was affected may be gathered from a telegraphic reply to a message from Mustafa Kemal himself in which he had verified the information that had reached India. This reply,[1] dated March 11, 1924, sent jointly by the Central Khilafat Committee and the *Jamiat-ul-Ulama-i-Hind*, reads as follows:

"The news so far received from Turkey regarding the abolition of the Khilafat has caused deep distress and consternation among young Indian Moslem brethren. The Mussulmans of India are not partisans favouring the retention of the Khilafat as the monopoly of any particular family or the perquisite of any individual. They entirely dissociate themselves from any desire to intervene in the national affairs of their Turkish brethren, who are quite competent to deal with them. But they are deeply concerned with the question of the retention or

[1] Associated Press message, published in *The Pioneer*, March 16, 1924.

the abolition of the office of Khalīfa itself, which is the very essence of the Islamic faith, and was designed to maintain and conserve the ideal of Islamic brotherhood through a definite and well-established institution. It is true that when, in the hour of his need, the Khalīfa called upon the members of the world-wide Moslem brotherhood to assist him and his nation, the response of the Moslem world was very poor; but it is equally true that this was for want of a properly and effectively functioning Khilafat organization. As a consequence of this not only Turkey, but the entire Moslem world, suffered grievously. But we learned our lesson in the terrible school of suffering, and awakened at last to a proper sense of the need of a reformed and renovated Khilafat.

"Indian Mussulmans expected that Your Highness, after achieving such a well-earned and signal success, would revive Islam's fundamental institution of the Khilafat, purging it of such excrescences as were not required by the Shariat, but were the growth of personal greed and dynastic ambitions, and re-establish it on a firm democratic basis. But the entire abolition of the institution of the Khilafat, just at the time when the Moslem world was showing unmistakable signs of an awakening, destroys all our expectations. We believe that the Khilafat and the Republic are not incompatible with each other, and that the continuation of the Khilafat after its reform will not only not be detrimental to the internal unity of Turkey, but will also be a source of strength to the Turkish nation in its relations abroad.

"We would, in any case, implore Your Highness and the National Assembly not to belittle the importance and advantages of the continuation of the institution of the Khilafat, and its re-establishment on true democratic foundations. The existence of the Khilafat does not, of course, depend upon the good-will of any particular Moslem nation or state, but Turkey, as the last great Moslem Power, is best fitted to remain associated with the Khilafat, and this connexion, we fervently trust, will benefit not only the rest of the Islamic world, but Turkey herself. If the National Assembly's decision abolishes the institution of the Khilafat itself, it is bound to cause a diversion and dissipation of energy and strength in the Moslem world, and would open the door to the mischievous ambitions of hosts of undeserving claimants. Seventy million Indian Mussulmans appeal to their brethren of the National Assembly to reconsider their decision, so far as it relates to the abolition of the office of the Khalīfa itself, and give an opportunity to the delegation of Indian Mussulmans, which desire to visit Angora, to make fuller representation on the subject."

This was the beginning of India's rude awakening, and ever since March 1924, Indian Moslems have been seeking for the proper mental adjustment that will enable them fully to understand what it is that Turkey has done to herself and to the Islamic world.

The more liberal-minded are inclined to agree that Kemal Pasha was right in removing the Caliphate from Turkey. They are quite prepared to admit that the Caliphate, as it has been constituted in the past, was inconsistent with the development of a modern republican form of government. Sir Muhammad Iqbal, the well-known philosopher-poet of India, defends the action of the Grand National Assembly in a scholarly essay on *Ijtihad*. In discussing the point whether it is contrary to the spirit of Islam to vest the Caliphate in an elected Assembly, rather than in a single person, this learned writer says:

"The religious doctors of Islam, in Egypt and India, as far as I know, have not yet expressed themselves on this point. Personally, I believe the Turkish view is perfectly sound. . . . The republican form of government is not only thoroughly consistent with the spirit of Islam, but has also become a necessity in view of the new forces that are set free in the world of Islam."[1]

Sir Muhammad and this school of political thinkers agree that the Caliphate, or Universal Imamate, has failed in practice, and that now the time has come for every nation of the Islamic world "to sink into her own deeper self, temporarily focus her vision on herself alone, until all are strong and powerful to form a living family of republics." Then he conceives that in due time the old Caliphate idea, born of Arabian imperialism of the earlier centuries of Islam, will be displaced by a League of Moslem Nations, "which recognizes artificial boundaries and racial distinctions for facility of reference only, and not for restricting the social horizon of its members."

The question that immediately began to be asked in India after the banishment of the Caliph, Abdul Mejid Khan, was, "Who is Caliph?" The first inclination was to hold to the view that the deposed Caliph was still Caliph *de jure*, and should be recognized as such, since he had been deposed, not by the world of Islam, but by only one part thereof. Messages expressing warm affection and allegiance were immediately sent to him, and in due course comfortable life-pensions totalling Rs. 6,000 *per mensem*, were granted him by the Nizam of Hyderabad and the Begum of Bhopal. It is now recognized, of course, that there is no Caliph, and accordingly reference to him is omitted from the Friday sermon.

The assumption of the title and office of Caliph by King Hussein of the Hejaz was met in India by prompt repudiation. The reasons for complete dislike of this

[1] The above and the following quotations from Sir M. Iqbal are from an unpublished essay on *Ijtihad* which he very kindly permitted the writer to use.

Hashimite family which are set forth in the following editorial from *The Muslim Herald*, Madras,[1] are alleged to be their dependence on British bayonets and gold for support of their pet schemes. The editor of the *Herald* says:

"The affairs in the Holy Land [Arabia] to-day demonstrate how unreal the Treaty Settlements in this portion of the world have proved themselves to be. These settlements aimed, it need hardly be said, at (1) the unification of Arabia into a strong confederation; . . . (2) the constitution of a strong and, nominally, at any rate, independent Muslim State such as would satisfy the Muslim sentiment that the Holy Places should not be under the protection of any but purely independent Muslim States. Neither of these objects, however, has the treaty fully secured. The Arab States are at present as far from developing into a strong, unified confederation under the auspices of the Sheriffians as they were ever before. Kingdoms are not made strong and independent at the mere wish of a foreign potentate. We see, therefore, the spectacle of all the three Sheriffian States—the Hejaz, Iraq, Trans-Jordania—declining into nominal dependencies at the mercy of an alien power for their very existence. The Trans-Jordanian administration has been dubbed incapable and corrupt; the Iraquian is weak, and, at any rate, there is no contentment in the land; while, in the Hejaz, Hussein's rule and his treatment of all the Hajis especially stink in the nostrils of the world at large. The Sheriffians' sanction for their rule is the British bayonet without which behind their back they would have been nowhere now, and this very support brings down upon them the execration of their people, and makes their positions as insecure as that of hated sovereigns can be with a people whose loyalty is dependent on the sword of a dominating ally."

[1] *The Muslim Herald*, September 20, 1924, p. 7.

Since the " traitor " Hussein is so cordially disliked by all persuasions of Indian Moslems, it is not surprising that the attack of Ibn Saud, King of Nejd, on the Hejaz was welcomed rather than deplored. True it was that bloodshed in the vicinity of the Holy Places was regarded with regret, but, when it became apparent that Ibn Saud was coming off victorious, feelings of regret were drowned in feelings of joy over the abdication of Hussein, and the King of Nejd was proclaimed the saviour of the Holy Places of Islam.

As for the future of the Caliphate, Indian Moslems are living in high hopes. Keen interest is being taken in the proposed Moslem world conference to discuss the future of the Caliphate, and to elect a Caliph. While King Fuad of Egypt, the Amir of Afghanistan, and Ibn Saud of Nejd are being mentioned as possibilities, yet a Turkish Caliph is still the desire of many Indian Moslems. As stated by the *Muslim Outlook*, Lahore, recently, " the chief reason why some Indian Muslims would like to see the Caliphate restored to Turkey is because the Turks are independent and able to defend their independence."

Before we go further in our study of the reaction of Moslem India to specific developments in Turkey and elsewhere, it is necessary to notice the Indian Moslem attitude toward the whole general break-up of old ideas and customs that have for long held sway, and have been considered indispensable to Islam. In other words, what is India's attitude toward the modern view of *Ijtihad*, or the " exercise of independent thought in Mohammedan Law," that is evidently prevalent among the powerful leaders of Turkey? Perhaps, as Sir Muhammad Iqbal suggests, " it is a bit too early to judge the reaction " in India, but at the same time, in his essay on *Ijtihad* above referred to, he makes some very pertinent remarks which are worth considering:

"We find that the idea of *Ijtihad*, reinforced and broadened by modern philosophical ideas, has long been working in the religious and political thought of the Turkish nation. We in India have practically no knowledge of the intellectual life of modern Turkey. Nobody in India knows, for instance, that Halim Sabit has developed a new theory of Muhammadan Law grounded on modern sociological concepts. The series of articles in which he developed this theory was, as far as I know, never translated in India. . . . The little knowledge that I possess of the thought-currents of Turkey is derived from German sources. . . . If the renaissance of Islam is a fact, and I believe it is a fact, we too, one day, like the Turks, will have to re-evaluate our intellectual inheritance, and, if we cannot make any original contribution to the general thought of Islam, we may, by healthy conservative criticism, serve, at least, as a check on the rapid movement of Turkish Liberalism."

The authority above mentioned, following the same line of thought as that developed by Moulaví Cherágh Ali, Sir Syed Ahmad Khan, and Sir Syed Ameer Ali, considers:

". . . That with the return of new life the inner catholicity of the spirit of Islam is bound to work itself out, in spite of the rigorous conservatism of our doctors. And I have no doubt that a deeper study of the enormous legal literature of Islam is sure to rid the modern critic of the superficial opinion that the Law of Islam is stationary and incapable of development. Unfortunately, the conservative Moslem public of this country is not quite ready for a critical discussion of *Fiqh* [canon law], which, if undertaken, is likely to displease most people and raise sectarian controversies."

This Indian advocate of liberal ideas declares further that the founders of the four schools of Moslem jurisprudence never did claim finality for their reasonings and interpretations. Therefore, he argues:

"The claim of the present generation of Moslem liberals to reinterpret the foundational legal principles in the light of their own experience and the altered conditions of modern life is perfectly justified."

On the question of the separation of Church and State, as carried out in Turkey, our Indian authorities are, generally speaking, true to the conservative tendency that Sir Muhammad Iqbal indicates in dealing with the whole subject of reform:

"There are at present in Turkey, two main lines of thought represented by (1) the Nationalist Party, and (2) the Party of Religious Reform. The point of supreme interest with the Nationalist Party is, above all, the State, and not religion. . . . They, therefore, reject old ideas about the function of State and religion and accentuate the separation of Church and State. . . . I think it is a mistake to suppose that the idea of State is more dominant and rules all other ideas embodied in the system of Islam. In Islam the spiritual and the temporal are not two distinct domains. . . . In Islam it is the same reality which appears as Church looked at from one point of view and State from another. . . . Islam is a single, unanalysable reality, which is one or the other as your point of view varies. The truth is that the Turkish Nationalists assimilated the idea of the separation of Church and State from the history of European political ideas, without understanding the nature of primitive Christianity which largely determined its evolution in Europe, where State and Church confronted each other as distinct powers with interminable boundary disputes between them. Such a thing could never happen in

Islam, for Islam was from the very beginning a civil society, having received from the Koran a set of simple legal principles which, as experience subsequently proved, carried great potentialities of expansion and development by interpretation. The nationalist theory of the State, therefore, is misleading, and open to grave objections from the Islamic standpoint, inasmuch as it suggests a duality between Church and State which does not exist in Islam."

The Nationalist Movement in Egypt and Turkey has begotten a marked response in India. But this interest seems to centre in the possible power that will be added to the world of Islam from the strengthening of the units in that world, rather than in the manner of actual national development itself. It is well known in India that the Turks are the leading nationalists of the world of Islam, and that they are even inclined to place love of country above love of religion. Maulana Muhammad Ali, the great nationalist and Khilafat worker in India, in an address in the Jama Masjid, Aligarh, immediately following the announcement of the banishment of the Caliph, expressed his disappointment in the Turkish attitude toward Islam when he said :

"During my stay in Paris had I not reason to weep when one of our best coadjutors, who was a Turk, had said to me at my own dinner-table, in all seriousness, that the Turks would have fared better if they had never embraced Islam ?" [1]

In India the attitude runs to the other extreme and it is common to hear the expression, "I am a Moslem first, and an Indian afterwards."

It is doubtful if many Indian Moslems appreciate at

[1] Associated Press Message of March 8, 1924.

all the strong national feelings of the Turks. Dr. Iqbal thinks that the supplanting of Arabic by Turkish in religious exercises is sure to be condemned by most Moslems in India, and the following sentiments expressed by Zia, the poet of Turkish Nationalism, as quoted by him, would be resented rather than applauded by his co-religionists in India :

> "The land where the call to prayer resounds in Turkish ; where those who pray understand the meaning of their religion ; the land where the Koran is learnt in Turkish ; where every man, big or small, knows full well the command of God ; O son of Turkey ! that land is thy fatherland ! "

In India Arabic still prevails as the language of religion, and any move to displace it with Urdu or any other vernacular would, as indicated above, be met with the highest disfavour, for this would savour of disloyalty to the universal Faith.

The Indian Moslem's strongest reaction to the nationalist movements in other parts of the Moslem world is to be found in the movement for the development of a strong communal spirit. In fact, the present indications are that the whole of the Moslem population in India is opposed to any further modification or extension of the Reforms Act in India granting a larger measure of Home Rule, unless and until the interests and position of the Moslem community are more carefully safeguarded than they are at present. The present position seems to be to stress the development of a strong community in league with the world forces of Islam above the development of a programme of Indian Nationalists. To this end, it is apparent, the present activity of the various organizations is dedicated. The Khilafat Committee is interested chiefly in (1) the coming Islamic World Congress that is to elect a Caliph and provide for the protection of the Holy Places in Arabia; (2) the removal of all foreign and non-Moslem influence from Arabia, Syria, Palestine, and Mesopotamia (a group of countries commonly called the Jazirat-ul-Arab); and (3) *tanzim*, or the organization and improvement of the Moslem community in India.

Much emphasis is being laid on the so-called National Islamic schools, chief of which is the *Jamia Millia Islamia*, or the National Moslem University of Aligarh. In these the aim, according to Maulana Muhammad Ali, the founder of the *Jamia*, is to turn out not only young men of culture according to modern standards, but also true Mussulmans imbued with the spirit of Islam, and possessing enough knowledge of their religion to be able to stand by themselves as sufficiently independent units in the army of Islam's missionaries.[1]

Therefore in this programme of "National" education an intimate knowledge of the Koran is regarded as a necessity, likewise a good knowledge of Arabic and the usual theological studies, including the commentaries on the Koran, the Traditions, Canon Law, Systematic Theology, and the History of Islam. In this connexion there is no development that is more truly national, while being at the same time Moslem, than the establishment of the Osmania University in Hyderabad, Deccan, where degree and post-graduate courses are taught entirely in Urdu, English being taught only as a second language. The Moslem University of Aligarh, the foundations of which were laid by Sir Syed Ahmad Khan in his Mohammedan Anglo-Oriental College, is still the

[1] Muhammad Ali, *A Scheme of Studies for National Muslim Educational Institutions in India*, pp. 4, 5.

premier Moslem educational institution of the country and may be said to derive no small share of its present-day interest in the progress and advancement of the Moslem community in India from the example being set by Turkey and Egypt.

The emancipation of woman, as it is being carried out in the lands of the Near East, is viewed with mixed feelings in India. There are many advocates of the larger freedom among Moslems, and the tendency is in some quarters for greater freedom to prevail. But it is significant of the clinging conservatism of India that, at the Bombay Provincial Moslem Ladies' Conference, held at Poona recently—

> "While the ladies decided on going in for enlightenment by resort to modern education, they did not lose sight of the fact that they had special functions to perform as distinct from those which the opposite sex were called on to do. The Poona ladies pressed for reform on cautious lines. They did not despise the *purdah* [veil]. Indeed, their chief function there was to show how enlightenment was not incompatible with the *purdah*, and how they could learn the most effectively to discharge the duties they had been called on by their Maker to undertake, without throwing themselves into the modern feminist movements in Europe and America. It was their ambition to be better mothers and wives [rather] than indifferent clerks or lawyers or statesmen." [1]

None the less, there are Moslem women who are fearlessly pushing forward the crusade to secure equal rights for themselves and their sisters, so that the day will come when Moslem women in India will be as free as they give promise of being in Turkey and Egypt. In

[1] *The Muslim Herald*, Madras, October 25, 1924, p. 6.

the matter of divorce, while in Turkey there is now equality for men and women before the law, yet in India, says Dr. Iqbal:

> "A Muslim woman who wishes to get rid of an undesirable husband cannot do so without becoming an apostate. Nothing could be more distant from the aims of a missionary religion."

Therefore, in his opinion, a radical revision of the Mohammedan law of divorce is badly needed.

From the foregoing discussion it is clear that Moslem India is at the cross-roads. She realizes that her life is vitally connected with the world-currents of Islam, and she has the conviction that somehow she is the special custodian of the faith of the fathers. Her liberal leaders are striving to be progressive, but not too progressive. The masses are, for the most part, still led by the orthodox mulvis, and reflect the mind of their leaders in strong aversion to radical reform and in the strictest adherence to all that is Moslem, so far as they understand the term. Moslem India is awake. The two things that have aroused her from her lethargy in the last half-century are unmistakably the revolutionary modern education movement, inaugurated by Sir Syed Ahmad Khan, coupled with the unfading vision of a federated world of Islam. Having the courage of their convictions, Indian Moslems are not content to sit in silence and let the world go by. They are ever ready to take part in international Islamic affairs of moment, and, in the words of William Lloyd Garrison, they are in earnest, they will not equivocate, they will not retreat a single inch, and they will be heard!

THE PRESENT ATTITUDE OF CHRISTENDOM TO THE PEOPLES OF THE MOSLEM WORLD

BY THE REV.

JOHN E. MERRILL, Ph.D.,

Principal, Boys' High School, Aleppo; formerly President, Central Turkey College, Aintab

CHAPTER VIII

THE PRESENT ATTITUDE OF CHRISTENDOM TO THE PEOPLES OF THE MOSLEM WORLD

THERE is throughout Christendom a growing interest in the peoples of foreign countries. Of its extent in America the success of publications like *The National Geographic Magazine* and *Asia* is an index, while in Europe it is of much longer standing. There is likewise in Christendom a growing readiness to view the customs and convictions of other peoples with toleration, and even with sympathy. Yet, in the background, there exist deep-rooted prejudices, and at any time a wave of nationalism may accentuate racial incompatibilities and sow afresh the seeds of distrust and ill-will.

Each of these tendencies has shared in forming the sentiment of Christendom regarding the Moslem peoples. During the war, and especially since the armistice, the attention of Christendom has been focussed upon Islam as never since those days when, in the sixteenth century, Europe was threatened with invasion by the Turks. The attitude toward the Moslem world which is to result from this new interest is a matter of prime concern to the future Christian Church.

For, in the first place, this attitude will determine the future action of the peoples of Christendom toward the peoples of Islam. A Christendom which sees in Islam a menace will prepare for self-defence. A Christendom which sees in Islam an enemy will plan how that enemy may be destroyed. A Christendom which sees in Islam a rival faith will gird itself to compete for world supremacy. Only a Christendom which sees in the Moslem peoples brothers and sisters in need of help will have the will to help them. The past is full of proofs that fear, hatred, and rivalry bear only bitter and costly fruits, demonstrating their own futility. Only in the path of helpfulness is there hopefulness, and we help sincerely only those whom we sincerely love.

This attitude will determine, also, the future disposition of the Moslem people toward Christendom. For, in a real degree, they may be expected to act toward us as we have acted toward them. It is common knowledge that Moslems everywhere are in reaction now against the imperialistic diplomacy of Christendom. Christendom is reaping that which it has sown.

Educated Moslems in India, in Egypt, in Syria, and in Turkey are reading books and articles written by Christians about Islam. Often translations from these publications appear in Moslem papers in the vernacular. The tenor of a single article or of a single citation may be regarded by Moslems as characteristic of the attitude of Christendom in general, with corresponding effect upon Moslem sentiment.

Further, there are in Christian countries many Moslem immigrants. They share the freedom of these countries, but they suffer from their inequalities, and they realize that often the best of these countries is withheld from them. Their hearts fill with resentment and bitterness at the exclusiveness and the unfriendly spirit manifested toward them. "We have nothing to say against the American Government," said a Moslem in conversation not long ago, "but we have many things to say against the American people." No doubt ignorance of the language of the country and difference in religion have contributed greatly to the peculiar isolation of the Moslems in America. Without doubt, also, many Christians could be found ready to extend a sincere and hearty welcome, if the need were understood and the necessary opportunity provided. Yet it remains true that the Ahmadiya Movement, with its missionary centre for America in Chicago, is able to conduct among the negro population of that city an effective propaganda for Islam, based upon the racial inequality which characterizes Christian civilization, as compared with the brotherhood of Islam which knows no colour line. When Moslem immigrants write of their experiences to their relatives and friends at home, the report of this prevalent unsympathetic attitude must have great weight in forming an opinion unfavourable to Christianity.

In the Moslem countries, likewise, there have been for centuries many representatives of Christianity, adherents of the ancient Churches and representatives of Western Christendom. The Moslems have not failed to study with care the spirit of these Christians. There have been happy instances in which Moslems have been attracted. Said a Moslem not long since to a native Christian in Turkey, "If all the Christians had been like you, these events [1915–19] would not have happened." It was a Moslem, attracted by the Gospel, who said years ago, "If the Christians lived the Gospel, we all should be Christians within fifty years." Christians often are not aware of the influence exerted silently by their lives. Only a crisis may reveal it. But wherever Christians, of whatever race, show themselves to the Moslems as grasping, unreliable, and insincere, they can but expect the Moslems to turn against Christianity.

It may be added that the attitude of Christendom toward Islam furnishes to Christendom an involuntary revelation of its own spirit. Only the Christ-like heart is perfectly Christian. The Moslem problem provides an automatic test of the conformity of Christendom to the mind of Christ.

The attitude of Christendom as a whole to the Moslem peoples is made up of the sentiment and attitude of a multitude of groups in Christendom. As typical, the attitude of diplomacy and commerce, the attitude of public opinion in general, and the missionary attitude of the Churches may be selected. Study of this composite attitude discloses the portentous fact that the attitude of Christian peoples to the peoples of Islam rests chiefly upon non-religious considerations, and that it is motivated by purposes which are not truly Christian.

The attitude of diplomatic and commercial Christendom toward the peoples of Islam is based confessedly upon non-religious considerations.

The political relationships existing between Christian Governments and their Moslem colonials, as well as between themselves and the independent Moslem Powers, necessitate the adoption by them of diplomatic policies toward the Moslems. Commercial relationships follow diplomatic, and result, likewise, in the adoption of policies on the part of commercial men. Many nations of Western Christendom are involved in such relations. Foremost are England in Egypt and other parts of Africa and in India, and France in Africa and in Syria. Italy has Moslem dependents in North Africa, Spain in Morocco, Holland in the East Indies, and the United States in the Philippine Islands. Russia includes Moslem peoples in Western and Central Asia. These and still other nations seek favourable relationships with Turkey, with

Persia, with the Arab States, and with Afghanistan. In these relationships the attitude assumed by diplomatic and commercial men is based usually and frankly upon self-interest. At its best, the self-interest seeks mutual welfare and is guided by mature judgment. The activities which result are not without advantage to the Moslem peoples, for the Christian Powers strive to maintain peace and order and to advance civilization. But it is well understood that the Christian Powers expect to retain a paramount influence, making secure their own position, and leaving themselves free to execute any project which they consider expedient.

In carrying out a policy based upon self-interest it is essential that the Christian Powers should adopt whatever methods of dealing with the Moslem peoples may appear most advantageous, and this is true not only in general but specifically in view of the religious characteristics of these peoples. For Islam as a religion enters deeply into the lives of its adherents, giving them an undertone of religious feeling, a unity, and a sensitiveness that may not be disregarded. Therefore diplomatic wisdom and commercial prudence are always at pains so to act toward the Moslems as to forestall religious opposition, and the oscillations of public feeling are studied with great care.

Unquestionably every Christian nation which bears responsibility for large numbers of Moslem colonials is compelled to face serious problems respecting them. Also, the most trifling incident may relate itself suddenly to a national or racial solidarity, which is rooted in turn in the international and interracial brotherhood of the world of Islam. Therefore the need is definite and urgent for the formulation by each of these nations of an adequate Islamic policy. Our present interest in these policies has to do only with the motives on which they may be based. And the significance of the fact cannot be overestimated that, in general, the political wisdom of Christendom, while recognizing the obligations of those who govern toward the governed, has acknowledged the determining factor in its treatment of the millions of the Moslem world to be self-interest. Add to this, also, the existence of urgent pressure from non-official quarters, demanding more intensive study of Moslem character, including its religious phases, in order thereby to facilitate political control of the Moslem peoples and their commercial exploitation.

Two references will serve as illustrations of this pressure. Let it be remembered that the Governments mentioned are regarded by the world of Islam as leading representatives of the spirit and practice of Christendom.

A comparatively recent book,[1] publication of which was not allowed during the war, summons the Governments of France and Italy to the study of Islam as a religious movement, in order to take advantage of the religious psychology of the Moslems, and so gain greater power among them. It is declared that England already has adopted such a policy in its dealings with Egypt, and that the plans made for the re-Islamization of that country show the highest degree of political wisdom. A more recent article in the *Revue du Monde Musulman* (1923) cites the success of German diplomacy in leading many of the Moslem peoples to see in Germany their only true friend among the Christian nations, a psychological asset of great political value. The article then asserts that this psychological propaganda has been continued by German commercial agents without abate-

[1] *L'Islam et la Politique des Alliés*, adapted from the Italian of Dr. Enrico Insabato. Paris, 1920.

ment, producing a corresponding advantage for German trade. France should appreciate the immense prospective volume of commerce with the Moslem peoples, and enter the same field.

The attitude of public opinion in Christendom regarding the Moslem peoples rests, partly, upon knowledge of them, and, partly, upon current presuppositions. Both are chiefly non-religious. There is a growing popular literature regarding the peoples of Islam, and it is evident that Christians desire to learn more about the Moslems.

This public opinion has no ulterior purpose as concerns the Moslem peoples beyond that of forming an honest judgment regarding them, and then alining itself accordingly upon public questions where they are involved. In attempting to do this, Christian public opinion fastens upon two classes of facts. One is the racial characteristics of some single Moslem nation. These characteristics are then transferred to all Moslems. The other is certain customs and characteristics which are supposed to mark every Moslem as a Moslem. Public opinion, for instance, has become confirmed regarding certain racial characteristics of the Turkish people, and these characteristics have coloured Christian imagination regarding all Moslems. But quite other racial traits distinguish the Arabs, the Malays, or the Chinese, who may be equally good Moslems. Or, a traveller reports some occurrence which has been observed by him in a Moslem land. The incident may have to do with polygamy, or slavery, or divorce, with observance of the hours of prayer or of the fast, with patient endurance of misfortune. A single event is generalized, and all Moslems are imagined to be like those described, while this may be far from the fact.

The substantial facts in view of which public opinion regarding the Moslems is formed are those regarding the degree of civilization in Moslem countries, the state of commerce and industries, the conditions of family and of social life, the administration of government, safety of life and property, the means of education, the honesty and morality of the people—facts other than those concerning religion. Religious considerations, however, are included, and there is a strong tendency to connect social conditions among the Moslems with the religion of the Moslems, as effect with cause. If the judgment of Moslem institutions is favourable, it may be accompanied by the statement that the excellences of these institutions are due to Islam. If the judgment is the reverse, all evils among the Moslems may be looked upon as the direct fruits of Islam. Going a step further, public opinion then passes judgment upon Islam itself. Islam may be declared a religion well suited to the character and needs of its adherents, provided that they are sincere. Or Islam and its adherents may be placed under the severest anathemas.

These various phases of public opinion are reflected constantly in the literature of Christendom. The most marked feature to-day is an increasing cleavage between those looking with toleration upon the Moslems and those looking with hostility. The former attitude is, in part, simply a reaction from extreme anti-Moslem propaganda. The harsher judgment arises especially from sympathy with Oriental Christians who have suffered so terribly at the hands of the Turks. The more tolerant judgment often reflects sympathetic study of Moslem literature and institutions or personal acquaintance with Moslems of worth. In either case, a fundamental understanding of Islam as a religion has little share in shaping the final judgment. Yet the essence of Islam is religiousness.

In so far as the missionary attitude of the Churches of Christendom rests upon a purely religious basis, it finds this basis largely in the traditional ideas regarding Islam. These ideas had their source among the Oriental Christians of the early Moslem centuries, and were passed on by them to the Christians of Europe in the Middle Ages, from whom they have been transmitted to us. These ideas see in Islam a rival religion, late born, false in its claims and in its teachings, evil in its licence and in its commands, the religion of an invading enemy, hostile to Christendom and to Christianity. The issue of these ideas is a crusade of arms, as in the Middle Ages, or a crusade of ideas, an anti-Moslem propaganda. This latter is to demonstrate the superiority of Christianity, to force Moslems to confession of their errors and to acceptance of the truth, and so to secure the downfall of Islam.

In the minds of many earnest Christians, such a missionary programme is looked upon as natural and right. It is open, however, to serious criticism, trenchant and vital. For such a purpose ignores deliberately the best that there is in Islam, making no attempt to ascertain the religious truth which it may contain. Such a purpose is charged with feelings of Christian superiority, not with Christian sympathy. Such a purpose wills the destruction of a religious faith which others hold sacred. How can such a purpose relate itself to the purpose of Jesus, who came "not to destroy, but to fulfil" the aspirations of the human heart in search of God, as truly as the premonitions of the Mosaic law?

This type of missionary effort has not met with great success, and the causes of its lack of success are inherent.

Had it succeeded, its success would have been as open to criticism as is the success of any Holy War. If spiritual success among the Moslem peoples is to be expected, the Christian missionary enterprise, in utter contrast to such a programme, must base itself upon sympathetic understanding of the religious life of Moslems, and upon loving service to them.

PRESENT-DAY JOURNALISM IN THE WORLD OF ISLAM

BY THE REV.

SAMUEL M. ZWEMER, D.D., LL.D., F.R.G.S.,

Editor, "The Moslem World"

CHAPTER IX

PRESENT-DAY JOURNALISM IN THE WORLD OF ISLAM

"FLEET STREET may well envy the young Afghan editors," said *The Times* of London in a notice of the Afghan Press; "it is the golden age of journalism when a nation is beginning to think, and truth is as fresh as dew, and there is no bugbear of banality." The present-day ubiquity, activity, enterprise, and enthusiasm of Moslem journalism have indeed created a new situation full of promise and a new mentality among the masses. Provincialism is on the wane even in the remote corners of the new world of Islam. Before me lies a Malay weekly published by Moslems in Borneo. On a single page there are: an article on Islam in America, another on the new mosque in Berlin, items regarding Aligarh College in India, nationalism in Bengal, and an advertisement of a Javanese Steamship Company that accommodates Borneo pilgrims going to Mecca if they will embark at Padang, Sumatra—a microcosm of interests.

The Press is at once a proof of the unity and solidarity of Islam, and an infallible index to the surging currents of thought in a sea of unrest. Moslem journalism is a thermometer on which we may read the rising or falling temperature of the spirit of Islam; a barometer that records the approaching storm of suspicion and fanaticism or the "set fair" of tolerance and diplomatic adjustment.

Some years ago Professor A. le Chatelier of Paris called attention to the fact that the Press was more important than the pilgrimage:

"Already the Press formulates the common thought between the Moslems of Mindanao and those of Adamaoua; between the Chinese Ahong and the Almamy Peul of Futa. The African Zawiya of Bir Alali in Kanem receives a newspaper from Irak, Arabia. The Cairo *Moayyad* circulates from Fez to Peking.

"The Shurufa of Mecca formerly exercised a more extended authority than that of the Khalif. People came to fulfil their vows of pilgrimage from all corners of the world. Pilgrims from China and pilgrims from the Sudan: great Indian rajahs, Turkish viziers, Arabian emirs. They came to the holy city to build themselves up in living and deep faith against the contaminations of the world. The pilgrimage had the value of a great act of world-wide policy. To-day it retains only the merits of a respected act of devotion. The pilgrimage by steamboat has introduced the great ensign of Cook and Co. into the religion of the Prophet. Although the Bedouins still form a religious barrier after their manner, by preventing European tourists from profiting by its agencies in accompanying their Moslem clients, the pilgrimage is not what it was. It has given up its political influence to the Press. One prays; one is exalted in making the round of the holy Kaaba; faith is revivified by the purity of the Ihram; one descends from Mina with firm resolutions against Satan the Accursed. But an article in the *Moayyad*, the *Sabah*, *Habl-al-Matin*, or even *The Observer* of Lahore has quickly replaced the opinions conceived in the isolated metropolis of the Hejaz, by the latest news from Cairo or Stamboul." [1]

The following brief survey of the periodical press in the world of Islam, its present-day character and ten-

[1] *The Moslem World*, 1911, p. 154.

dencies, confirms the judgment of le Chatelier, and may perhaps also justify the conclusions at the close of this paper.

Because of the polyglot character and the wide sweep of Islam, it is convenient to follow geographical divisions in our treatment of the subject:

I. The Extent of Present-day Journalism

1. *Turkey and Syria*

All journalism in Moslem lands is of comparatively recent date. The printing press was not introduced into Turkey until 1728. The very rumour of such an innovation spread alarm. Scribes saw that their profession would be imperilled; theologians thought the new project profane; and scholars who cherished literature were disturbed lest the art of calligraphy should be lost. A *fatwa* secured from the Sheikh al-Islam, authorizing the use of the press, is typical. It read as follows:

"*Question:* If Zaid, who pretends to have ability in the art of printing, says that he can engrave on molds the figures of letters and words of books edited on language, logic, philosophy, astronomy, and similar secular subjects, and produce copies of such books by pressing the paper on the molds, is the practice of such a process of printing permissible to Zaid by canon law? An opinion is asked on this matter.

"*Answer:* God knows it best. If a person who has ability in the art of printing engraves the letters and words of a corrected book correctly on a mold and produces many copies without difficulty in a short time by pressing the paper on that mold, the abundance of books might cheapen the price and result in their increased purchase. This being a tremendous benefit, the matter is a highly laudable one. Permission should be granted to that person, but some learned persons should be appointed to correct the book the figures of which are to be engraved."[1]

In Egypt, the Government began journalism. The first Arabic newspaper was published on November 20, 1828, at Cairo; its title was *Al Waqai al Misriya*. It appeared in Turkish and Arabic. The next newspaper was published twenty-nine years later, January 1, 1858, in Arabic-French under the title *Hadikat al Akhbar*, at Beirût, Syria. In 1869 *Al Bashir*, an Arabic journal, appeared at Beirût. In 1877 Butrus al Bustani, a Christian, published the first number of *Lisan-ul-Hal*. This became the leading newspaper, not only in Syria, but for the Near East. The American Mission began to publish a Christian newspaper and a magazine for children in 1880. After that date newspapers appeared in Egypt, Syria, and Palestine. The growth of journalism in Egypt may be judged from these facts: in 1892 there were 40 newspapers; in 1899, 167; in 1909, 144. There was comparative freedom of the Press in Egypt.

So difficult, however, were conditions in the Ottoman Empire that no attempt was made until 1832 to publish a Turkish newspaper. In 1843 an Englishman, N. Churchill by name, established a Turkish weekly, devoted to foreign politics. The first non-official self-supporting newspaper appeared in 1860. It was entitled *Terjumani-Ahval*.

"The publication of this newspaper marked an epoch. It was the first utterance of the Modern School, and in twenty years it swept from the stage the crumbling débris of five centuries of Asiaticism."[2]

[1] Ahmed Emin, *The Development of Modern Turkey as Measured by its Press*, New York, 1914, p. 23.

[2] E. J. W. Gibb, *A History of Ottoman Poetry*, edited by Edward G. Browne, London, 1907, vol. v, p. 26.

The Press, however, continued weak. In August 1877 one of the few Turkish newspapers expressed itself dissatisfied with the state of the Press, reminding its readers "that the Press can not only cause the progress of a country, as often stated, but can also bring about its ruin and destruction, if managed by short-sighted and favour-seeking men." In the Hamidian period (1876–1908), journalism suffered censorship and suspicion prevailed. In 1897 the Young Turks began to organize and to carry on their propaganda through the Press. Papers were published in Egypt, the Balkan States, France, and Switzerland. Most of them were short-lived, but they helped forward the movement toward liberty.

In 1891 the agitation against the Sultan became serious. Six daily newspapers, two political weeklies, and a military gazette appeared, but the reactionaries won out. Abdul Hamid's dread of the Press so increased that he would not authorize the publication of a single new periodical. The censorship became more severe, with the result that the number of papers circulating in 1901 was scarcely larger than that in 1873.[1]

July 25, 1908, marked the revival of the Press, and the dawn of a new day. The censorship ceased. There was an outcry of joy. Copies of the *Iqdam*, of which 60,000 had been sold at one cent each, could not be obtained for less than forty cents in the afternoon.[2] The number of publications, most of them of mushroom growth, was enormous. Not only newspapers, but monthly reviews of economics and sociology, popular magazines, papers advocating new liberty for womanhood, and humorous publications appeared. Liberty,

[1] *The Development of Modern Turkey as Measured by its Press*, p. 79.

[2] Ibid., p. 87.

equality, and fraternity, however, were not yet given to editors. The new Government held the Press responsible for the revolutionary outbreak of April 13, 1909. Papers were suppressed, editors exiled or imprisoned. The animosity between the old and the new parties was extremely strong, and is reflected in their journalism. But the new triumphed. Turkey's defeat in the Balkan War proved to be a moral victory for the liberty of the Press. The daily *Sabah* wrote, April 2, 1913:

> "Whatever the material losses of the war may have been, there can be no doubt about the moral benefits it brought about for us. It has created a new sort of self-realization, it has given a new direction to our national life, it has done away with the last barriers between us and modern progress. In short, our defeat means the final victory of modernism in Turkey." [1]

Political liberty was accompanied by a feminist movement, which found expression in such papers as *The Women's World*, and critically discussed the evils of social life under Islam. Recently one of the editors of this paper took a ride in a military aeroplane, scattering upon the assembled crowds feministic literature. She was afterwards lauded by the Press as a popular heroine and her portrait placed in the Military Museum.[2]

Religious liberty followed in the wake of political freedom. One newspaper published articles on such subjects as "Was Mohammed an Epileptic?" and "War on Theologians." In 1914 the number of Turkish newspapers and magazines in Constantinople was: six dailies, three humorous papers, five illustrated magazines, eleven publications for children, two publications for women, six religious journals, nine professional journals, five

[1] *The Development of Modern Turkey as Measured by its Press*, p. 109.

[2] Ibid., p. 110.

military journals, and eight scientific reviews. This does not include publications in non-Turkish languages. Other centres of the Press are Smyrna, Brusa, Konia, and Trebizond, each of which has its daily papers. The number in other provinces, published in Turkish and Arabic, is given as follows[1]:

	Turkish.	Arabic.
Adana	4	—
Adrianople	5	—
Aleppo	7	5
Angora	4	—
Baghdad	5	19
Basra	2	6
Beirût	1	41
Dardanelles	2	—
Diarbekr	5	—
Erzerûm	3	—
Hejaz (Mecca)	1 (Turkish and Arabic)	
Jerusalem	1	15
Kastamani	3	—
Kharput	3	1
Mosûl	3	2
Sivas	3	—
Syria	1	26
Van	1	—
Yemen	1	—

The actual number of periodicals at the end of 1913 in Turkey was 389.

"The present-day achievements of the Turkish Press," says Ahmed Emin, "the increasing specialization in review literature, the attainment of a nearly perfect equilibrium, and of possibilities for constructive work,

[1] *The Development of Modern Turkey as Measured by its Press*, p. 118.

10

only after four or five years of contest, struggle, and agitation, must be highly surprising to everyone who knows the previous conditions and realizes that there was not even one self-supporting Turkish paper as late as 1860, and that the development of the Press between 1876 and 1908 was coercively checked."[1]

A list of journals published in Turkey after the revolution[2] includes no fewer than 800 publications in Turkish, French, Arabic, Italian, and other languages. A small percentage of these, however, are not Moslem. The Turkish Press to-day, under the new Angora Government, is represented at Constantinople by four reviews: *Sebil-ar-Reshad* (a religious journal); *Mahfil* (devoted to mysticism); *Ijtihad* (positivist); and *Yeni Majmoua* (literary). Of the daily Press, the following newspapers are the more important: *Iqdam, Tanin, Tevhid-i-Efkiar, Ileri, Vaqit, Peyam-l-Sabah* (which was suppressed in 1922), *Vatan*, and *Aqsham*.

In 1924 there appeared in Constantinople a new progressive monthly Moslem periodical entitled *Al Mihrab*. It is in the Turkish language, and deals with religion, philosophy, and historical questions from the standpoint of reformed Islam. The editor of the magazine is a man of modern education and in touch with world movements.

At the new capital, Angora, the Press is also active and is represented by the following papers: *Hakim-i-Mellia, Yeni-Gun, Yeni-Turkija*, and *Shehir*.

2. *Egypt, Arabia, and Mesopotamia*

The number of Moslems who speak Arabic has been estimated at over 45,000,000. The Arabic Press, there-

[1] *The Development of Modern Turkey as Measured by its Press*, p. 139.

[2] *Revue du Monde Musulman*, 1909, pp. 97–139.

fore, is found not only in the great centres of Arabic learning, Cairo, Beirût, Damascus, Baghdad, and Mecca, but in nearly every great centre of the Moslem world and on its farthest border-marches. In Malta, for example, there are two Arabic papers, the first of which appeared as early as 1879; in Calcutta one appeared in 1924. The revolutionary and nationalistic activity of educated Moslems in the Near East, so often censored or suppressed at home, found expression among groups of Syrians and Egyptians abroad, who, as exiles, were ripe for propaganda purposes, to serve Pan-Islamism, to oppose the old Turkish régime, or to advocate Egyptian nationalism. Some of these papers were published in Cyprus, others at Constantinople, in Switzerland, or in South America. Arabic papers have also from time to time appeared in Italy, France, London, Tiflis, New York, and Philadelphia. Although over 95 per cent. of the population in the Arabic-speaking world is illiterate, yet the influence of the Press from its inception has been more vital and far more widespread than in Turkish lands. Egypt and Syria have set the pace as pioneers. Of the Arabic Press one might say, "Their line has gone out in all the earth, and their word to the end of the world." The February 1914 number of *Der Islam* contained some interesting notes by R. Mielck upon a collection of Arabic newspapers and journals gathered by Count de Terrazzi and recently purchased in Beirût for the Hamburg Kolonial Institut. This remarkable collection contained 474 specimen copies of daily newspapers, distributed as follows: Cairo 96, Alexandria 28, the rest of Egypt and the Sudan 6, Beirût 60, Jerusalem 5, Constantinople 16, Jaffa 3, Baghdad 33, Basra 9, Tripoli (Syria) 9, Damascus 22, Hama and Homs 11, Lebanon 24, Aleppo 15, Latikia 3, the rest of Turkey

13, Paris 12, Marseilles 1, London 4, Sardinia 1, Malta 1, Leningrad 21, Algiers 6, Morocco 3, Tunis 26, Tripoli 3, New York 12, Buenos Aires 5, São Paulo 8, Rio de Janeiro 3, Montreal 3, the rest of America 8, Zanzibar 2, Singapore 2. Also 239 journals distributed as follows: Cairo 121, Alexandria 24, the rest of Egypt 7, Beirût 34, Constantinople 1, Jaffa 1, Baghdad 4, Tripoli (Syria) 3, Damascus 5, Hama and Homs 4, Lebanon 8, Aleppo 2, the rest of Turkey 6, Marseilles 1, Algiers 1, Morocco 1, Tunis 4, Lucknow 1, New York 5, Buenos Aires 3, São Paulo 2, Montreal 1.

It is significant of the rapid development of the Arabic Press in Egypt that Hartmann, in 1898, gave the number of current newspapers and journals in that country as 169. In the Terrazzi collection alone there are 282 Egyptian papers; doubtless many others have started and failed within the intervening fifteen years. Such activity is the more remarkable when we remember that, in Egypt, strict censorship was exercised from 1914–22, or rather since 1909, as the law of 1881 for the control of the Press was vigorously enforced under Sir Eldon Gorst after a period of liberty under Lord Cromer.[1]

Not counting ephemeral productions, about ninety periodicals are now published regularly in Egypt, of which about fifty-seven are in Arabic (these, with a few exceptions, are all Moslem-edited); there are twelve in French, four in English, four in Italian, eight in Greek, three in Armenian, one in Maltese, and one in Hebrew. On account of their appeal to a larger public, the daily newspapers naturally occupy the first place, with consequently a wider circulation. Before

[1] "The Press in Egypt," by Lady Drummond Hay, in *The Near East*, August 21, 1924.

the war the circulation of an Arabic newspaper rarely exceeded 20,000 copies, but now 40,000 is the figure reached by one daily, although the most popular paper in English has less than 6,000 circulation.

The leading newspapers to-day are *Al-Ahram*, consistently supporting the Nationalist Movement; *Al-Mokattam*, until 1914 Anglophile and hostile to the Nationalist Movement; *Al-Balagh*, inspired by the Wafd (the extreme Nationalist so-called Delegation), and the policy of Zaghloul Pasha; *Wadinnil*, until the fall of the Government resolutely but moderately Zaghloulist; *Al-Mahroussa*, having changed its politics as often as its editors, now also Zaghloulist; and *Al-Akhbar*, though systematically opposing all and every Government, favouring the Egyptian Nationalist Movement. *Al-Siassa*, the organ of the Liberal-Constitutional Party, is anti-Zaghloulist.[1]

The leading monthly periodical is *Al Manar*, founded by the celebrated Mohammed 'Abdu, and continued after his death by his pupil and spiritual legatee, Rashid Ridha. Each number contains a section of a new commentary on the Koran, articles on social and moral reform, a question department, and book reviews. The magazine is ably edited, always polemic, and has a widespread, although rather limited, circulation.

The Press of Egypt was victim throughout the whole war-period of intrigue, instigation, propagandism, censorship, and suppression. The pulse of the Cairo Press quickly responded to that of the nationalists of India. It was sympathetic to Turkey, in spite of the censorship. But, had it not been for such censorship, the fanaticism

[1] "The Press in Egypt," by Lady Drummond Hay, in *The Near East*, August 21, 1924.

of the masses would have known no limit. Even a paper like *Al-Ahaly* often appeared with blank columns instead of text; nationalists tore up copies of the *Mokattam* from the hands of newsboys; newspaper offices were attacked, and windows smashed; other papers sold their birthright for a mess of pottage.[1]

Arabia depends almost entirely on Cairo for news. Until very recently no paper or magazine was published by Moslems anywhere in the peninsula with the exception of meagre Turkish-Arabic Government bulletins at Basra and Baghdad. In 1916, *Al Kibla* appeared, published at Mecca but, at first, printed in Cairo. Intended to represent the Arabs and their new kingdom, it was a political organ enthusiastically welcomed or violently opposed, according to the trust or distrust of the Hashimite lords of Mecca. With the Wahhabis under Ibn Saud occupying the Hejaz, the importance of *Al Kibla* has ceased for the present.

In Mesopotamia, Baghdad has five journals, Mosul and Basra each two. The Press of Iraq is awakening. *Al Mufid* and *Al Istiqlal* take sides in discussing the dangers or benefits of the Anglo-Iraq Treaty, in defending or attacking the new Ministry, and in pioneer effort at social reform.

3. *Africa*

The Barbary States were more tardy than Turkey. The first newspaper published in Tunis was in 1862, and

[1] Cf. "The Native Press of Egypt," *The Egyptian Mail*, October 1910, and "The Moslem Press and the War," *The Moslem World*, 1915, pp. 413–25.

the Press of Tunis has never been vigorous or important in its influence. We may mention, however, as a speciality, two Jewish-Arabic papers published in Hebrew script—*Al Bustani* and *Al Muhaiyr*. The only daily published in the country is called *Az Zoharah*, edited by Abdur Rahman as Sanaldali. The Young Tunis Party, corresponding to the Young Turkish Party or the Nationalist Party in Egypt, have an organ of their own called *At Tunisie*. This appears also in a French edition. Other papers are the *Hadhiri*, *Al Liwa*, *Ad Dhahak* (a humorous paper, as the title indicates), the *Murshid*, *Al Umma*, and *As Sawwab*. Extracts from these papers appear in the *Revue du Monde Musulman*.

Tripoli has only one or two Arabic newspapers, and these, until the Italian occupation, were the official organs of the Government.

In Algeria there is a vigorous daily Press at Algiers, Oran, and Tlemsen. Morocco is the most backward in regard to journalism. In 1905 the first newspaper was published at Tangier. The only Arabic paper published at Fez (1922) is a small four-page sheet, entitled *Akhbar Telegrafia* (Telegraphic News).

A monthly paper in Swahili appeared (1923) as a pioneer of the Press in that language. It is called *Mambo Leo*, the meaning of which is "News To-day." Yet this small paper had a circulation of 7,500.[1]

In South Africa there are one or two vernacular papers and a Gujarati-English paper, *The Indian Views*,[2] conducted by Moslems. It has a circulation in South and East Africa. Madagascar has no distinctively Moslem Press. A French paper is published by Moslems at Mauritius.

[1] *Central Africa* (Universities' Mission), September, 1923, p. 6.
[2] 137 Grey Street, Durban.

4. *Persia*

Journalism in this country has been treated fully in a monograph by Professor E. G. Browne.[1] Printing was introduced a century ago and the first newspaper appeared in 1851. Before the granting of the Constitution in 1906, however, only three or four papers appeared and journalism was of no importance. The only periodicals of value were published outside of Persia at Constantinople, Cairo, London, and Calcutta.[2] The Calcutta *Habl-ul-Matin* appeared in 1893, the *Thuraiya* (Pleiades) in Cairo in 1898 and the *Parwarish* replaced it in 1900. With the Revolution journalism sprang into frantic life led by the *Sur-i-Israfil* (Resurrection Trumpet), *Nasim-i-Shemal* (Breeze of the North), and *Nusawat* (Equality).

It would be a love's labour lost to record the rise, decline, and fall of the hundreds of newspapers, magazines, and journals that vied with one another in proclaiming the new era of liberty and the new day of education and reform. The curious reader will find in Browne's volume every detail, including a whole series of inimitable Persian political cartoons. He gives a list of all these earlier Persian papers to the number of 350.[3] Since November 1915, 47 papers and magazines have appeared. Tehran heads the list with 18 papers ; Shiraz has seven ; Tabriz and Resht four each, and Isfahan, Meshed, Kerman, Kermanshah, Khoi, Bushire, Herat, Kabul, and Jalalabad (the last three in Afghanistan) one or two each. But this list, published in *Kawa*,[4] a Persian newspaper printed

[1] *The Press and Poetry of Modern Persia*, Cambridge, 1914 ; also his later work, *A History of Persian Literature in Modern Times*, Cambridge, 1924.

[2] Edward Granville Browne, *The Persian Revolution of 1905–1909*, Cambridge, 1910, p. 242.

[3] Also the list in the *Revue du Monde Musulman*, December 1909, p. 682.

[4] No. 4, 1921.

in Berlin, is not altogether complete. Among the more important literary magazines are: *Armaghan*, *Bahar*, *Furugh-i-Tarbiyat*, *Danish* (Meshed), *Mimat-u-Hayat*, *Firdausi*, and *Iran Shahr* (Berlin).

According to recent information [1] many of the Communistic journals and those opposed to the new Government have been suppressed. Among the more important newspapers that remain are the following: *Iran*, *Ittihad*, *Bamdade-Roshan*, *Jahane*, *Zehan*. The last-named represents the feminist movement in Persia.

The boldness of the Press and its Pan-Islamic tendency may be judged from the following editorial which appeared in *Fakr-i-Azar* (Free Thought), a semi-weekly paper, Meshed, Persia (October 9, 1922):

"We are dead. The spirit of the nation and the spirit of Islam has bidden farewell to the body of our national life. If it is not so, where are the signs of life? Where are there any evidences of the presence of the spirit of Islam? When the good news came of the triumph of the victorious armies of Islam, where was our rejoicing? Where our glorious celebrations? Where is that assembly that sends a telegram of congratulations to our Mohammedan brothers in the name of Islamic feeling? What is the name of that party that invites their fellow countrymen to have a part in the universal joy in the world of Islam?

"The Mussulmans of India, who are under the firm heel of the English, and have no share in the blessing of liberty, in this time of victory of the Kemalists have had a whole series of celebrations, and face to face with the partisans of Greece they have raised to heaven a shout of joy over her defeat and degradation.

"Cries of congratulations and blessing are continually rising from the throats of the oppressed Mussulmans of

[1] *Revue du Monde Musulman*, 1922–3, p. 313.

Egypt, Mesopotamia, Morocco, Algiers, and elsewhere; and make the hearts of the enemies of the *Kibla* and the Koran tremble with fear and dread." [1]

5. *India, Ceylon, and Afghanistan*

The newspaper Press was introduced at the time of the British occupation of Bengal; yet at the time of the Mutiny there were only 19 Anglo-Indian papers and 25 in the vernacular for the whole of India. To-day, among 1,017 newspapers and 2,297 periodicals, the Moslem Press is represented by 222 periodicals and publications as follows: Madras Presidency, 26; Bombay Presidency, 37; the United Provinces, 44; the Central Provinces, 5; the Punjab, 84; Bengal, 24; Burma, 1; Bihar and Orissa, 1. According to languages these Moslem periodicals are divided as follows: Urdu heads the list with 149 newspapers and magazines edited by Moslems; 25 appear in Gujarati, 14 in English, 13 in Bengali, 8 in Malayalam, 6 in Sindhi, 4 in Tamil, and 1 in Arabic.

In Bengal the leading vernacular periodical is an illustrated monthly called *Al Islam*, of about seventy pages. A recent number contained articles on "The Canon of the Old Testament," "The Mohammedans in China," "The Library of Alexandria," and "Islam and the Race Problem." *The Muhammadi* is a weekly, often violently anti-Christian. This has a large circulation.[2]

India has several important Mohammedan papers published in the English language. *The Review of Religions*, published at Qadian, represents the original

[1] *The Moslem World*, 1923, p. 411.

[2] "The Moslem Press of Bengal," by William Goldsack, *The Moslem World*, 1917, p. 182.

Ahmadiya Movement, but has lost its old-time vigour. It has, however, a wide circulation outside of India. A recent number contained a list of contributors from Lagos, West Africa, to the building of the new mosque at Berlin. *The Comrade*, of Calcutta, was the leading English Moslem weekly until it was suppressed during the war. *The Muslim Outlook* is a daily published at Lahore, and *The Moslem Chronicle* appears at Madras. The influence of the Indian Press may be judged from the little magazine called *Peace* published in Dacca, which often speaks of Islamic solidarity in terms that would appear an exaggeration were it not that we find in the same paper a list of 19 Moslem magazines, exchanges which the editor receives. These magazines are published not only in India, but in South Africa, United States, Java, France, and England. Whatever else one may say about the Ahmadiyas of India, they are active. One of their latest methods of propaganda is found in *The Light*, a bi-weekly four-page journal published in English (Lahore). The editor is Mustafa Khan, B.A.

"The paper desires to disseminate Islamic doctrines, and to repudiate charges against Islam. Short articles, letters, and questions will also be welcome. Non-Moslems are also invited to send questions to be answered."

A list of the subjects treated in the number of August 16, 1924, will convey a fairly satisfactory idea of its character: "The Position of Christianity"; "Islam and Christianity in Africa"; "Moslem Mission in Germany"; "The Atonement"; "A Study of the Bible." The last page is devoted to questions and answers.

The Islamic World (Lahore) is a new quarterly journal "devoted to propagate and defend Islam against its hostile critics and to study the progress of Islamic thought, literature, art, and civilization in the world."

A complete list of all the Moslem newspapers published in India and Ceylon is given in an appendix.

The first Moslem journal published in Afghanistan appeared at Kabul in 1906. Under the progressive Amir Amanullah, Afghanistan is arousing herself from her sleep, and the two nationalist journals, the *Aman-i-Afghan*, of Kabul (1919), and the *Ittihad-i-Mashraqi* (Eastern Unity) (1920) of Jalalabad, aim at reflecting the national enlightenment. Both journals are published in Persian, and claim to be unofficial, though the inspiration and control of the Amir's Government are obvious, as is the Bolshevist hand behind it. Subscription to the *Aman-i-Afghan* is obligatory upon officials of a certain grade, and is deducted by the Royal Office from their salaries.

At one time Indian Moslems published a monthly in Tokyo, Japan, in the English language. It was entitled *The Islamic Fraternity.* The first number appeared April 15, 1910, but it was soon discontinued ; the editors were an Indian and an Egyptian Moslem. Islam has never gained a foothold in Japan, but this effort at propagandism is nevertheless suggestive. There is a small group of Indian Moslem students in Tokyo and also there are Moslem merchants in Yokohama and Kobe.

6. *Dutch East Indies and Malaysia*

The importance of the Netherlands Indies is evident when we remember its vast population—49,350,834 souls,—the present revival of Islam, and the increasing contacts between Insulinde and the Near East. Although the percentage of illiteracy is still high, it is decreasing. The number of literates in Java alone is estimated at over two million. The chief languages are Malay, Javanese, Sundanese, and Madurese. Various Moslem societies exist for the revival of religion or of nationalism on social and economic lines. All of these live by the Press. The Sarikat-Islam, the Boedi-Oetomo, and the Moehammadia are the best known, but there are many others. The centres of publication are at Surabaya and Batavia, but at many holy places and pilgrim rendezvous there is also considerable activity. Gressee and Demak are examples. A complete list of native newspapers and periodicals, secured from the Department of the Interior, gives the following Moslem papers and periodicals: Java newspapers, 8; Sumatra and other islands newspapers, 10; periodicals, Java, 24; periodicals in the outposts, 12; Moslem religious papers, 5; Arabic newspapers, 3. The titles of some of these periodicals are significant: *Light of Sumatra, Young Java, Young Sumatra, Light of India, Light of Minahassa, Light of Islam, The Revival of Islam, Agreement and Disagreement, The Area of Islam,* etc. Their variety and number, in a time of commercial depression and general crisis, are surely a proof that Islam is awake. Of the total, 16 are published at Weltevreden, Batavia, 10 each at Semarang and Padang, 9 at Jokyakarta, 7 at Solo, 5 each at Bandung, Surabaya, and Medan; the others are scattered. Some of the papers are frankly reactionary and advocate a return to the old Islam, but the majority are progressive and desire reform, educational and ethical. The contents of a single number[1] of the *Tjahaja-Islam* are typical. This paper is a diglot in Malay-Javanese. The advertisements, with one exception, relate to Moslem schools, booksellers, and eating-houses. After an editorial (which

[1] Issue of November 5, 1921.

closes with a threefold Amen), the leading article is on the Birthday of Mohammed. A second long article is on Islam and Democracy. Then follow an appeal for money to open a new Moslem school, a poem calling for the better observance of the five prayer periods, a proposal to unify the Moslem Press, and a reply by the editor, who says that three small papers reach a larger circle than one large one! The Javanese section has similar matter, and in addition a Koran exposition with reference to Thomas Carlyle's Essay on Mohammed.

Apart from a score of Chinese political newspapers and six Christian periodicals, there are over 90 newspapers and other periodicals which are Islamic in their outlook and influence, for even a general daily, under the control of a Moslem editor or committee, cannot help being an organ of propagandism.[1]

The Dutch East Indies are undergoing rapid evolution. The daily Press proclaims it in unmistakable accents. Processes which in Europe took long centuries are here taking place in a decade. In Sumatra you may see, side by side, the use of a needle fashioned from a thorn and a Singer sewing-machine; the smoking wool-wick and the electric bulb; the untrodden forest and the Ford car, with a Battak chauffeur whose grandfather was a cannibal! Single generations are separated by unbridgeable gulfs mental and spiritual, and in the new day of light, liberty, and more abundant life the Press is to the front as pioneer and cynosure.

A survey of the contents of the Press in the Dutch East Indies is regularly published by the Dutch Colonial Government. This is also done, from the missionary standpoint, by Dr. H. Kraemer from time to time in the magazine called *De Opwekker*, and also in *Mededeelingen*.

[1] For complete list see *The Moslem World*, 1923, pp. 39–49.

7. *China*

Although the Chinese people had newspapers before the discovery of printing in Europe, a Moslem Press did not exist until very recent years. At the time of our visit in 1917 we found only three or four Chinese-Mohammedan newspapers or magazines. A Chinese-Arabic periodical was then issued at Peking, but has been discontinued.

The Islamitic Review is a Chinese-Moslem newspaper, published in Yün-nan-fu, West China. A recent article therein, received from Peking, gives a view of Chinese Mohammedanism to-day:

"This is respectfully addressed to our . . . brethren of Islam. Do not slumber, all of you! Quickly awake! At the present time this Moslem religion of ours has in failure reached the extreme point; it appears that we are about to perish. O brethren of our Faith, all of you, make haste to think of some plan of remedy and rescue; otherwise, when our Moslem religion perishes, probably we shall not be able to preserve our places of worship and ablutions. . . .

"Brethren of our Faith, do not continue besotted in sleep! Up quickly, and save our religion! Look around at the present deplorable condition of our religion; it is day by day becoming more and more decadent." [1]

From India we learn of a new International Moslem Association (Shanghai) which has started a monthly journal, *The Light of Islam*, in Chinese, with some English and Japanese articles as well.

" . . . The principal object of this journal being to awaken the slumbering Chinese Muslims and acquaint them with the activities now widely spreading among

[1] Isaac Mason, in *The Moslem World*, 1923, p. 413.

their fellow disciples in the Western countries, and, on the other hand, to teach and propagate the Sacred Doctrines of Islam among the Chinese and the Japanese who are ignorant of them . . . and to stimulate and encourage our fellow Muslims of the Far East to form a close connexion with those of other parts of the world, so that we may ultimately establish a world-wide Association of pan-Islamism."[1]

The journal contains articles in Chinese, and many illustrations of Moslem leaders and the antiquities in China.

8. *Russia*

Here the chief centres of journalism are Bakhchisarai, Kazan, Baku, Orenburg, and Leningrad. Kazan, where several hundred books are published every year, is the educational and intellectual capital for the 17,000,000 Moslems under Russian governments. Ufa is the headquarters of the Mohammedan ecclesiastical Assembly. Orenburg, Tiflis, and Troitsk are also important.

Kazan has 6 Moslem newspapers, Tashkent 5, Ashqabad 3, Khoqand and Samarkand each 1. At Bukhara the Moslem Press is also fairly active in the Arabic, Persian, and Turki languages. Altogether about fifty Islamic newspapers have appeared in Russia.[2]

The most important, and one of the earliest Moslem journals, was the weekly paper entitled *Millet*, under the editorship of Ismail Bey Gasprinsky, the leader of education and reform. Another pioneer of the Press in Russia was Ahmad Bey Agayeff.

In the Crimea there is an important newspaper called *Tarjaman*, and published at Bakhchisarai, with a circula-

[1] *The Muslim Herald* (Madras), November 29, 1924.
[2] Hartmann, in *Encyclopædia of Islam*.

tion of over 5,000. It first appeared in 1879, also under the editorship of Ismail Bey Gasprinsky, but is now conducted by Jaafer Seyid Amet. In the Russian periodical *Mir Islama* (The Islamic World) reviews of the Moslem Press appear from time to time.[1]

In the Caucasus the Moslem Press has its chief centre at Baku.

In this connexion we may note that Islam in Bulgaria has, as its chief centres of literary activity : Varna, Rasgrad, Ruschuk, Shumla, Sofia, Philippopolis, and Burgas. At the present time the following Turkish papers are published there : *Echali*, *Zia*, *Trundscha*, and *Muwazene*.

9. *Europe, America, and Australia*

Moslem journalism has entered the Western World. The earliest magazine, which has continued publication, is *The Islamic Review*, published by the Ahmadiya Movement at Woking, England ; a Tamil edition appears at Madras, India, and an Urdu edition at Lahore. At Berlin a new Mohammedan magazine, called *Al Liwa*, appears in three languages, Persian, Arabic, and German. It gives a large amount of space to news regarding Central Asian politics and Bolshevism. A more recent publication, also issued at Berlin, is entitled *Moslemische Revue*, of which Vol. I, No. 1 appeared in April 1924. Three Islamic papers are published in France. In the bi-monthly organ published by the Bureau d'Information Islamique at Paris (24 Rue Taitbout), and entitled *Echos de l'Islam*, we find political news and propagandism in favour of Pan-Islam. This magazine circulates in Java and the Malay States.

There are one or two Mohammedan newspapers

[1] *Mir Islama*, 1912, pp. 257–87.

published in Brazil, the Argentine, and British Guiana; none in Trinidad. Five Syrian Arabic dailies are published in the United States of America, and three magazines. These are not all Moslem; yet the Arabic Press has a larger proportionate daily circulation than the Chinese, Greek, or Yiddish newspapers. The number of Arabic papers, beginning with 1 (1893–8), rose to 7 in 1911, and to 13 in 1917. It has since decreased. *Al Hoda* was established in 1898 as spokesman of Maronite Syrians. It is pro-Zionist. The *Kowkab America* was the first Arabic paper published. It was controlled by Turkish influence and fear of the Turkish Government. "The hand of the Turk was still heavy on me," says the editor, "even on Pearl Street, New York."[1]

Some of the magazines and papers referred to, however, although published in Arabic and read by Moslems, are edited by Christians. The first magazine published by Moslems in the English language in the United States of America bears the title of *The Moslem Sunrise*. This quarterly represents the Ahmadiya Movement. Its first number contained a new year greeting, a prayer for all its readers, followed by a transliteration and translation of Sura 31 : 13–20, the thirteen Commandments of Luqman to his son. There follow some sayings of Mohammed. An Australian Moslem tells how "prohibition is prohibited" in the United States. In the course of this article Jesus Christ is spoken of not only as a "wine-drinker" but also as a "wine-maker." The magazine has a large circulation outside of the United States. On the inside cover a list of its agents abroad is printed, and in a recent issue two pages are devoted to lists of converts made in the United States.

[1] Robert E. Park, *The Immigrant Press and its Control*, New York and London, 1922, p. 56.

For some time a similar publication, entitled *The Moslem Sunshine*, appeared at Perth, Australia.

II. The Character of Present-day Journalism

After our geographical survey of the Press in the new world of Islam, it remains to sketch briefly its character, its outlook, and programme.

First of all, and everywhere, it looks forward. Economic, social, intellectual, and spiritual movements are stirring thought everywhere, although the currents often run counter to one another and with terrific force. Zionism, Bolshevism, commercialism, nationalism, imperialism, all have interests centring in the undeveloped Moslem Near East, and each is a disintegrating factor in the old world of thought and life. No wonder Turkey is turning her back on the past and trampling on old traditions. The cry of the reactionary is, "Back to the Koran and to Mohammed!" The problem of the progressive Press is to get as far away from both as is decent and safe. The educational revival, the renaissance of Arabic as a world-language, the Feminist Movement—all are topics for Moslem journalists to-day. The shattering impact of the World War, race hatreds, the fall of the Caliphate, the increased government of Islamic peoples by European Powers, the impact of civilization and of missions, European scepticism, the rebellion against traditionalism and external authority, the hunger for knowledge of new scientific thought and invention, the canvassing of the status of Oriental womanhood—all yield the *furor scribendi* to the Moslem editors.

In Tunis, Turkey, Syria, and Egypt the Press has been furiously discussing polygamy, its prevalence, and its agreement or disagreement with Moslem ethics. One paper states that only 50 per cent. of the Egyptians are polygamists! Another newspaper suggests the promulgation of a law against polygamy on lines following the precepts of the Koran, which require the husband to support his wives without discrimination; and suggests that this law should make it compulsory for the husband to give evidence, before a second marriage, that he is able to support more wives than one.

In commenting on the Feminist Movement in Egypt, *Al Kibla*, the semi-official organ of the Hejaz Government, expresses indignation at the publication of a portrait of Madame Zaghloul, in which she is seen unveiled and seated among European and Egyptian men. *Al Kibla* also criticizes Mustafa Kemal for allowing his wife to accompany him on a military parade unveiled and riding a horse. The article concludes by warning Moslems not to violate Sharia, which forbids Moslem women to show themselves unveiled except to their husbands.

In the second place, Moslem journalism is religious—that is, it cannot get away from Islam. It challenges Lord Cromer's verdict that reformed Islam is Islam no longer. The new wine is always put into the old wine-skins. Thus, according to the Moslem Press, the Koran has become "holy"; Mohammed never conducted aggressive warfare; he was practically a monogamist, and inculcated tolerance. Likewise, the Bible yields proof-texts to establish the doctrines of Islam; Western civilization and Christianity are submitted to its acid test. On December 24, 1920, a Cairo daily (*Al-Ahaly*) wrote:

"How curious and strange is the nature of man! Tomorrow Westerners will celebrate Christmas Day, the day when forbearance was born with the birth of Jesus, when the mercy of heaven came down to earth as He came to it, and when the good news was heralded to all that fraternity, love, and peace had come. One may imagine, as one casts a look on them while they celebrate this blessed day, and exchange good wishes and greetings on its occasion, that the principles of Christ are still in the hearts of His peoples, and that His generous commandments are strictly obeyed by these peoples; whereas, if one looks well, one clearly sees that they are in one valley, and the principles of Christ in another.

"Injustice is up and justice is down; slavery is permanent; the mighty continue to consume the rights of the weak, and without feeling any remorse; the influential trespass upon the humble, without feeling any shame; the wealthy, who only care to fill their safes with money, look as if they would suck up the blood of the poor without feeling any pain in their hearts."

On the other hand, the Press often speaks in terms of the highest praise of Jesus Christ. On Christmas Day, 1921, *Al Iraq*, Baghdad, had an editorial beginning:

"On the morning of December 25, nineteen hundred and twenty-one years ago, the ray that leads to the right path appeared in Bethlehem as a bright star, and His light spread over the East and the West. On that day was born the Image of Love and the Great Child.

"He spent His days calling people to the Truth and guiding them to the right path. He was a good shepherd who sheltered His sheep and defended them against the wolves. He was pure of heart, and His hidden thoughts were clear. He was humble, like a blessed ear full of wheat-grains, and that in an age when error had a universal rule, and when the wolves longed to be ferocious lions so as to enslave others. Man's innermost thoughts had been covered with a tissue, the warp and woof of which were pride and arrogance.

"All His life He was loved by the poor and the good, and was shunned by the arrogant and the proud. He showed love to the poor and to the weary, and revolted against the tyrants and oppressors. He devoted His life to the assistance of humanity, which was suffering from persecution, colonization, and that warfare which man wages against his brother.

"Neither the greatness of the Cæsars nor the sophistry of the priests could turn Him away from His purpose, for how can perishable greatness and apostate priesthood wrestle with immortal glory?

"The greatness of Cæsar has passed away, the Nero's page in history is a dark one; but time has failed to efface the greatness of the Apostle of Love, and His page in history remains white, with no spots on it."

A small section of the Moslem Press (especially the Ahmadiya) uses the arguments of liberal Christianity and Western infidelity to combat the Scriptures and Christian missions.[1] The sinlessness of Jesus is assailed, His virgin birth ridiculed, His death, resurrection, and ascension caricatured. Paul invented the Christianity of the Churches; Jesus was a true Moslem. *Al Manar*, Cairo, recently gave an account of the Modern Churchmen's Conference held in Cambridge, August 1921, and maintained:

"... That the thinking clergy of England and America have been approaching almost automatically the theological position of the Unity of God, so that there has been no need, as in the days of old, for Islam to resort to the sword and the battle. ... And so, of course, the day is not far distant when idols will be demolished and churches razed, while true piles will be erected to the worship of Amighty Unity in accordance with the laws of Mohammed, the master of men."

Vituperation of Christian missions and of certain Christian doctrines is still found in some religious perio-

[1] Cf. "A Moslem View of Christianity," by Samuel M. Zwemer, in *The Missionary Review of the World*, November 1924.

dicals of India and Egypt, but it is far less common than a decade ago.

Some editors proclaim an Islamic renaissance, and others sound its death-knell. It depends on temperament and temperature. What a contrast between the voice of *The Crescent*, Colombo, and that of *The Islamic Review*, Woking, almost of the same date! The former draws this roseate picture:

" The Islamic world seems to be on the threshold of a great renaissance. For long, mysterious murmurs, presages of a coming revolution, have been echoing from the colourful cafés of Stamboul through the vaulted halls of Al Azhar and of Aligarh to more Eastern climes where the followers of the Prophet congregate into Brotherhoods of Purity. Under the impact of Western civilization, the East is slowly awakening to a consciousness of its own soul, and the time cannot be far distant when it shall once more resume its own self-appointed search for the Holy Grail, with something of the high, ancient earnestness that brought forth religions and philosophies and stayed the flight of time."

But *The Woking Monthly*, quoting from a mosque sermon at Woking, said:

" There has been many a dark hour in the history of Islam, but never any so dark as the present. We, the present-day Moslems, have indeed fallen on evil days. Our past glory has forsaken us. Our might, our honour, have deserted us. To our rivals, our days are already numbered. It is true that, to a certain extent, we have awakened and realized the critical nature of the situation in which we find ourselves; but, like a man who has been enjoying a deep slumber and is awakened, all of a sudden, by some turmoil around him, we are rushing about in utter darkness to avoid what we perceive to be an imminent danger. Confusion has seized our senses;

and, though the danger is within our purview, yet we cannot properly locate it. Death is staring us in the face, and the struggle for self-preservation has just begun."

While this call for social and religious reform occupies so large a place in present-day journalism, we note an alarming feature. According to Joseph Castagné, the Russian Soviet has obtained control of some of the leading Russian Moslem newspapers, and since 1921 has been engaged in a systematic effort to make Islam the ally of Bolshevism, not only in Russia, but also in all Central Asia. Two Usbek journals, *Inqilab* (Revolution) and *Kyzyl Bairak* (The Red Flag), both published at Tashkent under Mohammedan editors, preach Communism to all Turkistan. The last-named paper appears in Tatar, Kirghize, and Russian, as well as in the Usbek language, and the total circulation in these four languages is over 37,000.[1]

In Java the Russian Soviet has its secret agents and succeeded once and again in winning over certain leaders of the Sarikat-Islam and their Press to the Third International programme.[2]

In Persia Soviet propaganda has been active in the Moslem Press since the appointment of a Bolshevik Minister at Tehran in 1921. At Resht a Communist paper called *The Red Revolution* is distributed gratuitously. Georges Ducrocq mentions many other Bolshevist-Moslem journals, such as *Hallaj*, *Badr*, *Toufan* (The Deluge), etc.[3] Some of these were ephemeral and others were suppressed, but the Soviet influence continues in

[1] Joseph Castagné, "Le Bolshevisme et l'Islam," in *Revue du Monde Musulman*, October 1922, pp. 68–73.

[2] Idem, December 1922, pp. 70–81.

[3] Ibid., pp. 127–33.

the Persian Press. Two Turkish papers are also mentioned, *Yeni-Dunya* (Baku), edited by a follower of Karl Marx, and *Yeni-Hayat* (Angora), a Communist journal.[1] Strict censorship and government precautions have hitherto prevented an alliance of Bolshevism with Islam in the Press of India and Egypt.[2]

In conclusion, we emphasize the importance of modern journalism in moulding not only everyday thought but the language and literature of nations. The newspaper has freed the Arabic language from much of its old bombastic and affected style, has adopted or invented new words, and broken through religious prejudices by its illustrations and advertisements.

Literature itself has entered upon a new career of beauty and power by the fructifying mind of great races awakened by modern science, art, and culture in the Press.

Poetry and the fine arts, history, archæology, and the natural sciences are coming to their own in modern Moslem journalism. The child has a larger place than in the old world of Islam. Womanhood has secured a forum and popular education its great advocate in the daily newspaper. In many reforms—for example, the Prohibition Movement—the Moslem Press is an ally of Christian missions. It is, therefore, increasingly important to make a careful and sympathetic study of the contents of the daily papers and periodicals. We must cultivate friendly relationships with the large and influential body of editors and journalists. They are the leaders of the leaders, and control the thought of the masses.

[1] Joseph Castagné, " Le Bolshevisme et l'Islam," in *Revue du Monde Musulman*, December 1922, pp. 207–10.

[2] Ibid., pp. 218–21.

Of present-day journalism in the new world of Islam the words of Kipling are also true :

> " The Pope may launch his Interdict,
>   The Union its decree,
> But the bubble is blown and the bubble is pricked
>   By Us and such as We.
> Remember the battle and stand aside
>   While Thrones and Powers confess
> That King over all the children of pride
>   Is the Press—the Press—the Press ! "

SOME TYPES OF LITERATURE IN THE WORLD OF ISLAM

BY

CONSTANCE E. PADWICK,

Church Missionary Society, Cairo

CHAPTER X

SOME TYPES OF LITERATURE IN THE WORLD OF ISLAM

In Amman, the Arab capital of Trans-Jordan, one can never forget the Arabian desert where the heart of Islam beats. The little city lies in a cleft made by the Jabbok through the breezy Moab uplands, and these bare pastures are an ill-defined barrier between the settled pastures of Palestine and that untamed desert. Three miles away the railway, with uncontrollable passengers who travel on the roof if they feel so minded, makes a tangible link between Amman and the Hejaz itself. The greater houses have ladies or slaves from Mecca or Medina. In the market street, full of flashes of gold and orange head-draperies, tawny figures talk the purest language-of-the-desert Arabic as they watch the mending of harness or the making of a pair of yellow boots under personal supervision. There, in the Amman market, the desert man finds links with the outside world. The train that goes to Ma'an comes from Damascus with gossip of the French official world. It takes up a load from Haifa with cheap clocks, cheap crockery, tin toys, and even sweetstuff made in Europe. The rudimentary brown road (mended last summer by prisoners who were Wahhabi warriors raiding from Nejd) takes cars to Jerusalem with its tourists and the daily train for Egypt.

That market street of gunsmiths, camel-harness makers, and cafés is not a literary centre, and what books are sold there are sold in a luxury-shop along with cheap mirrors, tin trains, masks, bottles of scent, and slabs of unutterably stale chocolate. Yet, when books are rare, each one read counts the more, and, after inquiry as to where books were sold in the capital, I stood among the dusty rattle-traps and had the pile of literature pulled down, that I might finger it and see what that corner of the Moslem world was reading, when it read at all.

The Korans were left on the shelf. The shopman explained that it would have been counted a shameful deed in the Amman market to offer one to me, a Christian woman; and I could but agree to the deprivation, though I should have liked to see whether the presses of Stamboul or of Cairo were supplying that part of the Arab world. The pile of books before me was quickly classified. There were a few grubby linguistic works on the Arabic language, with instructions for writing letters in good Arabic style, and flowery examples of figures of speech. These came to Amman from Damascus, that home of Arabic belles-lettres. There was a little, a very little poetry—true poetry of the desert from the days before Mohammed, songs of one 'Antar, son of a warrior of Nejd by a black slave-girl, his spoil of war. 'Antar, so the books say, spent his youth as a camel-herd among slaves, and only forced his way to his father's recognition by deeds of daring in a tribal war. His sixth-century poems are fierce songs of desert loves and desert raids that have an antique flavour when read among the electric trams of Cairo, but do not read as out of date among the Arabs in the Amman market. These were printed in Beirût. But the greater part of the pile before me was made of stories in leaflet form. Right well I recognized them, with their poor paper and their poorer type. They were the same stories of crime and venture that are sold for a cent or two at the tram terminus of Cairo; poor in language, very poor in thought; grubby enough sometimes in morals as in exterior; but stories, and therefore beloved on the desert borders as in the public gardens or the tramcars of Cairo.

Damascus, Beirût, and Cairo had thus contributed to the spiritual culture of Amman; but perhaps the most significant contribution came from Stamboul. I grew insistent that there must be some books concerned with higher things, and, under pressure and secretly, another little pile was revealed to me. A Syrian friend barricaded it with his body from the public view while the infidel woman turned over the pages of a specially blessed book. It was a prayer-manual compiled by a sheikh who died some three hundred years ago and was buried at Mecca, as his book does not fail to state. His Arabic work, with a few Turkish marginal notes as introduction, is a book of those devotions wherein lies the religious strength of Islam. There are directions to the worshipper as to the times at which the prayers are most beneficial, and the ritual and number of repetitions, with ejaculations, and the benefits to be obtained from blessing the name of the Prophet. There are the ninety and nine names of Allah, and the two hundred and one names of Mohammed for devout repetition. There are litanies of obsecration:

"I pray to Thee by the greatness and majesty and glory and power and might which Thy Throne upholds.

"I pray to Thee by the power of Thy guarded secret Names which none of Thy creatures know.

"I pray to Thee by the power of the Name which Thou didst lay upon the night and it darkened, and upon the day and it was called forth. . . .

"I pray to Thee by Thy great and Greatest Name by which Thou hast called Thyself. . . .

"I pray to Thee by the Names by which Thou hast called Moses, upon whom be peace.

"I pray to Thee by the Names by which Thou hast called Aaron, upon whom be peace. . . ."

So it runs on, full of the ancient sense of the magic power of a Name, and full of pieties, for this is a book of personal devotions in the singular number, just such a book as Berber doorkeepers of Cairo croon over to themselves on the benches before their lords' gates. It meets the human need for something more warm and personal than the official worship of Islam. And it meets it by lavishing honour and devotion upon the person of Mohammed. The manual warms up to hymns of which the closing note is, "And this our Mohammed, he is our Lord."

This little, cheap, popular work of devotion could not in Amman market-place be sold to a Christian for fear of the indignation of passers-by. It was, however, after a little parleying, laid in my hands as a "gift," I in my turn making the shopman a "gift" of money. And so we exhausted the literature offered to that corner of the Moslem world, yet not quite all its literary contacts; for some of the official class are of Turkish extraction and education, and have in their houses libraries in French, from which they bring out for the Christian's benefit objections to his Faith based on modern philosophy and modern scientific or economic theories. And again an influence, semi-literary since it demands the art of reading and looking at pictures, is the cinema show, which takes place every night hard by the mosque, in the centre of the town. Strange and lurid must be the view which the Arab audience receives of the life of Western and so-called Christian lands!

That tiny trickle of literature into the out-of-the-way Moslem town has been described thus in detail because it is strangely representative of great streams of literary influence poured out upon the whole Moslem world, and more especially upon the Arabic heart of it, each stream constituting a several challenge to those who believe that Christ is the rightful Master of the thought of men.

And, first, the Korans on the shelf that were held sacred from the touch of a Christian are the representatives of all that prolific output of Koranic literature, text, comment, law, theology, which the Moslem presses of Cairo (to name only the greatest of many renowned centres) steadily grind out, and which travels thence to Java or South Africa, to India or Brazil, or to a score of other lands. This literature, be it remembered, is directly responsible in its spiritual attitude (though not in any particular precept on that point) for that estimate of the Faith of Christ which made it seem outrageous for a Christian woman to touch the sacred book. This literature, which trains men in amassing texts and authorities and in a certain dialectic skill in using them, offers to the Christian Church intellectual positions to be captured, but yet more, a spiritual attitude to be changed and prejudices to be broken down for the rightful Lord of human thought.

But next, those elegant letter-writers and poetry books may stand for all the world of Arabic belles-lettres, a world sometimes of naïve charm, sometimes of piled-up luxuriant verbiage. It is a strange phenomenon, this polite literature of the great Moslem tongue whose periods exercise such fascination over her children. It would sometimes seem as though the intellect of Arabic creators had gone all to the elaboration of this magnificent vehicle for human thought and then had failed of thoughts worthy of such a language. Certain it is that an education in such literature tends to breed readers who are content to be paid in words and to gloat over fine periods rather than over fine thought. If books of Moslem theology give the sense of intellectual positions to be won and spiritual attitudes to be changed, books of Arabic belles-lettres suggest rather a great instrument waiting until the rightful Master shall play upon it. The people of Christ in East and West have been strangely without ambition here. Some have coveted for Him the use of the Arabic tongue because of the area it covers and the number of souls who speak it. Shall we not add to that aspiration another, based on the very magnificence of the language? Who but He can raise this great instrument to its fullest beauty and nobility by taxing it to express the thoughts of One who spake as never man spake? Would that all institutions of Christian learning besought the Lord daily to inspire some genius among His people of the East to bend this language to His will.

The stories were the largest element in the pile of books—forlorn-looking street-leaflet stories. And that fact speaks loudly of a human need. The other books, the Koranic works, the high Arabic literature, the sheikh's prayer-manual, have a group or an order to praise, support, and recommend them. But these little street stories there are none to praise. They found their way from Cairo to the desert border simply because of the human desire for a story. Who will awaken the Church to the meaning of this situation? Moslem lands to-day, with the modern increase of primary education, have a new population of half-readers or stuttering readers who cannot attain to the glories of high literature, but who are, like all normal human beings, hungry for stories. The recent survey of literature conditions in Moslem lands brought in strong appeals for more story-books, Christian in spirit and message, from Egypt, Syria, Arabia, Algeria, Turkey, Azerbaijan, Persia, India, Java. Even while this chapter was in the writing a letter arrived from a government education official in Jerusalem, a Palestinian, who writes:

> " One of the sad points one cannot help noticing about the schools of all types in the Near East is that the pupils are slaves to the textbooks, and I believe that one of the chief reasons for this slavery is the great shortage of light reading-matter."

Scores of the schools of the Near East are conducted in Christ's name by missionary societies, and " slavery to textbooks " is a strange result of education in the name of One who said, " The truth shall make you free " !

Here, then, is a situation and a challenge. A challenge first to the Church in the West that provides and controls mission finance. It would seem a hard thing for the Western man even to picture the difference that would have been made in his life if the story element that surrounded his youth had been anti-Christian in its influence. It is hard for him to realize how many unconscious impulses to admire and love the right would go with the stories that inspired them. The influence of stories has been so overlooked that the man they trained will, as a supporter of missions, often refuse to feed Christ's lambs with them, forgetting that the teaching methods of his Saviour honoured the human love of a story, and desiring to publish in that Saviour's Name no literature but tracts. Or the same Western man, as a missionary in the East, will be assaulted again with distrust of the value of a story, and will leave—nay, has left—his Eastern co-workers no sense of the vocation of the Christian story-teller and story-writer. When will the Eastern world see an order of Christian story-tellers gathering groups by the wayside? And when will she see an output, generous in spirit and quantity, of cheap, engaging stories in print with pictures to match?

That last hidden element in the bookseller's stock, the prayer-manual, represents the most deep and spiritual influence of Islam on its children. It recalls to us the whole network throughout the Moslem world of sheikh or guru and pupils, grouped often in one of the numerous and far-spread dervish orders. At its best the literature of these movements has expressed the mystical faith and given hints of the ecstasy of the saints of Moslem mysticism. But such books, mostly mediæval, are for the very few. On its more ordinary levels this literature meets the need of the common man for direction and fellowship of the spirit, even though it be but fellowship in common rhythmic movements for self-hypnotism. This whole literature, whether in its rarely frequented heights or in its common manifestations—in the *puthi* of the Bengali villager or the *wird* of the dervish order, murmured over in odd moments by an Egyptian shop-keeper—all this stands as an almost unheeded challenge to a Church which easily forgets how normal, frequent, and full of rich meaning in her life at its best are the words "I was in the Spirit." Where, in the Church's whole approach to the Moslem world, is the man or woman deliberately set apart to write the message of the Inward Way?

Challenging, then, in their way are all of the handful of Moslem books found that day in Amman. Challenging, too, is the witness that they bear to the cosmopolitan life within the cosmos of Islam. The Arab of Amman was drawing his reading from Mecca, Damascus, Cairo, and Stamboul. It is this fact of the unity of product and consumption within Islam which gives special point to the proposals mooted at the General Conference at Jerusalem, 1924, for a bureau to promote co-operation among all Christian writers and circulation agencies in the Moslem world. Christians must be shamed into acting together in this matter when the counter unity is a fact.

But still more challenging to the man who is Christ's are those two non-Moslem strains of influence that reach Amman, as they reach the whole Near Eastern world, through the European books from which anti-Christian arguments were drawn, and through the cinema, which has come to stay. Through book and picture the West is giving its message to the East. Shall books and pictures carry every message but the message of Christ?

WESTERN EDUCATION IN THE MOSLEM WORLD —FORCES, PURPOSE, AND RESULTS

BY THE REV.

WILLIAM H. HALL, M.A., D.D.,

Principal, Preparatory School, American University of Beirût

CHAPTER XI

WESTERN EDUCATION IN THE MOSLEM WORLD —FORCES, PURPOSE, AND RESULTS

THIS chapter is divided into three parts: the first, historical, in which is set forth something of the intellectual debt which Western peoples owe to Moslem lands; the second, an outline of the Western educational forces at present at work in Moslem lands; and the third, some comments on the purpose and results of Western education in Moslem lands.

THE INTELLECTUAL DEBT

In Muir's *Annals of the Early Caliphate*[1] occurs this statement:

" It was through the labours of these learned men [certain scholars of Baghdad] that the nations of Europe, then shrouded in the darkness of the Middle Ages, became again acquainted with their own proper, but unused and forgotten, patrimony of Grecian science and philosophy."

In like manner Coppée, in his *Conquest of Spain by the Arab Moors*,[2] maintains:

" These Arabian adventurers were to achieve a moral triumph far nobler [than arms], to make an intellectual

[1] Sir William Muir, *Annals of the Early Caliphate*, London, 1883, p. 453.

[2] Henry Coppée, *History of the Conquest of Spain by the Arab Moors*, Boston, 1881, vol. 2, pp. 297-8.

incursion which was to be acknowledged with gratitude in the schools of Oxford, and to be permanently felt 'as far as the confines of Poland and the Highlands of Scotland.' They were now to throw a flood of light upon the darkness of western Europe; and while, directly, they were imparting secular knowledge, they were . . . indirectly to rouse Christendom, and bind all its components together in a grand rally for the Christian faith,—positively to instruct and thus negatively to strengthen."

Just what forces combined to rouse Western Europe from its Dark Ages and bring on the Renaissance no one can finally state. But certain it is that the influence of Arab learning played no small part in the great awakening. There were three main channels through which this learning of Moslem lands penetrated to the countries of Europe: the pilgrims and Crusaders returning from Palestine; the Arab scholars and schools of Sicily; and the Arab Moors of Spain. Through these three sources Europe came in touch with the philosophy, science, mathematics, and medicine of Moslem lands.

While Europe was slumbering in the darkness of ignorance brought on by the barbarian invasion that overthrew the culture of Rome, learning of all kinds was flourishing in the lands of the Caliphs. The city of Baghdad became an intellectual centre to which were drawn the scholars of all lands and faiths. Harun al-Rashid, of *Arabian Nights* fame, and his successors patronized every form of learning. They caused books to be gathered from all countries into a great library at Baghdad. Scholars from Persia and India, from Syria and Egypt, were encouraged by royal favour. The works of Aristotle, lost to the Western world, were translated into Arabic, and in this form passed on to Europe. Ibn Sina, known to Europe as Avicenna, born in far-away Bukhara about 980, was the recognized authority in the interpretation of Aristotle.

Medicine and medical science flourished. It is said that in the eleventh century there were 6,000 students of medicine in Baghdad alone. There were well-ordered hospitals in Cairo, Damascus, and Baghdad. Geography and mathematics were developed to a high degree. These Arab scientists had conceived of the spherical shape of the earth, had measured the angle of the ecliptic, had studied algebra, trigonometry, and analytical geometry. They had brought from India the so-called Arabic numerals on which our present decimal system is based, thus displacing the cumbersome Roman notation. In short, to such an extent did the study of science advance and so enthusiastically was it encouraged by the Abbasid Caliphs, that they were accused of infidelity to religion and the Koran.

While this intellectual activity was going on amongst Moslem people, Western Europe was sleeping under the spell of the Dark Ages. A portion, at least, of the awakening was due to the scholars and the learning of Arab lands.

Then, by the turn of fortune's wheel, came the invasion of Turk and Tatar, and the Dark Ages, lifted from Europe, settled over the Arab people who recently had done so much for the bringing of dawn in the West. And thus there has been left to the West an intellectual debt, an inheritance of obligation to "send the light" of education to lands that were once the centre of learning.

Dr. E. G. Browne closes his lectures on Arabian Medicine[1] with this observation :

"Above all there has grown in me, while communing

[1] Edward G. Browne, *Arabian Medicine*, Cambridge, 1921, p. 126.

with the minds of these old Arabian and Persian physicians, a realization of the solidarity of the human intelligence beyond all limitations of race, space, or time."

It is the preservation of this solidarity that is the call to-day for "Western education in Moslem lands."

Western Educational Forces at Work in Moslem Lands

In estimating the evangelizing agencies in non-Christian lands one is prone to think solely in terms of Protestant mission institutions, and to overlook the educative influences that radiate from the non-Protestant missions, the commercial enterprises, the connexion established by emigration, and the government school systems. All of these, it must be remembered, are contributing their portion, whether great or small, to the transforming of life and thought.

There are three special lines along which the developments of Western lands are now, in turn, helping to pay to the Moslem lands the educational debt contracted during the mediæval Dark Ages. First, there are the government systems of education; second, the non-Protestant missions of Europe; and third, the school systems under the patronage of American and European Protestant missions.

Within less than a century there has been a general awakening throughout the Moslem world to the need of introducing Western systems and Western methods of education. As governments of these lands have been brought into closer relations with the governments of Europe they have realized the vast difference that has separated their people from those of the West. With the introduction of modern machinery and modern commercial productions they have come to realize that, if they are to compete on anything like even terms, their youth must receive a training similar to that given the youth of Europe.

This realization has led to the formulation of educational laws, the appointment of ministers of education in cabinets, the making of plans for national systems of education, and the appropriation of funds for school purposes. Hence we find in practically every Moslem country of the Near East—North Africa, Egypt, Palestine, Syria, Turkey, Persia, Mesopotamia—a system of public education well outlined, provided for by national laws, and supported by the public treasury. In practically every case these public systems are based on some European system. The grading of the schools, the content of the course of study, the departments of the university, and the granting of degrees are all reproductions, in the main, of the French system.

Where these countries have been under the guidance of some foreign Power the systems have become more efficient in operation, as in Egypt and Palestine and portions of North Africa. In the more independent districts, as in Turkey and Persia, the systems exist chiefly on paper. But in every country the desirability of the Western system is recognized by the enactment of the law and the organization of the system, at least on paper. Too often the promoters of these systems seem to think that their value lies in the university alone, take great pains for its establishment, and give too little thought to the long years of primary education upon which, as a foundation, the university must be built. But, nevertheless, there is the positive and official recognition of the value of the Western method. The laboratory, hospital, library, and museum are recognized as the proper means of instruction. An official seal has been placed on the value of the scientific method of education as developed in the West, in contrast with the method of tradition as practised in the religious schools of the East. And in this the educational leaders are but receiving back again their own method after nine centuries.

In evaluating the educational progress of Moslem lands during the past fifty years and in forecasting its probable influence in the years to come, proper weight must be given to these governmental systems, fashioned on Western models. As in Palestine, where there is a comprehensive school system, efficiently administered, with teachers trained and schools inspected, the impact of this government programme must be the same power for elevation of the people as is public education in America or Europe. An efficient educational system and superstition cannot long exist side by side.

After the government school systems should be considered those educational systems established and maintained by numerous non-Protestant bodies. In nearly all the Moslem lands there will be found such schools as those of the Jesuit Fathers, the Frères, the Mission Laïque, or the Italian schools. Whether or not we approve in all cases of their methods, or agree with the content of their curricula, we must concede that no study of Western education in Moslem lands would be complete which did not take account of the fact that earnest men and women, confident of the uplifting value of their mission, are making their contribution to the mental development of the youth of the East and have a part in the thought-growth of the people.

The Bull of Pope Paul III in 1540, which first formally

recognized the order of the Jesuits, specified the teaching of boys and ignorant persons as part of the work for which they were established. Throughout the history of the order teaching has been prominent. At one time they were the schoolmasters of Europe. Later, banished from France, they became active in the conduct of schools in the colonies. In Moslem lands they have been promoters of education in language, history, and science. There are many fine scholars amongst them, and their educational influence has been widely extended.

A clerical teaching order known as the Frères maintains a very extensive system of schools throughout the entire Near East. Their schools are well attended, and their course of instruction is one of the best of all the Western systems working in the East. Side by side with them, and not always, one regrets to state, in the greatest harmony, is a French lay order, the Mission Laïque. This mission believes that Western, and especially French, culture is worth extending to other people. It is a non-religious but not an unreligious body of teachers.

Other orders and missions might be enumerated, but those mentioned suffice to show that many educators from Europe are giving their lives to the work of instructing the people of Moslem lands in the thought and method of the West.

"A church on every hill-top and a school-house in every valley," used to be the boast of Puritan New England. This same sentiment might well be echoed by Protestant missions the world over. Education has ever been taken for granted as a first result of mission work.

Christian mission work in Moslem lands began a little over a century ago. That century has been an era of miraculous growth in world communication. The rapid development of these means of communication and transportation, the enormous increase in emigration with the attendant reports sent back to friends, the penetration of commercial products—these, together with other contacts with the West, have given an increasing demand for the knowledge and training that could come only through schools of the Western type.

Protestant missions have not been slow in meeting this demand. At first education seemed about the only means of contact with a people who were practically closed to appeal in any other way, save perhaps through medicine. As a result, the educational phase of mission work amongst Moslems has assumed rather a larger proportion of attention than in other fields. There have been developed complete systems of schools beginning with the kindergarten and extending through the high school, college, and professional schools, systems so complete that they afford a boy or girl as thorough a training as can be obtained in many a Western land, even up through the medical profession in its various branches, or the fitting for a teacher, preacher, business man, or engineer.

Purpose and Results of Western Education in Moslem Lands

Western Education is chiefly distinguished by the application of "the scientific method" to all departments of human knowledge. This method is the following out of the Pauline text, "Prove all things, hold fast that which is good." In this it is directly opposed to the Oriental method of memorizing texts and traditions. The one is advancing with face to the future, believing that the best of truth is still to be discovered; the other advances with its face to the past, believing that the golden age lies in the years gone by.

It is a dictum of Western education that the final goal of education is the formation of character. Oriental education demanded the memorizing of catechisms and commentaries, but made no impact on character. In contrast with this, Western education emphasizes reality—the taking of beliefs and theories and making them vital in the practice of every-day living, and in the formation of character. Moreover, Western Christianity says, "Character can best be developed when the spirit of Jesus is dominant in an individual life."

When Western education comes into Eastern lands it does not try to make Westerners of Eastern peoples, but rather to give them the Western scientific method recast in the Eastern moulds. Western Christian education, instead of permitting the "scientific method to run rampant and undirected, leaving a train of doubt, takes the scientific method and interprets it in the light of faith and devotion."

The findings of the Jerusalem Conference, 1924, state that in the past the chief use of mission schools has been as an approach, a means of entrance for other forms of mission work. But, now that changing conditions have rendered this no longer necessary, the school "has been set free for its direct educational task." They further state that, in view of the new self-consciousness aroused by the war-years, the new purpose of Moslem peoples to demonstrate their ability to make proper use of Western appliances and methods of thought—

" . . . It seems necessary, not only to re-emphasize our former aims of educational work, but also to state the necessity of sympathetically guiding students in their historical and scientific studies."[1]

The regional conference for Syria and Palestine expressed the chief object of educational work as follows:

"This Conference would reaffirm that the prime object of educational work should be to train men and women of such Christian character that they will be able to help their people develop a proper social and economic life, both national and international, to lay a firm foundation of honest, upright moral character, and to find the source of that character in Jesus Christ as Saviour from sin and Lord of life. But the specific object should be the training of intellectual leaders who, untrammelled by the traditions of the past, whether Christian, Moslem, or Jewish, shall do their thinking freely for themselves. They do not need dogma and convention so much as the mind of Jesus of Nazareth, so that they may awake to the eternal fact of truth in Him."[2]

From these quotations it will be seen that Western Christian education in Moslem lands has a far wider task than to use its schools primarily for developing a point of contact. Everywhere the contact has already been made. "Reports from all fields indicate an increasing desire on the part of Moslems for the education given in missionary institutions." They have come to believe in and to trust the results of the physical, intellectual, and moral training of the students committed to these schools. That confidence should not be betrayed by use of the schools for narrow propaganda. Rather should they be devoted to training in the understanding and use of the methods and results of modern scholarship.

[1] *Conferences of Christian Workers among Moslems, 1924*, New York, 1924, p. 21.
[2] Ibid., pp. 111–2.

Western education, with its Western spirit of democracy, its belief in the open mind, its questioning of all forms of knowledge, and its insistence that all things must be tested and proved, is already an established fact in Moslem lands. The government systems of education are modelled on this pattern. Many young men and women have been sent to the universities of Europe and America and are returning to their homes with the method and spirit of the West. Extended commercial and political relations are rapidly aiding in spreading this Western method, as opposed to the unquestioning acceptance of traditional dogma and dictum. Forces with untold possibilities are thus being released. Just here comes the opportunity of Western Christian missionary education.

Amid this rising tide of inquiry, doubt, and infidelity, there must appear men and women of faith and training who will be as light-houses guiding to a future of sanity, tolerance, and truth. "In no case will it be possible to compete quantitatively with government and other institutions," says the Jerusalem Conference. For the educational institutions that are established is recommended, therefore, "the thorough and scientific organization of Christian schools and their adequate equipment so that they may be equal or superior to any non-Christian schools in the community."[1]

The curriculum and teaching in these schools should accept fearlessly the method of the day. The mission institution will lose its opportunity if it in any degree adopts the Oriental system of authority, of "This is the creed," or "Thus it has been written." Whether in questions of science, in questions of history, or in

[1] *Conferences of Christian Workers among Moslems, 1924*, New York, 1924, p. 22.

questions of religion, it must be in the lead in the inquiry after truth. It cannot apply one method in the class-room of science and another in the class-room of religion. It dare not apply the tests of the "scientific method" to the claims of Islam, and refuse the same application to the claims of Christianity. It must face the facts in fairness and faith. It must resolve that its students shall go forth to be the lighthouses, respected for their learning, trusted for their honesty and frankness, followed for their forward look, and beloved for their likeness to Christ.

Education is, in itself, a primary missionary force. The North Africa Conference recorded that "the government schools are preparing our way by breaking down prejudices and opening out new horizons." This is the effect of all systems of modern education. The Western Christian mission schools should be in the lead in exercising this leadership; they should at all times retain Jesus' outlook on the abundant life.

When one seeks for the results of Western education in Moslem lands he will find them not primarily in tables of statistics, but in a constant increase of those who can read and write; in higher ideals of social and political life; in more hygienic conditions for the community; in horizons that stretch out beyond the village, the sect, and the race, and begin to include mankind; in the breaking down of superstition, prejudices, and intolerance; in thoughts lifted above the routine task of living, to the glory of life. The processes are slow; the results are difficult to calculate; but they are just as worth while for the youth of Moslem lands as for the youth of Western lands, and just as real.

WESTERN EDUCATION IN THE MOSLEM WORLD —CHANGING FACTORS

BY

PROFESSOR PAUL MONROE, Ph.D., LL.D.,

Director, International Institute, Teachers' College, Columbia University, New York

CHAPTER XII

WESTERN EDUCATION IN THE MOSLEM WORLD —CHANGING FACTORS

A DISCUSSION of Western education in Moslem lands involves the consideration of several factors which would not have entered into the situation a few years ago.

The first of these is the fact that there now exists among Arabic peoples, both Christian and Moslem, a well-defined renaissance of Arabic culture and hence of Arabic education. This renaissance reveals itself in a revival of literary activity; in the publication of numerous newspapers, periodicals, and pamphlets; in the establishment and more generous support of schools; in increased school attendance; and in stimulation of the political agitation now occurring throughout these lands. It is also shown in a more suspicious or even a hostile attitude towards Western educational institutions. At the same time, there may exist in some of these lands an intensified interest in Western culture or in certain aspects of it and consequently in the schools which represent it.

It is quite possible that the Arab overestimates the importance of this new cultural movement, especially in terms of the old learning. The Arab is inclined to say that because algebra and chemistry originated with his forefathers, and because they were the transmitters of Aristotelian learning to the West, therefore the Arab student in this present movement can rapidly become the peer of the scientists and the scholars of the West. But it is just as possible that the Western educator may underestimate the significance of this renaissance and the strength of the attachment which the Arab—or any member of a suppressed race or people—may have for his own culture. The Westerner is inclined to underestimate the stimulus which the renewed vitality of Arabic culture may give to the Moslem people. He may fail to realize that such a revival is likely to arouse hostility to his own culture, for Western culture, more forceful and aggressive, tends to ignore and suppress that of any weaker or backward people. Above all, he may fail to see how much assistance the apostle of Western culture or religion may gain by admitting the inherent value of the native culture and the significance of its renewed vitality. An infusion of this new vitality into his own work, through sympathetic appreciation and co-operation, may afford a way out of an awkward situation where the two cultures seem to have reached a hostile *vis-à-vis*.

This Arab renaissance affects Syria, Palestine, Mesopotamia, Egypt, and, by indirection, the other Moslem lands.

The second factor demanding consideration is that all Moslem lands and all Moslem peoples have received a new political stimulus, are striving for political organization in modern form, and are endeavouring to throw off any political restraint or control exercised over them by the Western Powers. This political renaissance began perhaps a generation ago, certainly as early as the Young Turk movement in 1909. It was greatly stimulated during and immediately after the World War and by the *impasse* later reached by the French and British policies.

It was recognized as a vital political fact by the Conference of Lausanne. This political development assumes its own peculiar form in each country and with each people.

In Turkey this has taken the form of a nominal Republic under a dictator and controlled by a small but determined faction. This faction, conscious that the Western Powers had made prey of the East by dividing its forces, have now retaliated by dividing the forces of the West and thus obtaining independence. Chagrined by the failures and the weaknesses of their own people, as well as resentful of their oppression and exploitation by the West, the Turks have determined to succeed even at the cost of their ancient capital, one of the great historic cities, now seemingly dying. In the endeavour to get rid of elements of political weakness, they have sacrificed some of the most important economic elements in their social structure through the exchange of population and the elimination of the Greek and Armenian peoples.

In Egypt a new constitutional monarchy is replacing the English occupation. Notwithstanding the obvious advantages conferred by English rule, these rulers themselves have recognized the inevitability of the political forces at work. This long training under the English, together with taxable assets sufficient to support any fairly efficient government, gives greater promise for the political future of Egypt than can be hoped for in the case of any other new political entities of the Moslem world.

Palestine is restive under a British protectorate or mandate which gives nominal control of the local government to 15 per cent. of the population. Syria is even more restive under a French protectorate which has not yet made evident, to the Syrians at least, that its chief interest is in the welfare of the people living under the mandate.

The ancient Empire of Persia is dallying with the idea of a republic. With judgment unusual in these days of political phantasies, she chooses, for the present at least, a constitutional monarchy tempered by a dictatorship rather than a dictatorship clothed in the disguise of a republic. For a true republic she certainly will not be ready before a generation of modern schooling.

Iraq—home of ancient monarchies—is experimenting with a constitutional monarchy, with a king and a very active legislative assembly, under the military protectorate of a British mandate sanctioned by a negotiated treaty.

In addition to the cultural and political forces a third factor is to be taken into account. In all these lands there is a distinct movement towards the separation of the State and the Church. Since in the old Turkish Empire, which covered most of the territory under consideration, State and Church were identical, and in the other lands were closely associated, this change is of profound significance.

As has been the case in all such instances of Church and State closely bound together and of schools in the hands of the Church, this transition is of special significance to education. In the Protestant Reformation of Western Europe, where the Church became an established Church, as it did in most lands, education long remained under its supervision. Where the Reformation was largely political, as in England, educational foundations as well as ecclesiastical foundations were destroyed for political ends, and learning suffered greatly in consequence.

The immediate effect of the disestablishment of the

Church in Moslem lands must inevitably be a great curtailment of education, due to the destruction of the old system, with its trust funds held by the Church. To balance that loss stands the effort of the Government to furnish facilities for modern education. These efforts are likely to be woefully inadequate, yet will be jealously guarded, especially from any encroachment by ecclesiastical authorities, either native or foreign.

The changes produced by these three new factors are so profound that it must be recognized that the past of Western education in Moslem lands is now a closed chapter. This fact is perfectly obvious to all concerned in the work in Turkey. It is little less obvious, but perhaps as profoundly true, in all the other lands under discussion.

Western education in these Moslem lands of the Near East entered a new epoch with the close of the World War. There are now demanded a new policy and a new programme which call for the most serious consideration. Much thought is now being given to the problem by all concerned.

For those not on the ground, but interested in the problem, one further factor must be borne in mind. The various Moslem countries present very diverse situations. In Turkey there is a hostility to all Western Governments and all Western enterprises, due to her experiences of a century past. There is a suspicion of, if not a direct hostility to, Western education, especially mission education, owing to the fact that it has been directed toward the minority peoples and not toward the Turks. Whether or not this suspicion is justified, it undoubtedly exists. Furthermore, there exists a hostility to these schools on the part of the Turkish people as well as of the Turkish authorities, based upon the belief that they have been directly responsible, in part at least, for the political misfortunes of Turkey. And while it can be proved that such schools have taken no part whatever in agitation, or in any overt act against the established authorities, it cannot be denied that there is in Western education, as interpreted by Americans, even by American missionaries, a political bias hostile to the traditional political ideals and practices of the East. It cannot be maintained that this education produced the modern Bulgaria without admitting that it had some influence on the political ideas and aspirations of the other minority peoples of the old Turkish Empire. This situation, however, is of the past, even if the hostility is not. The present problems are entirely new. Turkey, with the form of a modern republic, with the social minorities eliminated and the Moslem Church disestablished, presents an entirely new situation and demands on the part of Western educators an entirely new policy. What shall this policy be? How shall the West disarm hostility or suspicion? What shall it aim to contribute to the Turks? What shall it aim to accomplish for Western culture and for Christianity?

These same questions arise but with varying incidence in the other Moslem lands. In Egypt the hostility toward mission educational work is less pronounced. This may be due to the facts that in this country contacts with the West have been chiefly political, have been for many years past with one Government only, and have been of a benevolent and beneficial character. It may be due in part to the fact that there has always been a minority Christian population, native to the land, and causing little or no political difficulty.

In Syria the immediate problem lies chiefly in the adjustment of policy and the political mandatory power.

The French plan in the mandate territory is to work out their educational programme chiefly through the Church, which means chiefly through the Roman Catholic religious orders. At present, then, there are two distinct problems of adjustment in this area. The one is with the native population. Since this is part Christian, part Moslem, the situation is much easier than where the native population is entirely Moslem. The other problem is adjustment with a mandatory Power accustomed to use the Church as an instrument of government and to this end to give the Church large authority over education.

The most that can be asked or expected is a working agreement of tolerance. The situation is very greatly eased by the facts that the one leading mission educational institution has long been cosmopolitan in the composition of its student body and staff and that it has sent its graduates into important positions of social and government service throughout the Near East. Furthermore, it has served the Arabic peoples of the old Turkish Empire and has for its backing the Arabic sentiment in so far as this is indifferent or hostile to the old Turkish political domination.

In Persia also a more friendly attitude is found toward the Western schools. Despite the fanaticism and ignorance of the masses of the people, the mission schools are patronized by the families of the best classes; not only by those of the landed gentry, as is chiefly the case in Egypt, but also by the official class.

Altogether the new conditions, political, cultural, and religious, call for a policy differing in many respects from that of the past, and present a new opportunity throughout the Moslem lands. While antagonisms, hostility, and suspicion are still present, yet there is nevertheless a greater opportunity.

The Turkish authorities may restrict the privileges of the mission school; they at least recognize its influence even with the Moslem population. They may try to sever all religious instruction and influence from the schools; they are at least doing the same thing with the schools for Moslems. The profound political, ecclesiastical, and cultural changes which have taken place indicate a willingness to learn or at least a willingness to consider new evidence and to change from immemorial custom. Hostility to Western power and culture, even in India, does not imply an unwillingness to learn from these contacts and to profit by them. While it must be recognized that there is a new sensitiveness and a renewal of fanatical intolerance throughout the Moslem world, felt even as far away as with the Moros of the Philippines, this again is but the reaction of the masses to the conviction of their leaders that Western culture and Western schools, and even Western religion, are making, or have the opportunity of making, a new and a more forceful appeal to the Moslem world.

A few of the changes in policy made necessary, or at least desirable, by the new situation may be indicated.

Obviously, all non-governmental work will have to be carried on under closer government supervision than heretofore. It would, therefore, seem desirable that Western education should seek to adapt itself more closely to government standards than in the past. The essential things in mission education are its purpose, spirit, and method. Institutional organization and arrangement of curriculum materials are not so essential. It seems unwise for mission educators to sacrifice so much of their main purpose for the preservation of those externals to which they had been accustomed in the West.

Education is now recognized as a great political power, just as heretofore it has been recognized as a great religious power. It is but natural that all these new organizations, not yet assured of their stability, should seek to control education as a means of strengthening their hold on the people. Western education, mission education, should further this end by assisting public education wherever possible, by complying cheerfully with minimum political requirements which perhaps are seldom required in our own country, and by seeking to demonstrate to the political authorities and to the public at large that private initiative in education, including the enterprises of mission or Western education, can contribute to general progress and welfare. Such contribution may be made by experiment, by demonstration of superiority in certain lines, by caring for special ability, and by the introduction of elements which the Government can never control or command.

In Persia, where there is a receptive attitude on the part of the officials to Western ideas, this can readily be done. In Turkey, where the attitude is suspicious, if not hostile, it will be far more difficult. In Egypt, and wherever there is a desire to learn from democracy, even though democracy is only partially conceived, the position just outlined can easily be taken by Western education with profit to both parties.

A second need is adjustment to the actual life and needs of the community, to the culture of the people. This is more difficult because it is less tangible than is adjustment to the policy of the Government. The latter may call for diplomacy and modification of externals; the former demands close study, great insight, and modification of essentials. It may be that approach to the life of the people, now more open and sensitive than ever before, can be better made through agriculture and industry than through the learned professions. It may be that the school-teacher or the trained agriculturist or artisan is a far more important person to produce than the physician, the government official, the diplomat, the lawyer, or the merchant.

It is even possible that investigation of the daily routine of life in home conditions, in industrial process, in rural custom, followed by judicious attempts to improve this routine, is more important, and a more direct way to the end sought than the production of a few religious teachers who follow the traditional formal routine.

The concept of salvation as the saving health of a community, or of society, or of a people, as well as of selected individuals, has been slow to dawn upon the religious world. Its dawn is even more retarded in the smaller world of religious or mission education. Perhaps the new day of opportunity in the Near East awaits such a dawn. Certainly the new opportunity for such a closer approach to the people now exists. They are conscious of their many defects, conscious that their own Government cannot fully meet these deficiencies. In many instances they are awaiting just such leadership. The significance of the educational work of the Near East Relief enterprises lies in its intimate connexion with the whole life of the child and hence with the entire life of the communities of which these children become members. This seeking the good of society rather than merely that of the person educated is particularly the thing which mission education should demonstrate for the members of retarded groups.

Looked at from another point of view, the present situation offers a third aspect of the new opportunity and the need for a new policy. Clearly the chief contribution which Western education can offer to native education is to lead the way by experimentation and demonstration. Its endeavours should be more novel, its achievements more specialized, than those of the usual governmental and private native efforts. It can never compete in quantity; it should excel in quality, not only of products but also of types of endeavour. Western education in the Orient should not be tied down too closely to an imitation of the traditional models. Western educators abroad should be conscious of the fact that what was standard in their own experience is rapidly being changed in the homeland through subsequent experience; that educational conditions at home are not static if they are vitally alive; so that Western education abroad should not be static. Efficiency or success in the conventional is not sufficient. It may be adequate for the individual student; it does not suffice for the society to which this education is on mission.

In this closer approach to the life of the people it is evident that the educational work itself should be shared in by the people of the country concerned. Not only on the teaching staff, but in administration and control, native co-operation should be more largely sought. This is not so simple a proposition in the Near East as it is in the Far East, though even there it is far from simple. The point is, that so long as this mission education remains wholly alien, so long does it miss its main purpose of entering fully into the life of the people, and thus ceasing to be wholly Western or alien, but becoming a common Christian product and possession.

One final point of profound change may be mentioned although its possibility may be a debated question. It is closely related to the point previously made. If education should seek to influence the entire life of the community, then one of the best ways of doing this would be to demonstrate its efficiency in the entire life of certain small communities, just as now it seeks to accomplish its main purpose by influencing a few individuals. Especially with mission education, which seeks to make a demonstration of the superiority of a life of reason, of faith, and of right conduct—of the unity of life, physical, economic, social, spiritual—it would seem that the most effective way of doing this is to show changes wrought in the life of some entire community. Strangely enough, this has seldom been attempted, and that only recently. Progress in rural life, in agriculture, in health conditions, in industrial relations, has been improved in our Western world by such group demonstrations. It is high time that Western education in Eastern lands made serious attempts of this kind.

Whether old or new in policy is urged, there arises the more fundamental question of the place and function of a mission education in Moslem lands. Why should Christian men and woman devote either their funds or their lives to this work? What is its need, its justification? What are its results? The answer given by those native leaders who patronize or favour the schools, and that given by the Western educator experienced in the work, are fundamentally the same. The one outstanding responsibility, the one outstanding contribution, of mission education is character-building. While strong moral traits may be developed by the Oriental home, or even by the Oriental religion or social life, this is not usually the case. And, even if it is, the school has little to do with the result. The home and social organization may furnish efficiency; the native religion may furnish social motives and moral ideas; the school may furnish knowledge. But it is the vital organic union of these factors which constitutes character, and that union the mission school can and does bring about far oftener than does any indigenous agency. For this reason thoughtful native teachers welcome the mission school.

In addition, the Western school contributes a number of other results which the East consciously needs. One is a training in democratic ideas and practices, for which all these people are now reaching out. Another is the idea of efficiency, the working over of knowledge into conduct, of which the native schools have little conception. Another is that of the harmonious co-operation of several national and religious groups which in their natural condition are always hostile. Still another is the concept of education as affecting the life of the community, its concept as the vital social or political influence in contrast with the external or physical force represented by public officials or soldiery. In this last respect Western education needs to assume a more definite leadership in agriculture and in the direction of commerce and public health than it has hitherto done.

Whether viewed from the standpoint of opportunity, of policy, of achievement, or of function, Western education in Moslem lands is now facing a crisis, and both needs and deserves the sympathetic interest and support of the homeland.

INFLUENCES TOWARDS A NEW ART IN EGYPT AND PALESTINE

BY

W. A. STEWART, F.R.S.A.,

Director of the Egyptian School of Arts and Crafts, Cairo; Inspector of Industrial Arts and Crafts to the Egyptian Government

CHAPTER XIII

INFLUENCES TOWARDS A NEW ART IN EGYPT AND PALESTINE

ALTHOUGH it may not be quite correct to say that Moslem art has never been creative, it is generally admitted that it has always shown great powers of absorption ; it has made use of whatever forms of art came to it and has moulded them to its special requirements.

This is very evident in India and in Egypt. Both countries had a pronounced native art much older than the earliest Moslem work, and in both countries there are traces of the influence of this older work in the Moslem ornament and architecture. In Egypt the Early Fatimid work is strongly reminiscent of the Greek, Roman, and Byzantine ornament upon which it is undoubtedly based. The ornamentation of the mosque of Ibn Tulun in Cairo is almost a frank importation of the decoration of the mosque at Samarra which Ibn Tulun had seen when a boy, and this again is very Byzantine in character.

In much earlier work there is a use of living forms of birds, animals, and human figures which still further indicates the Byzantine parentage, and this use of figures, though discontinued in the Saracen art of Egypt, continues in that of Persia and India, and becomes quite a characteristic feature, particularly in the art of painting, which was never so highly developed in Egypt as in the more eastern Moslem countries. Egypt has never developed the art of the painted picture as an end in itself. All Egyptian art has ever had a basis of utility. In ancient Egypt the tomb and the many sides of a complex religion connected with the ritual of burial and the welfare of the soul in the after-world of the spirit demanded a form of decoration that was more in the nature of a pictorial list of necessary objects and events than of an æsthetic interpretation of nature.

It is true that in the long series of tomb reliefs and paintings we find work that reaches great heights of artistic achievement, but such work is the exception, not the rule, and is proof of the poetic and imaginative temperament of the craftsman overcoming the difficulties and limitations of his routine work. In Saracen work also we find that all art seems to have had a basis of utility. It is the art of the craftsman rather than that of the artist as we think of him to-day, an art concerned with the decoration of buildings, books, and articles of domestic use, not with pictures.

A ceiling becomes a wonderful maze of complex arabesques in colour and gold; a brass bowl is adorned with scrolls in engraving and silver inlay; a Koran is beautiful with pages marvellously illuminated, with details of form and colour so delicately worked that we are amazed at the patience and skill that produced it. But the decoration is always decoration. We look in vain for the picture painted for its own sake, or for the sculptured figure that was an end in itself. It follows, therefore, that Moslem art, as it has continued to our times, should have become more and more the art of the craftsman. It no longer exists in Egypt outside the native workshops, where indeed the traditions are still alive but linger on in a feeble condition, degenerating more and more into a copying and repetition of what has been done before.

Egypt is awaiting another influence from outside, and it is certain that that influence will come, or is already coming, from Europe.

If we examine the educational system in force in Egypt, it is not difficult to understand why art has not developed. Art has been almost entirely neglected. Drawing, in an elementary form, is part of the curriculum of primary and secondary education; but æsthetics, the history of art, and its influence upon mankind, have never been dealt with.

Pictures and music have in the past been looked upon as frivolous and unnecessary. The average young Moslem is not concerned with these things, and has no conception of the ennobling influence of creative art upon life. The craftsman who may be still capable of producing something fine is looked upon as a workman, a member of the lower classes, and is rarely given the encouragement or payment which real skill deserves. The painting is regarded as little better than a photograph, and its essential qualities are but rarely understood.

We see, then, that there are no traditions of art, and that the rising generation has none of the artistic influences which surround the European and American child in the house and in the school, to stimulate and guide it.

We must now examine what is being done to remedy these conditions. For many years students from Egyptian schools have been sent on educational missions to Europe, where they have imbibed a little of the culture and refinement of life in the great educational centres. These young men, on returning to Cairo, miss the exhibitions, the music, and the theatres to which they have grown accustomed in Europe, and this rising demand for something more than the usual café life of Cairo has produced the beginnings of a local drama which promises to develop rapidly into a fine local art of the theatre. Already plays are being produced in Arabic which are genuine creations based on the social life and problems of the people, not merely translations of European plays. The new drama has brought with it a little group of local scene-painters, some of them trained in Italy and France, and they are taking their part in the revival of theatrical art. Egyptians have much natural talent as actors, and a really living drama shows signs of healthy growth.

A school of fine arts and a school of artistic crafts have been established. Nothing great has so far been achieved, but several students from these schools have been sent to France and England and have done work which is full of promise. A little group of local student painters has held exhibitions in Cairo which had sufficient interest to justify the formation of an arts society. This society holds an annual exhibition of painting, sculpture, and decorative arts, to which any local artist, of whatever nationality, may contribute. The last exhibition was officially opened by His Majesty King Fuad, whose kindly sympathy in the movement is doing much to make it officially recognized by the Government as of considerable educational importance. The barriers of prejudice and official neglect are being broken down by the force of public opinion, and in this there is great hope for the future.

The Arts Society has for president H.H. Prince Yousef Kamāl, a man whose wide knowledge of Oriental art is a great help. He is an enthusiastic collector, and his palace at Mataria is a treasure-house of beautiful objects which will some day become the property of the national museum. His Highness is keenly interested in the society, has himself endowed the school of fine arts, and has sent the best students for further training in Paris.

But all efforts to train artists will be futile without more general local patronage, and this is at present the great difficulty. Education has been so lacking in the arts that the general public does not yet appreciate the work of the artists. To overcome this difficulty a special Committee of Fine Arts has been recently formed to advise the Ministry of Education on changes in its courses of study, and to encourage in every possible way the local artists and craftsmen. A sum of £10,000 (Egyptian) was voted by Parliament to this Committee, and with this sum several students have already been sent to Europe. Grants have been voted to local music and drama, and a book on the history of art is being translated into Arabic. The history of art is to be introduced into the curriculum of primary and secondary schools, and music and eurythmics are to be taught.

Large sums of money are allocated for further developments in the industrial schools, particularly for the weaving and carpet-making industries, and it is proposed to set up a modern dye-works in order to improve this very important industry, upon which the beauty of so many other crafts depends. It is intended to build as soon as possible specially designed schools for the fine arts and for the arts and crafts. Both these schools are at present housed in old buildings which are unsuitable and badly lighted.

A proposal has been made to the Public Works Ministry that some control be exercised over the designs for all buildings in the city to ensure that they maintain a standard of dignity and beauty and conform to a general scheme; also, that state buildings include decoration of the interiors in order to give local artists an opportunity for exercising their art in mural painting. With some such state patronage and encouragement a lead will be given to the public, for without patronage art cannot exist. Hitherto there has been no control of private building other than that required by certain regulations of sanitation and public safety. Styles of every description have been erected, and the confused effect and general lack of taste and suitability to climate and traditions is very lamentable. State buildings also have, so far, shown no tendency to adopt a local style of architecture, with the exception of the court-house at Asyût. In this building a most praiseworthy effort has been made to use a modified Arabic style of architecture with the limitations imposed by the materials of construction, namely, sand-bricks. The result is a dignified, unostentatious structure whose decorative features are the logical outcome of a right use of material.

In Lord Kitchener's period of office a scheme was drawn up to impose the Arabic style on all buildings erected in the vicinity of the ancient mosque of Sultan Hassan in order that this noble monument should have a fitting setting. Some of the work was completed, and the houses approach the old Arabic buildings in beauty and dignity. With so many examples of the flower of Moslem architecture in the city of Cairo, it is a pity that more effort has not been made to keep up the tradition and to adopt a style of state architecture that, while allowing for the requirements of modern conditions, would be in keeping with the old monuments which are the charm of Cairo. Unfortunately, Egyptian authorities prefer the more florid styles of the French Louis, and have used these styles in both public and private buildings.

They cannot bring themselves to decide upon the Arabic style as an official state architecture. It is looked upon by most of them as out-of-date and unsuitable to modern conditions of life; but that this is not the case is amply proved by the experiments of one or two Europeans who have built houses in the Arabic style with great success. The French authorities in Morocco have used the Arabic style for their public buildings, and the style has been adopted by local notables for their private houses. This has led to a revival of ceramic art and of Arabic carving in wood and stone, and the example might very well be followed in Egypt, where so many fine models already exist.

There has been much discussion as to the style of art which should be encouraged in Egypt. There are many people who regret that the Arabic style is dying out, and who urge that European art should not be encouraged. There is a certain amount of work being done in the style of ancient Egypt, but this period of history is further from, and more foreign to, the modern Egyptians than Arabic art. Again, painting, as represented by the picture, does not exist in Arabic art. It is, therefore, somewhat difficult to decide what should be done. In my opinion, it is advisable to give every possible opportunity for the development of talent, to make the scheme of training very wide, and to base it upon the study of historic examples and upon nature, but to leave style severely alone. Style will come by itself, and will be the expression of what the people themselves bring to their art. It cannot be imposed from outside, and it is a mistake to attempt to do so. Already some of the local painters who have come under the influence of French impressionist art show signs of becoming mere copyists of this style of painting. They do not know that the work of Monet, for example, is based upon a very sound knowledge of drawing. The quick and easy brushwork attracts them, and their own efforts to imitate this show a sad lack of knowledge of real structure.

The national library contains a rich collection of fine oriental miniatures which could well be studied. They are as important in their way as are the paintings of Europe, and they should have their influence in the making of a native school of Egyptian art.

The country needs an art gallery. It has fine museums of Arabic, Coptic, and Egyptian work, but no general art gallery where students who cannot afford to travel may study the various schools of painting. The Art Society intends to do something to this end by holding occasional international exhibitions by invitation, from which it hopes to make purchases towards a national collection. It also proposes to offer awards to local artists and craftsmen. There is, therefore, considerable activity towards a revival of art in Egypt. Undoubtedly there are two vital needs: further propaganda to stimulate the public appreciation for the finer things of beauty in life, and more general education in æsthetics.

There is no doubt that the Egyptians have artistic ability. Within certain limits they show very considerable taste. In native costume, for example, one seldom finds a mistake. The colours of the silk caftans of the sheikhs are beautiful; the silk-weaving craft of Cairo is still one of very real excellence, and should be encouraged in every possible way. It depends upon the continuance of native costume; and this is tending year by year toward the vanishing point. By the younger students, who wear European dress, it is looked upon as old-fashioned and almost a symbol of lack of civilization; but it is still the official dress for sheikhs at the Houses of Parliament and at court receptions. This is as it should be, and one hopes that the King will maintain a regulation which gives dignity to so valuable a national possession. In Egypt and Palestine almost every district has some characteristic feature of its own, either of colour or of form. The production of the special materials and colours is in many cases a local industry with age-long traditions, and it would be a real loss to the interest and beauty of Eastern life if European costume, with its monotony of form and colour, became universal.

We have noted that education in crafts is already going on, but it will be a long time before the students now being educated in artistic crafts begin to influence the actual output of local workshops.

The conditions of these shops are most primitive. In the provinces, jewellers, brass workers, makers of inlay work, and weavers use the most elementary tools and methods, sometimes even still those that must have been employed in the days of the Pharaohs. One does not regret that the tools and methods are primitive, but there seems to be no inspiration in design and very little skill in drawing. Old Arabic geometrical patterns are often so broken and badly drawn as to be almost unrecognizable, and copies of old Egyptian forms have lost all the beauty and refinement of line that make them so interesting in the originals.

Woven patterns are produced by the draw-loom system of the Middle Ages and the patterns are, in consequence, very limited in size of repeat. The increasing use of the Jacquard loom will gradually open the way to greater variety of design, but education in drawing is very necessary for all the crafts in order to raise them to higher artistic excellence. Improved methods of work must also be introduced or many of the crafts will be unable to compete with the imported products from Europe and Japan. In the weaving industry, for example, there is a great deal of wasted and costly hand-labour in all the preparatory processes, which could be done by modern machinery to cheapen the final product.

Egypt has no need to go through the long, slow development of Europe in the textile industries. Her weavers are very skilled in the essentials of their craft, and there seems to be no reason why up-to-date machinery should not be introduced. The traditions and Oriental character of her products could be retained, but modern methods must, sooner or later, be introduced or one of her largest industries will shortly be unable to exist.

Whatever religious objections ever existed against the representation of living or human forms in art are gradually dying out. There is a growing interest in the art of portraiture, and portraits, often of native ladies, are frequently shown in the exhibitions of the Society of Arts. Egyptian ladies are taking a very prominent part in the revival of art. They helped to organize and support the first exhibition of pictures, and several of them contribute work, both in painting and in sculpture. By their propaganda in the homes they are doing a great deal to widen the interest in art among their people, and one hopes that the Government will take a more serious interest in a revival that is already proved to spring from the desires of the people themselves.

Further stimulus from outside will doubtless be needed, but the germs are already planted, and, with sympathetic support and encouragement, the future should be full of hope.

MOVEMENTS IN THE LIFE OF WOMEN IN THE ISLAMIC WORLD—THE NEAR AND MIDDLE EAST

BY

CAROLINE M. BUCHANAN, Litt.D.,
American Girls' College, Cairo

CHAPTER XIV

MOVEMENTS IN THE LIFE OF WOMEN IN THE ISLAMIC WORLD—THE NEAR AND MIDDLE EAST

IN the station square at Cairo there stands a statue to commemorate the renaissance of Egypt. The artist has carved a marble sphinx as a fitting reminder of Egypt's ancient glories and a symbol of her age-long sleep. At the side of the sphinx is an Egyptian woman, her hand stretched forth to end that slumber by her arousing touch. Looking at that outstretched hand, and into the beautiful face, one is thrilled by the thought of the part that the Oriental woman is already playing, and the greater part she may still play, in the awakening not of Egypt only, but of the whole of the Near East. What could she not achieve, faith whispers, if out of her eyes looked the spirit of Jesus, and, exchanging the yoke of Islam for His blessed yoke, she attained in His service true liberty of soul, " the liberty wherewith Christ hath made us free " !

From Morocco, Algeria, and Tunisia; from Egypt, the Sudan, and Abyssinia; from Arabia, Palestine, Syria, and Turkey; from Mesopotamia, Persia, and Central Turkistan to the Dutch East Indies, we hear the confident voices of the few women who have stepped out into a degree of social liberty; the cries of those who are struggling to be free; and the unhappy murmur of the women and girls who are, as yet, ignorant of any world outside of their four walls. We get far more than glimmerings of progress along educational, literary, political, social, and religious lines.

In direct opposition to Islamic tradition and practice, Moslem women in the Near East are beginning to demand an education. A definite organized movement has gone forward in Turkey; and a compulsory education clause, which includes girls, was placed in the Constitution of Egypt in April 1923, when the first complete Constitution was secured, although neither country, as yet, has been able, because of lack of teachers, buildings, and equipment, fully to enforce the education laws.

In Turkey, especially, there have been rapid strides toward the goal. In a Teachers' Association which met in 1924 in Angora, Constantinople alone supplied 1,000 women delegates, and Angora 200. In Smyrna there is the fine large Training School for Girls, and the public schools are devoting much time and money to the normal, or teacher-training, departments.

There is a growing desire for a liberal, thoroughgoing education. No longer do the best families depend upon governesses: the girls are sent to school, and later to the Constantinople College for Women or to the University, where women are now on an equal footing with men. In this co-educational institution there are women students in science, literature, and law. Twelve women entered the medical class in 1924. The same year there were three women candidates for degrees in law. Many women have studied abroad, among them several prominent Turkish women doctors of medicine. Without doubt the women of Turkey lead in the educational movement of the Islamic world.

Egypt is travelling along rapidly in the footsteps of

Turkey. The first girl to be sent abroad for her education went in 1901, and in 1924 there were, in England alone, twenty-one young women students sent from Egypt by the Ministry of Education. Besides these, many are studying at their own or their parents' expense, in France, England, and Germany, and a few in the United States. Art, domestic science, physical training, medicine, nursing, kindergarten, special teacher training, and law are the subjects which are studied.

In October 1924, Miss Nebaweeya Moosa, one of the young women who were educated abroad, was made Superintendent of Girls' Schools in Egypt, a position never before occupied by a woman. This remarkable woman quite independently some time ago opened her "model school." She is the only woman who has been decorated by the King with "The Order of the Nile." Her book, *Woman and Work*, in Arabic, is of unusual merit. The Educational Council, which consists of four men inspectors and Miss Nebaweeya Moosa, meets with the Minister of Education to discuss the conduct of the schools.

From the time of the establishment of the first girls' school by the American Mission in 1856, up to 1903, that mission and others led in girls' education. Even in 1906, there were in all Egypt, with its 11,000,000 inhabitants, only 33,280 girls in government schools. Now the Government has opened girls' schools in every city and in almost all the towns along the Nile, and the number of pupils has increased to 99,402. The American Girls' College in Cairo graduated its first Moslem student in 1916, and since that time young women are remaining in the college in increasing numbers until they complete the course. Men no longer fear to marry educated wives. Neither are the fathers and mothers afraid of Christian schools, and Moslem young women are sent to mission schools in Egypt with absolute freedom. The number of women who can read (seven out of every thousand in 1919) is rapidly increasing, although the proportion of literates is still pitifully small (fifteen out of every thousand in 1921–22). One of the most hopeful signs of progress is the willingness of the Moslem girl to become a teacher. We see this even among the richer class. Women are pushing their daughters into the medical professions also. The spirit of service has come only to the few in Egypt, it is true; but these few are leaders, and in consequence benevolent and industrial schools for girls are springing up.

In Persia education for girls is now being successfully promoted by the Persians themselves. Bishop Linton says: "Christian schools have always been in the forefront in education in Persia, and setting a standard which Persian schools have sought to reach."

From the new Mesopotamia comes word of a great thirst for education, including the education of girls. A member of the family of the Naqīb of Baghdad, head of the religious aristocracy, approached a missionary, saying, "If you will establish a school for girls in Baghdad I will guarantee you sixty girls from the Naqīb family." To have the Arabs realize the value of an education for their daughters indeed gives one a real thrill.

Syria is much to the front in the Moslem woman's educational movement. Even from conservative Damascus girls are being sent to Beirût for their education, a thing much condemned a few years ago. A writer from Syria says:

"It is impossible to give statistics, but the proportion of educated women in Syria is much higher than it was ten years ago. The girls are crowding into our schools, and the fathers say they are sending them to our mission schools because of the moral training the school gives."

From Dr. J. Kelly Giffen, a pioneer missionary in the Sudan, comes the word that even there, in the black belt, women and girls from Islamic homes are learning the value of education, and making great sacrifices for it. He gives many striking examples.

A missionary from Atbara writes of a Sudanese woman who was left a widow when her children were young:

"She works hard in order to earn enough money not only to feed her children, but also to send them to school. These schools and their methods of education are spoken of very appreciatively by Sudanese women. And it is not only the material advantages of a good education for which they look. Those who have had a mission education are very anxious for their children to come to Christian schools and to receive the same teaching which they found to be an inspiration and help to themselves, a teaching of which they see the effect in character and in life."

A missionary who has laboured long in the Near East says:

"I am convinced that the emancipation of the Oriental woman, that is, raising her status to that of her Western Christian sisters, carries the key to the whole Islamic situation."

Again, quoting one who has studied the situation in Turkey:

"Those who watch the march of events both in Constantinople and in Angora are amazed at the swiftness of the development. Unveiled faces were seen for the first time in 1908, following the first revolution. To-day, in Angora, the chic modern wives of the members of the Grand National Assembly, headed by Latife Hanoum, the accomplished and progressive wife of Mustafa Kemal Pasha, dress in European garb, visit the movies with their husbands, and have their 'at homes' where men and women, Turkish, European, and American, freely mingle.

"In Stamboul one finds about seven in eight of the Moslem women going unveiled to and fro through the streets. Even a school-girl can go alone through the streets without exciting remark or attracting criticism. Husbands and wives walk arm-in-arm, and young men and women may be seen intent upon jaunts here and there.

"In public vehicles the dividing curtains and partitions have been removed and women may sit where they choose, though custom is still sufficiently strong to hold them rather closely to the older places. There are some who enjoy breaking away and venturing into the hitherto forbidden sections."

When Aishat at Temour, the poetess, wrote her first book in 1896, the Feminist Movement in Egypt was born. Her poetry expressed in beautiful cadence the upward struggles of a woman's soul. She wrote in Arabic, Persian, and Turkish with equal ease. Then came Ḳāsim Amīn, a daring writer whose first book, on *The Emancipation of Woman,* was published in 1898. For this he was criticized, ostracized, and considered almost a madman. Among his faithful friends was Saad Pasha Zaghloul, to whom was dedicated his second book, *The New Woman,* written in 1900 and rewritten in 1911. No doubt this book has done more than any other single agency in bringing about the strong movement which is pushing everything before it to-day. Another strong reformer was Jamāl ad-Dīn al-Afghānī, who was exiled for his views on the emancipation of woman and other changes in the Sharia. Mansur Fahmy wrote denouncing the Prophet because he was not in favour of women's advancement, thus making himself unpopular with the conservatives.

All this time the reader must see a background of girls' schools filled with Western influence. This would not be a true picture without that background. In 1873 the first government girls' school was opened, and it belonged to the *Wakf* (private religious endowment) of the third wife of the Khedive Ismail Pasha, who gave it to the Ministry. In 1908 the Lady Cromer Dispensaries were opened, and, acting on this incentive, the Egyptian ladies formed an association which established at Abdin in 1911 a dispensary called, after its founder, "Ain al Hayatt." In March 1914 Lady Byng formed an International Club for women in Cairo. Again, the "Egyptian ladies wished a society which would be more exclusively for Egyptians," and in May 1914, with the princesses heading the movement, they formed "The Association of Egyptian Women for Social and Intellectual Improvement." It had but one meeting; then came the war.

In 1919, after the political upheaval and the excitement which followed had subsided a little, women began to see that there were at least two ways in which they could help their countrywomen: by forming societies and by publishing magazines entirely dedicated to their own interests. Three societies were formed, "The New Woman," "The Young Woman's Club," and "Al Nahda al Nisaiya" (The Feminist Movement), with a magazine of its own by the same name. In joining this last-named society each member must dedicate herself by oath to the cause of virtue, patriotism, and service.

From Iraq comes the word by a trusty messenger:

"The Woman's Movement here is getting under weigh. Our latest development on these lines is a woman's club which is now being organized and to which, it is said, all the leading Moslem ladies of Baghdad have promised to belong. The rules of the new association have been published in the local press and have aroused much interest and one or two heated editorials. At present, it may be said that the more conservative Moslems are marking time and watching what the next move will be before preparing their counter-move.

"Meanwhile, a little flutter has been occasioned by one of the government girls' schools asking to be allowed to start a troop of Girl Guides. The Boy Scout Movement has been remarkably successful, and the infection has now apparently spread to the other sex. The idea of young girls marching through the streets and bazaars with arms swinging, and banners flying, has sent a thrill of horror through the old conservative circles. 'The young civilization of the West' [from our girls' schools], bitterly complains the *Mufid*, the Baghdad Arabic daily, 'which is not in line with the traditions and good breeding of our women, is slowly poisoning the nation. The Girl Guide Movement is wholly alien to our ideas, and in a country which has been backward for five hundred years these innovations are inadvisable. The Minister of Education ought to draw up a curriculum of instruction for the girls' schools which is in keeping with our beliefs and traditions and in consonance with the noble honour of the Arab people.'

"And so the battle rages. But, in view of the success of the Boy Scout Movement, one feels that it is extremely likely that the girls will get their way."

The veil, which for many years was worn by Christian women, is now rapidly disappearing in most of the cities. The sight of unveiled Christian Egyptian ladies has become so common that Moslem ladies may appear in the same way without attracting attention or criticism.

Ever since their establishment, the American Mission girls' schools in Egypt have held their commencements without any reference to harem customs. No screens or curtains separate the large audiences of men and women; princesses, pashas' wives, mothers and sisters of the "sweet girl graduate" sit in plain sight of the princes, pashas, beys, and ministers, fathers and brothers. Here, with face unveiled, the young woman who is to receive her diploma takes her place upon a raised platform with her fellow students and performs her part in the programme. Because this is an established custom for this particular day in her life, all accept it as right and proper, with never a word of criticism.

A writer from Syria says:

"There is a very marked Woman's Movement in Syria, including Moslem, Druze, and Christian women. A large society of women of different religious faiths meets once a month in Beirût to discuss matters of interest to women. The president is a devoted Protestant, and the society was started by Syrian Protestant women.

"The women still wear the veil, and seem to be stricter in this particular than in other Moslem countries. This summer, however, young Moslem women in the Christian villages in the Lebanon went about everywhere with their veils back, carrying sticks and walking freely with an athletic stride. One young Moslem woman, smart and educated, is taking her freshman college year at the American Girls' School in Beirût. She hopes to go to America next year and study medicine; then she plans to come back and work for the emancipation of other Moslem women."

In Palestine the women seem not much interested in the political situation, and are more exclusive than in some other countries. From one of the Christian girls' schools we have the following:

"Our girls attend the religious services gladly. The brothers and fathers are liberal, also some of the relatives, particularly those who are educated. There is decided progress in the homes, which are much cleaner ; the food is better cooked, and the general living on a much higher level."

In our information from physicians in Eastern lands we find but two bright pictures. One, the readiness of the women to come to the hospitals, and to bring their girls, to listen to the word of the doctors, and even to submit willingly to necessary operations ; and the other, brighter still, is the relief which promises to come from the distinct movement to raise the age of marriage. The background in all their writings is so black that in some cases one can but faintly see the outline. Dare we insert one dark picture here in this hopeful chapter ? If we do, let it be from the pen of that great-hearted Bishop Linton, of Persia, who has given us his book of wondrously clear Persian sketches [1] :

" Those shadows ! They are so intensely deep that it hurts even to attempt to sketch them in here. Some cannot be put in, not at any rate by a man. Here is what a hospital nurse in Persia once wrote ; only, perhaps, it would be better if you would read it when you are alone. You may want to kneel down and pray. It is too unutterably sad to be read and lightly forgotten. The part that is not written is the saddest.

" ' Just for the day or two petted and feasted, pleased and decked with bridal robes—a happy little queen. The next ? . . . May God forgive ! . . .

" ' Her mother brought the little child to see if foreign skill could even then restore the little trembling frame ; knowing that he who owned her could, if he chose, cast her out as a useless, broken toy—divorced, dishonoured, and by all despised.

" ' A little child ! I saw her as she waited in the

[1] The Rt. Rev. J. H. Linton, *Persian Sketches*, London, 1923, pp. 118–21.

C.M.S. hospital, and never can I forget her piteous cries, the horror staring from her fear-glazed eyes, from which all childishness had fled. She crouched, like some wild, tortured animal, trust in everyone, all childish hopes, forever gone. A quivering, outraged form; a broken, wounded life; a terror-stricken heart! Surely that was enough for any child to bear. No, not enough; for still that mother (was she worthy of the name?) refused to promise that for two short years a time of respite should be given to the girl for healing of the body and mind.

" 'So from the hospital that little one was borne, with piteous cries and frantic pleas for help, back to that husband in whose heart was not one drop of pity, back to a life far worse than death. A little child of nine!'

" And now it is the hour of prayer; I listen as that husband approaches his God and I hear him say, 'O God, the merciful, the compassionate'!!! There is clearly something wrong somewhere!

" Suppose that it were your little girl of nine! If you are a parent I think you will understand. . . .

" One day a Persian boy came to me and said: 'I wish, sir, you would come to our house and help us.' I asked what he wanted me to do. He said: 'You know my little sister?' I did. She was a little girl apparently seven or eight years of age, just like any English girl of that age, bright, happy, joyous. He went on: 'Well, she is to be married next week; I wish you would come and see my father and try to stop it.'

" I went to the father, and spent a whole afternoon pleading and arguing with him. In the end he turned to me and said: 'She is eight years old, and it is time she was married!' And the boy burst in with, 'She is not yet eight years old!'

" So she was married—to a man of thirty-five, whom she had never yet seen! And all the light was darkened, all the joy and innocence of childhood were blotted out. And 'she is not yet eight years old. . . .'

"But here, again, is a light across the shadows. I want to guard against misconception. There is a growing feeling against child marriage, and I know of a small society among Persian women whose members are pledged not to give their own daughters in marriage till they are sixteen years old. Old schoolboys, too, have told me that they will neither marry a child wife nor give their own children in marriage till they are grown up. But, with the example of their Prophet before them, the struggle is an uphill one. Nevertheless, the social problem in Persia is beginning to cut deep into the hearts of her thinking men and women, and herein is great hope for the future. The best of her people are asking whether there is any solution, and, if so, where it lies."

Just here it is of great interest to note that recent legislation in different Eastern countries will greatly benefit women and girls when put into execution, and it will grant privileges of justice and equality of which we never dreamed a few years ago. This is notably true of Turkey. In Egypt also there has been like progress. On March 16, 1923, at a meeting of ladies at the house of Madame (or *Hoda*) Charaawi Pasha, it was decided to form a new society, to be called "The Egyptian Feminist Union for Woman Suffrage." Nine points were drawn up as the definite aims of the union, and presented at the International Woman's Convention by Hoda Charaawi in Rome, and later in the woman's delegation in Paris. They were then presented to serve as a basis for laws in the new Constitution. The nine points are as follows:

1. To raise the moral and intellectual level of woman in order to realize her political and social equalities with men from the point of view of laws and manners.
2. To ask for free access to higher schools for all

girls desiring to study, and equal privileges to be given with the boys and young men.

3. To reform customs relating to the arranging of marriages so as to allow the two parties to know each other before betrothal.

4. To reform laws in regard to marriage so that the real spirit of the Koran might be interpreted, and thus preserve woman from the injustice caused by bigamy exercised without reason, and from repudiation taking place without serious motive.

5. By laws to limit the age of consent to marriage for a young girl to sixteen years.

6. To open active propaganda for public hygiene, particularly with reference to child welfare.

7. To encourage virtue and to fight against immorality.

8. To fight against superstition and certain customs which do not accord with reason, even though mentioned in the Hadith (like the Zar, Charms, etc.).

9. To open propaganda in the Press on the aims of the society.

Already five of these points have been under consideration in Parliament. It will be seen that these aims cover a comprehensive field: intellectual and moral equality, education, marriage reforms, hygiene and sanitation, and a battle against superstition and immorality. There is a voiceless reproach in these moderate demands plainly stated—ghosts of old sorrows seem to lurk in them.

Through the help of the League of Nations, Bishop Linton, of Persia, was able to secure laws for the benefit of the little carpet-weavers. These reforms have more than an indirect influence upon the health and happiness of the poor wee mothers of that land. These laws, especially No. 4 and No. 5, are significant: (4) that the minimum age of workers in the factories be eight years for boys and ten for girls; (5) that no children under fourteen work more than eight hours a day. These laws prevent the bodies of the little girls, who formerly were married when only eight or nine years of age, from becoming deformed.

Even from Chinese Turkistan around Kashgar, we have the word that there is a little forward movement in the life of women and girls. They have begun to be tidier in person and in their home, and they really seem to love to work. They are more self-respecting, and are beginning to thirst for knowledge. The custom of giving away their small girls in marriage is slowly disappearing under the influence of Christianity. The missionary adds:

"Our Turkistan women have the liberty of joining dervish sisterhoods and of going to these meetings, but otherwise they have no religious or social liberty and are not advanced sufficiently to care anything about politics."

In answer to the question, Is polygamy still the rule among all classes, and what kind of family life is prevalent? there come answers varied as the different countries of the Near East.

In Turkey, as might be expected, we get the word:

"Polygamy is practically prohibited. We are inclined to believe that it is much less common than is supposed. Practical economic difficulties arise in carrying out polygamy; also its unpopularity among the women themselves is probably a deterrent factor. But the easy divorce laws result in something approximating to polygamy."

In Egypt, polygamy is practically a thing of the past among the educated and high-class Moslems. But among the simple people in the villages one finds that the custom still prevails. Here there are many plural marriages because it is easy to take on another wife when economic conditions allow it. Perhaps one-third of the men of the peasant class either have more than one legal wife or at least are living with more than one woman. The desire to have a big family of children is still common with them. A man's idea of affluence is to marry another wife as soon as he has sold his cotton, and until education reaches the class in which this view prevails polygamy will still hold sway in Egypt.

If the law of marriage now under consideration is actually passed it will be a serious matter for Moslem social life, if not for the religious prestige of Islam, which is most sensitive to any attack on the position of women, simply because it is conscious of the weakness of its position. Hence the progress made shows victories which at first do not appear to Western eyes.[1]

From several sources in Persia come answers which show that, as regards polygamy and family life, conditions are just the reverse of those in Egypt. There is no strongly organized movement toward reform.

"In all wealthy houses polygamy is prevalent. This may not cause as much sorrow as one could expect, owing to the absence of higher ideals. On the other hand, in one chief's household the head wife went through agonies of jealousy and grief because she could not get her husband to hold the ideal of monogamy which she, independent of Christian thought, cherished."

"Among the poor people one wife is much more usual. But this does not do away with the evils of divorce and temporary marriages. Family life under these conditions cannot reach a very high standard, and yet it is surprising what a lot of family affection there is. According to the religious law, girls are of

[1] See *The Moslem World*, July, 1923, p. 309.

marriageable age at nine, but among the more enlightened people there is a feeling against this, and many girls do not marry until fourteen or fifteen."

From Syria and Palestine we have the reliable information that, although there is much heart-breaking complaint against the marriage and easy divorce system, nothing as yet has been attempted by the women in the way of petitions to change the code. A missionary who has lived and worked long in Syria says:

"Polygamy is not prevalent, but successive divorce is appallingly common. I know one sixteen-year-old girl who was married three times and divorced twice within a year. She had been married and divorced once before I knew her. Of course, under such conditions there is almost nothing of what we can call family life."

From Arabia we have the word of a high government official and of a missionary who has spent nearly half a century in that land. The latter says:

"While polygamy is rare, frequent marriage and divorce are prevalent. One man who had been married and divorced eighteen times brought his young wife of fifteen to the doctor for examination. When the result of the examination showed that she was not in fit condition to become a mother, the man wished to divorce her. Since I left he had divorced his nineteenth and married his twentieth wife."

From Turkistan it is said:

"Polygamy is the rule only among those who can afford to have more than one wife at a time. The family life is patriarchal, but divorces are very common."

From the Sudan and Abyssinia we find that polygamy is still the rule. Quoting from one who is perhaps the best authority from the Sudan we have:

"There is an existing state of things in social life that makes family life, as we understand it, an impossibility. Then, too, there is the keeping of concubines and their children that makes anything but the herding of women and children impossible. It is not a family, but a flock, a herd, to which the women must submit without choice. This will probably give way eventually with the entire abolition of slavery."

From Iraq, the new Mesopotamia, we find the same brave fight going on against polygamy as we have in Turkey and Egypt. Perhaps this last country to awaken shall be the first in attainment.

From Dr. Kelly Giffen we have the summing up:

"The psychology of the situation is not easily understood, but the explanation which seems most reasonable is, first, that the Moslems of the Sudan, and perhaps of the whole Moslem world, have been longing for something more satisfying than the Koran and the religion of Mohammed bring into their lives. This longing probably existed quite generally before the war, as we know that it did in many cases. Then came the war, and there was a releasing of all previous bonds in religious and moral conduct. I make no attempt to explain what it was that broke these bonds, but certainly we must recognize that there is a new liberty and the people have a new vision. It may not be the one we wish for them, but it is a new vision, and indicates a turning from their age-old beliefs, either for better or for worse. This brings new opportunity, and increased responsibility to lift Christ into the field of the vision of the soul which longs and looks for something but knows not what. But we know it is Christ."

MOVEMENTS IN THE LIFE OF WOMEN IN THE ISLAMIC WORLD—NORTH-WEST AFRICA

BY

I. LILIAS TROTTER,

Honorary Secretary to the Algiers Mission Band

CHAPTER XV

MOVEMENTS IN THE LIFE OF WOMEN IN THE ISLAMIC WORLD—NORTH-WEST AFRICA

ELEVEN or twelve words, carrying a dim sense of a needy throng—the title means little more to those who have never crossed the Mediterranean ; it carries no pictures. And as in our nursery days the pictures come first, then their meaning, so come and look at a few of them.

Turn over two or three pages of the picture-book. The first is a long blank wall in a city street, unbroken save for a barred slit here and there, and an arched doorway, roofed with painted rafters, red and green. Within is a dark vestibule with stone seats, tiled to the vaulting in quaint colouring. Then another door, which may not be opened by any of the men residents above the age of ten or twelve, without a warning cough. That cough enables all the women to fly to their rooms except those of the family of the entering male.

If you are a woman you may walk straight in with the one sentence, " O mistresses of the house ! " Then you are in a court, marble-tiled, recessed with Moorish arches and twisted pillars. Grouped together or scattered here and there are delicate-featured women, in robes of every tint, egg-shell-blue and silver, apricot and pale-green, trying to forget yesterday's sorrows and to-morrow's fears in laughter and gossip, as they work at their household tasks.

Then turn the page, and up and away through the fig-trees and the dim peacock-colour of the prickly-pear hedges, you will see a troop of mountain-women swinging down the path, lifting a hand now and then to steady the earthen water-jars on their heads, and draped like Roman matrons, in flowing crimson of woollen material, hanging from the shoulders on heavy silver brooches. The little girls who trot alongside have imitated the brooches by means of a bit of orange-peel, with a mimosa-thorn thrust through as fastening.

Turn another page, and, far back, where the mountain land dips to the desert, you will find the womenkind in mud houses, proportioned like palaces, with palm trunks for their pillars. Women in indigo cotton robes are silhouetted against the tan walls. A touch of pea-green or orange gleams here and there, and a glitter of silver from massive amulets slung on the breast. Dear coffee-coloured babies in one scanty garment tumble about the sand floor.

Out and away once more, where the palms scatter in a thin line, you will find the tent-woman, heavy-featured and dense as compared with the others limited in her horizon to the little camp that is her world, and with hardly a chance of hearing of another one, even of the earthly type. Out and away again, in regions ever more remote, these Bedouin live and die.

Multiply all these groups by the hundred thousand and add as many other contrasting ones, and you still will not have seen " the women of North-West Africa." They number, so far as they can be numbered, well over 7,000,000 from Tripoli to Morocco, including the Sahara.

Athwart these lands is being driven the plough of Europe. The regions of the inaccessible shrink year by year. Autos thread the defiles and climb the plateaux to link the markets, the camel sways bewildered from the jarring Citroën car that breaks up the peace of the sand-dunes. It will all serve, in due time, we believe, in opening highways for God's service. And it may well be that this ploughing, as it touches the lives of the girls, will bring the same result.

This upheaval is as yet in its initial stage, and, as with the work of the literal ploughshare, it is not to the outward beautifying of the field. The gorgeous wild-flower colouring of the East is destroyed and buried, and a curious crop of anomalies tends to spring up in its place. The former sense of native demureness is crossed with the first seeds of liberty; the roots of superstition twine still under the surface, and threaten to strangle the new ideas of a universe that is governed by law, not by demons. These and a dozen other incongruous elements go along with the hat and pinafore that surmount the old-time robe of the go-to-school child.

We are truly glad she is learning to read. Her husband of the future may or may not be glad that she knows how to write; we remember cases where such knowledge is feared, for the troubles of the new home can no longer be hidden from father and brother as of yore. We hope that the up-turned soil of her mind may yield a harvest in days to come, but at present she is in a transition stage that is full of risks, with centuries behind her of womankind kept in leash and now being suddenly freed in the midst of coast towns where the worst elements of East and West flourish together.

We are only at the very outset of the problem, so we cannot as yet judge its issues. Before the war scarcely a girl obtained any education; now, on all sides, excellently organized schools are being opened in Algeria and Tunisia, and others are being started in Morocco.

With true discernment of the make-up of the little Eastern maidens, mental training is given only in the morning hours, and the afternoon brings rest to the unaccustomed brain by employment in needle-craft and weaving.

In the inland towns, where the streets are less full of danger than in the coast cities, our workers feel that the immense awakening of latent possibilities in the keen-witted young lives more than counterbalances all that can be said against the venture.

Farther south, Islam still holds practically undisputed sway, and the girl is kept in permanent ignorance of anything beyond the household lore that has been passed down from mother to daughter since the days of Eve. In deference to their official superiors, the Arab postman and policeman and two or three others will send their daughters to the newly opened girls' school, and there it stops. The highest estimate of the literacy of woman (putting its standard at reading and writing, and including French education as well as Arabic) would be about 2 per cent. in Algeria, less in Tunisia, and almost nil in Morocco. But whatever results have been attained are the achievements of the last ten years only.

The two factors that have worked towards this sudden stride have been, first, governors of the land who have laid themselves out to meet the needs of the natives on far more understanding lines than of old, and, second, a consciousness of those needs awakened in the native men by contact with Europe during the war. Young Arabs and Kabyles in large numbers went off to the fighting line or to help in the work that lay behind the trenches. Even now, if you cross to France, you will find the decks thronged with them, and, if you watch through the last half-hour before landing, you will see in Marseilles harbour the strange sight of one red fez after another flung into the water and left floating there, to be replaced by the cap that will make its owner indistinguishable from the European. What this means, as a symbol of riddance from the cramp of Islam, those will realize who know all that the fez implies to dwellers in this land.

First and foremost, the vision of Europe has brought a dawning desire for changed conditions in domestic life. The North African has seen there the civilized home, with husband and wife sharing their interests and their friendships, the girls in free enjoyment of their 'teens, the growing lads still sheltered instead of being flung out into the pollution of the streets. The Algerian native does not contemplate any such upheaval of social conditions, of course, but he would like a wife with some outlook on this new world with which he has become familiar—some intercourse beyond the scandal of the compound and the alternate coaxing and screaming about new finery and leave to go to a fête.

So, before long, the demand for wives with the elements of education will create a supply in such regions of the country as are in touch with the European shore. The young schoolmasters and the pensioned non-commissioned officers of the native regiments share this new outlook towards woman's education, though in their case it is through a less direct contact with France.

It is among these surroundings that we expect the lead to be given. The bourgeois class and that of officialdom above it do not seem to us at present aroused on the subject. At any rate, their womenkind take slack interest in the movement towards liberty in the Near East. Egypt and Turkey are in disfavour—the former among the authorities on account of its subversive tendencies, the latter among the Arabs through ancient tyranny—and their influence does not tell. The high tide of progress in these houses of the well-to-do seems to have reached only the mark of reading French newspapers and novels, with an occasional taxi-drive, incognito, in French costume, and in exceptional cases a journey to Paris with the husband under the same conditions. No leader has ever arisen among them suggesting anything further; so the trend towards progress seems likely to arise from the class below.

The land is peopled by two different kindreds: the well-known Arabs and the mysterious aborigines, Berbers as they are generally named, whom the Arab cornered when he overran the coast, but never conquered. Cornered they are still, in certain districts of mountain and desert, with an origin unknown, a tongue unrelated to any other, and an industry and independence that stand in sharp contrast with the lazy easy-going of the Arab usurper. In the plains the two groups intermingle.

Those most in evidence of the Berber races are the Kabyles, in possession of the hill country that borders the Bay of Algiers to the east. Here alone do we come in contact with their women. Another detachment of their tribes inhabits the Aurès Mountains, near Biskra, and is known to us only by photographs, showing stately creatures with a massive outline of brow and chin. Farther south, among the Beni M'zab, no woman is allowed to stir from the tribal cities, and not an individual of her sex has ever reached the northern towns. Farther still, in the recesses of the desert, lies another branch, the Touaregs, and here the innate forcibleness of the Berber women has thrown to the winds the lightly borne yoke of Islam, and they keep the archives in quaint square characters, bring up the children, sit on the councils, obtain respect for the unmarried girls under the soubriquet of "little queens," while their men, in black muffler veils, and on their running camels, go out to pillage and to fight. The first gleam of God's dawn has not reached these women yet.

But the Kabyle woman we know well, and from the grandmother, her white hair dyed carrot-red with henna, to the smallest specimen of girlhood, forcefulness marks them all. A woman has more than once held a brotherhood together during the interregnum caused by her husband's death: Lella Khadija, Kabylia's snow-crested peak, is named after one of these.

Material for Christ is surely there, and it is being steadily sought, for the land of the Kabyles is the best worked for God's Kingdom along these coasts. It remains to be seen how they might rise to leadership if they had right of way, though numerically they are far below the Arabs.

As yet the women, taking them all in all, are queens in slavery. A feast is being held in the stone hut, and the men sit shoulder to shoulder round the wide wooden footstool that serves for table; the bowl of semolina is crowned by a stewed fowl. From this the neck and claws are thrown to the woman huddled in the corner. That is her legitimate portion. She has fed the chicken with her own scraps; she has modelled the bowl with its quaint criss-cross of orange and black and red colours pounded from stones that she knows. She has rolled and steamed the raw grain for hours. So be it: she shall have the neck and the claws.

Well for her if contempt such as this were all: it is but the drifting straw that marks the undertow; and when we know something of the force of the stream of injustice against these rock-like characters, we wonder that life in their villages can pass as quietly as it does.

" Her general make-up is strong through suffering," writes one who has passed half a life-time in those villages. " Her native humour and brightness come touchingly to the surface, but tears lie just beneath."

For the tribal code that frames her destiny is considerably more drastic than the Koranic law of the Arabs. Here are a few of its pronouncements. Remember, as you read them, that the so-called " woman " may be a child of nine or ten.

" The Kabyle woman has no hereditary right." " She has no right of property except to the clothes she wears."

" In marriage she is sold by her father, or, failing him, by his nearest male relative, who receives the price."

" She has no consent to formulate. Marriage can be imposed on her even by force by the man having authority over her."

" The husband may repudiate his wife when he pleases without being obliged to formulate a reason." " She has not the right to repudiate her husband," and in no case, under any pretext, can she claim divorce from the law. She may leave her married home, however, and take refuge with her father if he consents to receive her. She then declares herself in a " state of insurrection " against her husband.

" The Kabyle husband can, in repudiating his wife, declare that he ' sets a price on her head.' In this case, the woman, although repudiated, cannot marry another man unless the latter pays first to the former husband this integral sum, as ransom. Meanwhile she is ' put out of circulation.' "

" The children belong to the father. During marriage the mother attends to them. If she is put away she becomes a stranger to them."

" As part of the marriage ceremony, the husband beats the young bride over the threshold, in token that she is now under his power."

" The husband feeds and clothes his wife as he pleases. The complaint of the woman is not admitted."

" If a married man dies, his wife becomes part of his succession. She is transmitted with it. She remains 'hung to his death.' "

The tragedies of these mountains go unbroken into the dim depths of the past. Will a break in them come now? It may be, for a brave French magistrate here and there, and an answering sense of chivalry awaking in some of the younger Kabyles, have produced successful appeal to law more than once of late.

Meantime, among both Kabyle and Arab womanhood (and, even among the latter, this begins in the early 'teens) one of the most intense needs is that shelter-homes and rescue-homes should be opened from end to end of the land for the shattered young lives that result from ruthless marriage and divorce and tossing from household to household that we cannot call homes. No such shelter exists to our knowledge, and the cry of one little lost sheep after another, as it slides down the moral precipice, must reach the ear of the Good Shepherd. Surely He will soon be calling some to go with Him " to seek and to save " from among them.

Polygamy cannot be said to be the rule. It is not principle that tells against it, but expense, for often the wives, especially in the coast towns, require each to have a separate establishment. Probably in the shopkeeper class two wives would be the common thing, and in the classes above this plurality would be the rule rather than the exception, sometimes extending to three or four. In the houses of the well-to-do, and in the interior, it is usual for all to live under one roof with separate apartments. As to family life, in the villages, especially in Kabylia, it is at its lowest ebb, men, women, children, poultry, and even sometimes sheep and goats sharing one hut. In the towns, among the poorer classes, one room is still the rule, and often with bad over-crowding. Especially among the Kabyles we have known of as many as eighteen in one room, four or five families, each of which has its own corner. Where a whole house is owned, it is generally shared in patriarchal fashion with sons and their wives, the whole being usually under the dominance of the old grandmother, who rules the house forcibly and resists innovations of any kind.

In the sorrows of their lot, the Kabyle women and the Arab women meet, and they share the darkness of mind and spirit of which we shall speak anon. In character they differ widely. The Arab woman is vivacious, affectionate, supple, often *rusée*—seeking to go round a difficult position that the Kabyle women would set out to take by storm—marvellously intelligent, when we look at the age-long limitations of her past.

The Arab woman does not strike one as so tragic as the Kabyle, for the Arab has adapted herself comfortably to the creed which the Kabyle feels was forced on her people by the sword of old. The Arab toys with her chains, and is proud to be secluded. The power of fatalism, so deeply rooted in Islam, helps her to live on with her heart buried in the graves of her babies—often laid there through the foolish love that refused them nothing—or torn over the wretchedness of the daughter, concerning whose marriage she had spent months of intrigue; or broken over the waywardness of the son of whom she was so proud when he first showed his manliness by beating her. She cannot reason about these things—cause and effect are in an unrecognized realm; she smothers and stamps all questioning under the fiat,

"It is decreed," and goes on mechanically preparing her own woes over again.

The religious life of the Arab woman, as you follow her into the inland districts, becomes more and more marked by a crude intensity. It looks like fanaticism; it is really concentration. She will take you by the shoulders, in the desert villages, and cry "Shehedi, shehedi," that you may be induced to repeat the formula of witness to Mohammed which she believes to be the passport into heaven. She is interested in you; she likes you; surely she should win you to go there too. Beyond that, she knows nothing but that she should fast throughout the Ramadhan moon, and this she does with touching faithfulness. Where the sense of spiritual need is numb or dead, these two elements, representing faith and works, are her pride, as a good Moslem. Where a spark is awake she holds on intensely to these same two points, not daring to let them go, for she has nothing more. Is that her fault, or ours?

It is only where the brotherhoods of mystics hold sway, in mountain and desert, that the women seem to get any farther in dim seeking for God. We are only just beginning to get into contact with these movements on the women's side, though we knew that certain orders had organized sisterhoods attached. A glimpse of a tiny *zikr* of women in the desert, a day spent in the mother-house of a sisterhood in a holy city, a friendship with a beautiful "Marabouta" soul in the mountains, who gave herself to God in gratitude for restoration from illness, and spends her time in comforting and helping others—these come within a year's experiences. They only make us feel our ignorance of the unseen brooding of the Spirit over this chaos of darkness.

When it comes to the cities and the inland towns, the

religious life of the women becomes diluted, so to speak. There is now, for the most part, no intensity at all. The social element predominates at the cemetery rendezvous on Fridays and still more at the "Ziara" pilgrimage to the Saint's tomb where the country-side gathers periodically. Nothing more is expected till she reaches the age of forty; then, if so minded, she begins to tell her beads and to attend the mosque services in the women's gallery in preparation for the world to come.

Even then, as before, there is no thought of religion having any bearing on daily life; love as "the fulfilling of the law"—neighbour-love in its true sense—has little place. They give to each other, it is true, only it is on a co-operative system. "I gave her three duros at her baby's seventh-day feast; may the sea be upon her if she does not the same by me at my son's wedding." And the quick wits and idle days and complicated households all serve as tinder to the Southern fire of jealousy, and intrigues are kindled without end until no one can trust her neighbour. They become used to playing a double game all round till a curious duality of mind and character becomes a part of their make-up.

It is only the tender mother-love that shines true and clear, though so ignorantly applied that the little ones will be exposed to moral risks such as to make innocence practically impossible after babyhood. All the time the mother will be torturing herself with fears concerning the invisible demon powers that she imagines are making for their ruin.

If we are asked what is the prevailing background in the heart of a native woman of these coasts, from childhood to old age, and in every rank and condition, we should say it is the grip of fear. There are fears well founded, and enough of them—the fear of her husband's anger and consequent divorce, fear of the day when old age will bring contempt and neglect, fear of the power of venomous tongues around her and their effect on the mother-in-law who grudges her the position in which she herself has placed her, or on the autocratic grandmother who dominates the household. But these are less terrible than the haunting of the charms and spells that may be thrown over her and the untoward chance that may arouse the wrath of the demons towards her and her children. We know a young wife who is being deliberately and purposely driven into insanity by the constant suggestion that it is threatening her through the powers of darkness.

So much has been written of late concerning the prevalence of animism in Islam that there is no need to relate instances. A chapter could easily be filled with them, but we are dealing now with the broad outlines of the Arab woman's life, not with details, and there is yet more to be said about these outlines.

We have traced the shadows of her character, but have not told what a lovable thing she is, and what powers of mind and character have lain dormant through the bleak centuries of Islam, awaiting God's spring. Brightness and endurance of life-long injury and wrong, powers of hard work and patient self-sacrifice, are all there, sometimes latent, often visible, and the girls, if they had the chance of being trained, might be developed as keen students or as good housewives, with a civilized standard of cleanliness, infant welfare, and health culture. All these are impossible while Moslem rule prevails and while girls are shut away at twelve or thirteen for the short interval before marriage. Their powers of being and doing are stunted past recall in the stiff soil of Islam.

So we rejoice in the breaking up that lets in God's free light and air.

Let us hold the simile clearly in our minds, however. The ploughshare is one thing, the seed is another. Civilization, education, the trend towards liberty—all serve to prepare the way with their sharp thrusts into the age-long wilderness; but they are not the seed, they have no vitalizing power for man's spiritual being. "He that soweth good seed is the Son of Man."

That sowing by the Son of Man through His servants began only a generation ago, and in these lands, constituting for the most part a French colony or protectorate, the seed-basket of hospital and school work has been in little use. Direct evangelism is wide open, and only limited by the time and strength of the few workers; industrial effort and hostels are supplementing it, and already the first green shoots are coming through.

All is as yet in that initial stage. "First the blade," and the fear is always that, by reason of the fallow ground of Islam around, it will stay there, undeveloped. The women converts, unless they can be married to Christian husbands, must continue secret disciples. Each one belongs, in the eye of the law, to her nearest male relative, and, if he is still a Moslem, he will not dream of the disgrace of letting her stand out for Christ in his home. Throughout the country, around the mission stations, there are souls whose trust and allegiance have been transferred to Him, and who dimly try to please Him; but the stages of "the ear," and "after that the full corn in the ear," await the time when God's power reaches the men. The future of the women is bound together spiritually as well as socially with that of their fathers, brothers, husbands. The colporteur who brings the books to the men and the boy-lover who wins a hearing from the lads, are steadily helping on the day of grace for the women.

While we wait for that dawn, who can tell what can be done by mere presence, bringing them into touch with Christ's love shed through human hearts and lives. To "lay down" for their sakes time and strength and inclination, every day and all day long—that is the only way in which we can show Him to them in a fashion that they can understand. "He saved others, Himself He cannot save"—the highest missionary calling lies in a faint, far-off reflection of those words.

And when the soil has been softened and prepared by earthly love, the vision of Christ crucified may break in far and wide on the men and women of North-West Africa, awaking the life-springs that will work on through blade and ear into a multiplying power around them that will bring the sheaves at last.

MOVEMENTS IN THE LIFE OF WOMEN IN THE ISLAMIC WORLD—INDIA

BY

RUTH E. ROBINSON, B.A., M.A.,

Editor, " The Treasure Chest," Bangalore

CHAPTER XVI

MOVEMENTS IN THE LIFE OF WOMEN IN THE ISLAMIC WORLD—INDIA

THOUGH it is sometimes dangerous to generalize about conditions in so large a country as India, there is on the whole surprising agreement regarding the changes that are taking place in the life of Moslem women in all parts of the land. Prolonged contact with England's civilization, subtle currents of influence, pressure of new ideas—all these have produced a restlessness, a vague discontent, and a desire for escape into a world that fills the mind and heart. The war, the Caliphate agitation, the Nationalist Movement in India, the emancipation of women in Egypt and Turkey, have penetrated to the zenanas, and have given the women an interest in a world outside their own.

One of the noticeable features of recent years is the awakening of the Moslems to a consciousness of the distance they lag behind the other communities. Especially startling is their illiteracy. For Christians the proportion of literates is 32 per cent. among men and 18 per cent. among women; for Hindus it is 15 per cent. among men and 1½ per cent. among women; but for Moslems it is only 8 per cent. among men and a half of one per cent. among women. In this matter the traditional Islamic prejudice against women's education is a determining factor. The Census Report of 1921 contains an admirable statement on this point [1]:

"Though the number of literate women throughout India is still small and their proportion very low . . . the fact remains that there has been steady advance in the education of girls in the last twenty years. Literacy is an indication rather of culture than of civilization, and, while there is nothing inherent in the Indian tradition that should prevent the development of the education of the male population, the case is . . . different in regard to women. The spirit both of Brahmanism and of Islam is distinctly opposed to the education of the female sex; and there is little doubt that the women of India owe the growing facilities offered them for acquiring literacy to the influence on the male section of the community of foreign standards and ideals. That the education of women is unnecessary, unorthodox, and dangerous, is still the standpoint of a large section of Indian society. It is still the predominant attitude of the Mohammedans of the better class, though, in the case of their men, the ability to read and write is . . . a religious obligation. . . . The scheme of life which orthodox tradition imposes on the women of India presents obstacles to education which, if not insuperable, are at least formidable. The customs of *purdah* [2] and of early marriage limit the number of girls in the schools and necessitate the withdrawal of the majority before they have had a fair opportunity to acquire any lasting knowledge of letters, while the orthodox attitude of society towards women who accept any public position accentuates the difficulty of obtaining the necessary supply of professional teachers. It is only, or at least chiefly, when the general advance of

[1] *Census of India, 1921*, vol. 1, part 1, p. 179.

[2] Literally, a curtain. A word used in India to express the seclusion in which the high-class women live. They see no men but those who are relatives, and never go outside of the women's quarters.

male culture has reached well beyond the stage of mere vernacular literacy that the atmosphere becomes favourable to real progress in the instruction of women; and, if the extent and progress of literacy among females usually follows closely the statistics for males, it is because the higher cultural advance of the latter, which causes the improvement of the condition of women, is built up on the basis of elementary literacy."

That there can be no great improvement of the community until some of the cruel and wasteful limitations have been removed from the life of its women is a slowly penetrating idea which, more than any other, has produced the spirit of unrest. Two classes of women have hitherto been comparatively untouched by this movement: the very poor and the very rich. The lower classes are for the most part too preoccupied with the daily problem of how to make a living to give attention to education. The women of wealth and high position are in general quite satisfied with their comfortable, settled existence, and are besides firmly bound by convention.

The older women of all classes are almost without exception strongly conservative. The spirit of progress finds its expression in a comparatively small handful of the younger generation—some hundreds, or possibly thousands at most, out of 35,000,000 women. These are confined almost entirely to the middle classes, being chiefly daughters of professional men and lower-grade government officials. Their protest takes three directions: the demand for an opportunity to study, the demand for an opportunity for self-expression through taking part in the world's work, and a demand for freedom from humiliating and intolerable social disabilities.

The demand for an opportunity to study is meeting

with a steadily widening acceptance. Thousands of girls are now studying in primary and middle schools; scores are in high schools; two are in Queen Mary's College, Madras; thirteen in the Isabella Thoburn College, Lucknow; one has received the degree of M.A. from the Aligarh University, and another from the Lucknow University; one has taken a medical degree from King George's Medical College, Lucknow, and, after going to England for further study, has been given charge of a Dufferin Hospital in India, and her four sisters are now studying in King George's Medical College. Several others are studying privately for degrees.

Moslem men as well as women are so waking up to the necessity of education for girls that, in view of the paucity of good schools of their own, they are willing to place their daughters in Christian institutions. This applies to towns and cities, not to rural areas. In Madras there are not sufficient schools at present to meet the demand from Moslems. A missionary in Gujarat says that if she had had the funds to open a school when the head mulvi approached her on the subject a short time ago, she would have had all the Moslem girls in the town as pupils, although it was understood that Christian teaching would be given. A missionary in Colombo believes that numbers would attend boarding-schools specially opened for Moslem girls. Even in places where the number now attending school is small, missionaries say that the attendance would be increased if Arabic were taught as well as the vernacular. The present educational opportunity is almost limitless.

The younger generation's attitude towards education is indicated by one of the speeches at the first session of the Bombay Presidency Moslem Ladies' Conference held at Poona in October 1924. In the report given in

The Daily Telegraph and Deccan Herald (Poona) we read:

" Mrs. Moulvi, proposing a resolution, made a stirring speech on Moslem female education. She deplored that Moslem men had wronged Mohammedan women by neglecting their education, treating them at the most as a fine delicate piece of household furniture, unfit to be moved about. Moslem men were under the impression that Mohammedan women possessed neither head nor heart, and were meant for nothing more than serving their husbands as cooks, and hence were treated worse than domestic slaves. They had been given to understand that such services were the only part they were fitted to play, and, marvel of marvels, most of them were quite satisfied with their miserable fate. She therefore appealed to the women of Islam to open their eyes and follow the revolutionary changes in female society in Egypt and Turkey. She concluded by asserting that, purdah or no purdah, what was wanted was education. Purdah was sure to disappear sooner or later if education was widely spread amongst the ladies of Mohammedanism."

It is inevitable that along with education should be mentioned progress in literature. Very little exists especially written for women. A prominent Moslem lady of Lahore edits *Tahzib-un-Niswan* for women, and the wife of the treasurer of the Aligarh University edits *Phul* for children. A missionary in Bengal mentions a newly started magazine in Bengali for Moslem women. " It contains no political or religious articles so far, but seems to aim at arousing women to prove themselves not the slaves of men, but their equals." The same missionary says that, in work among the ignorant villagers, she has found the ordinary Bengali books too difficult, and so has prepared simple Bible stories for them in their own village dialect, which is known as Mussalmani-Bengali. "They willingly buy these books to serve as readers, and so gain knowledge of the truth with every reading-lesson. Even middle-aged women beg us to take them on as pupils, and our opportunities in this direction are almost unlimited." A missionary in Delhi emphasizes the need of books for women of the better class "written from a Moslem point of view by one steeped in the life of the women themselves." Probably no form of work would have so powerful an influence as a well-planned literature of this kind.

The demand for self-expression through engaging in the real work of the world has resulted in such achievements, when given opportunity, as place women's ability beyond question. The most conspicuous example of leadership among Moslem women is that of the Begum of Bhopal, whose enlightened government of her State and whose courage in prohibiting liquor in its territory (1923) have ranked her among the most progressive of Indian rulers, while the educational and social reforms in her own State and her influence over all Moslem India through her position as Chancellor of the Aligarh University mark her as a pioneer in those fields. Other women have taken part in social service, particularly child welfare work. Women like Lady Mohammed Shafi of Simla and the late Begum Bibi Amman, the mother of the Ali brothers, have done much to bring women forward by addressing women's meetings and organizing purdah parties. A Moslem woman was appointed in 1924 an honorary magistrate in Bombay.

The fields so far entered by Moslem women have been chiefly education and medicine. The larger number have become teachers, but some have been appointed educational inspectresses in Indian States. Nursing claims the largest number of those in the medical department, but several have become assistant doctors, and at least one has become a dentist. A few have also entered the field of journalism by contributing magazine articles of interest to women, writing novels, and editing papers.

To women such as these the miseries of genteel leisure are only too apparent. Even though, in some cases, learning and professionalism are carried on in the seclusion of the zenana, life has become to them a thing of richness and colour through their many interests and preoccupations. Although to others the idea of a woman's earning her living is still distasteful, these have come to the conclusion that women who live the parasitic life are a cause of weakness, economically and intellectually, to their community.

It is in the answer to the third demand, for freedom from social disabilities, that those have most reason to rejoice who long to see Moslem women given a chance to live in a liveable way all the relations of life. For this demand is resulting in the setting up of new social standards for woman in Islam. We need to remind ourselves of her enormous handicaps—a minimum of education; a marriage contract wholly determined by man, to which she does not give her assent, but simply submits; a marriage relation in which the relationship is not fixed by any rule of life, but is dependent on to-day's caprice and to-morrow's mood; and finally, subordination to a whole system of society in which law, organization, and custom have all combined to fix her in a position of inferiority. Is it any wonder that she is slow in coming out of her shell and realizing herself as an independent force? The interests opposed to her have secured for themselves so long a start that the Moslem woman will have a longer road to travel than most to secure her rights. But it is heartening to see the steps already taken.

The first of her social disabilities polygamy, has met with such criticism from outsiders that twenty years ago Mr. (now Sir) Syed Ameer Ali was led to offer his interpretation of the law of the Koran which says that a man may marry two, three, or four wives if he can be just to them; but, if he cannot, then he should marry only one. The new view offered, it will be remembered, was that the word "just" means conscientiously just, and, since no man can possibly be conscientiously just to more than one wife, Mohammed intended that he should have but one.[1] This is one of a number of instances of the way in which Moslem thinkers have faced circumstances and endeavoured to harmonize the precepts of Islam with the progressive conditions of modern civilization and life—courageous efforts at reform which command our deep interest and sympathy. Partly as a result of this liberal interpretation, public opinion against polygamy has been growing. Often a man of high position refuses to give his daughter as second or third wife to a man. At the All-India Moslem Ladies' Conference of 1924 a resolution was passed by the members declaring that they would not countenance the marriage of their daughters to men already married, and that they would try to persuade their friends to take a similar stand. It is interesting to note that, five years before, a similar resolution failed to be passed by this organization. A young woman who then advanced this view was opposed by some of the other members and bitterly denounced by the local Moslem Press.[2]

Divorce is still lamentably common, especially among

[1] Syed Ameer Ali, *The Spirit of Islam*, p. 190.
[2] See *The Moslem World*, April 1919, p. 172.

the poorer classes and in village communities. In no respect do their social limitations bear more heavily on the women than in this. Although theoretically protected by the provision made for divorce in the marriage settlement, it often proves impossible in practice to collect the sum so promised. Not only are the women too ignorant and inexperienced to fight for their rights because of their narrow up-bringing, but they are also far more afraid of public opinion than men, and the very act of appearing in court is usually enough to put them beyond the pale of respectability, since that is considered "coming out of purdah." Hence, a divorced woman—divorced in many cases for the most trifling reason—is a helpless outcast, conspicuously unwelcome in any home. But among the educated classes a man who divorces his wife is coming to be regarded with disapproval, and the practice is not so common as it was a generation ago.

On one point, that of the purdah system, or the seclusion of women, Moslem society still refuses to give way, though there is an increasing volume of opposition to it. The upper classes cling tenaciously to it, the women regarding it as a badge of aristocracy. At the Bombay Presidency Moslem Ladies' Conference, 1924, the president warmly defended the system, though she is said to have been the only reactionary among the three hundred delegates. A constantly increasing number of women in cities appear at lectures and public gatherings, but almost invariably veiled if it is a mixed audience. A missionary mentions having been at a dinner-party in Aligarh at which the wives of some of the professors in the Aligarh University appeared unveiled and moved with the greatest freedom and sociability among the guests. But such episodes are all too rare. Almost the sole exception hitherto made is in the case of girls attending school and college at a distance from their homes. The purdah is abandoned by them during the school term, but resumed when they return home for their holidays or after completing their education. It is naturally these girls who, having had a taste of freedom, resent being forced back into seclusion, and it is probable that their daughters will enjoy the liberty that they now so much desire. There is a certain justification for conservatism on this point. Even those men who, in theory, are in favour of abolishing the purdah (and the men are as a rule much less conservative on social questions than the women) fear that its sudden withdrawal would result in widespread abuse of liberty and in social disintegration. It is natural to wish that such a change should come gradually. But the breeze of new ideas stirring among old time-worn restrictions and conventions tells us that the system cannot live long. It is already doomed, and must go.

The emancipation of Moslem women is proceeding along lines intellectual, economic, and social. Is it also proceeding along the line of religion? This is less evident than the other three, yet even here are signs not without significance. There is unquestionably an appreciable number of unbaptized Christians in Moslem homes, and a still larger group of sincere inquirers. But there is also opposition. Remembering the natural conservatism of the Moslem woman and her extreme pride in her faith, remembering also the admirable traits of that faith and her belief in its vital contribution to the religious life of the world, we cannot find it surprising that she usually glories in Islam or tries to prove that it is essentially the same as Christianity. Especially in circumstances where she feels that her religion is challenged, however indirectly, there is a natural desire to put herself on the defensive. At the Isabella Thoburn College nine Moslem students banded themselves together in 1922 into a club called the "Anjuman Nau-Nihalan Islam" ("The Association of Nine Young Plants of Islam"), whose purpose was to foster loyalty to their religion. Such a reaction is almost invariably the first result of the impact of Christianity against Islam. But here and there some who have been touched more deeply than others through some experience of life have expressed their dissatisfaction with Islam and their sense of its emptiness and formalism. The story of the death of Christ touches the hearts of such women, and Christian ideals of love and service make an undeniable appeal to them. To deepen these impressions until through their surrender to Christ Moslem women reach their highest freedom must be the endeavour of those who sympathize most intensely with their longing for intellectual and social freedom. It is impossible to forget that their aspirations will never be fully satisfied until they have realized the higher freedom of the spirit.

We shall probably have to wait a while for the big things to happen. It is, after all, only a tiny fraction of the whole that has been touched by the new spirit. The movement is virtually leaderless, though it has the enormous asset of an idealistic impulse. But the revolution it implies is tremendous. Its making good rests with the women themselves. Will they have sufficient insight and foresight to ally themselves with that which will give each individual personality its truest freedom?

THE ANCIENT ORIENTAL CHURCHES AND ISLAM

BY THE RIGHT REV.

RENNIE MAC INNES, D.D.,

Anglican Bishop in Jerusalem,

IN COLLABORATION WITH THE REV.

CANON HERBERT DANBY, D.D.

CHAPTER XVII

THE ANCIENT ORIENTAL CHURCHES AND ISLAM

WHEN estimating the resources at our disposal for spreading the Gospel throughout the Moslem world, few Western Christians think, and then only as an afterthought, of including the ancient Oriental Churches.[1] Not only is it the exception to look upon these ancient branches of the Catholic Church as assets in the Christian cause: some would even regard them as liabilities. This attitude of mind, though not incomprehensible, is to be regretted.

Soldiers who have guarded the outposts and suffered the first shocks and full force of the enemy's onslaught, and, though all but exterminated and cut off from all outside material support and moral encouragement, have yet held tight to their posts—such soldiers, however wounded and helpless, however limited in outlook and enterprise, and however lacking in resource and initiative, can only inspire feelings of respect and veneration in the hearts of fellow-fighters in happier, more successful, and—let it not be forgotten—easier fields. Such soldiers

[1] Under the vague heading, "Ancient Oriental Churches," we include the Orthodox Eastern Church (commonly but quite erroneously known as the "Greek Church")—and particularly those portions of it included in the pre-war Ottoman Empire, the Armenian Church, the Coptic (including the Abyssinian) Church, the "Nestorian" Church, and the Jacobite ("Syrian Orthodox") Church.

in our Lord's cause are the ancient Oriental Churches. They are all that is left of the Christian outposts in Western Asia, Egypt, and Mesopotamia, on which fell the first, freshest, and most powerful blows of the recurrent Moslem campaigns from Khâlid to Tamerlane. Their Christian brethren in the West could not, and, sad to relate, at a later stage would not, help them: the battered remnants have remained where they fell, wounded by the wayside, neglected and isolated, and despised by their earthly rulers. Neglect, isolation, and contempt have been their lot these thousand years and more; the world had no other reward to offer them for their adherence to Christianity, though ease and worldly honour might have been theirs by the simple process of acknowledging the Prophet; yet they held to the faith, endured the cross, and despised the shame. It is thoughtless presumption in Christians of the West to pass by such age-long devotion to our Lord and Master, or to give a condescending glance at these Oriental Churches as "interesting historical survivals." The lot of the Christian of the West, compared with that of the Christian of the East, has been cast in a fair ground: his life has been easy and well-ordered, his suffering in the cause of Christ has been negligible. He has scant right, in the sight of history, to any claim of proved superiority over his Christian brother of the East.

In the double light of experience and faith we shall be blind indeed if we do not see in the ancient Oriental Churches potential allies and valuable assets in our work of rewinning to Christ the peoples of Egypt and Western Asia, now under the sway of Islam. Those outposts of the Christian Faith, so long isolated and even forgotten, are no longer left to fight alone their grim struggle for survival: the West, very late in the day, moved by the missionary ideal, has, in groping around the un-Christian East, regained touch with these worn and weathered pickets. Time has had its effect on them. Their moral and material resources have been exhausted almost to the limit of endurance. But they have endured. They are now in the condition of a relieved garrison: no longer need they remain in the same state of acute tension, with every fibre of their being strained to its utmost in the simple effort to exist. That strain is for the most part gone. They are free once more to take their true place in the ranks of the Church Militant and to reinvigorate their almost atrophied powers of spiritual growth and progress. Theirs need no longer be a purely passive and defensive rôle. The younger, fresher fighter from the West must devote himself with loving care towards re-equipping his veteran brother fighter: there is the strongest possible call for the outpouring of sympathy and inspiration to wipe away the enforced lethargy of ages which has cramped the aggressive possibilities of these Eastern Churches, hemmed in and overpowered by sheer numbers and political oppression.

Now, throughout a large part of the East—with some grievous exceptions—the more positive political oppression is past. In place of a ruling power instinctively hostile, is found a power friendly or, at the least, neutral in its sympathies. There is little to stand in the way of the hoped-for reaction of the ancient Eastern Churches to the fresher idealism which is the contribution of the Christian West to the despairing languor of the Christian East. It is in our power to offer moral encouragement and material aid—but not conditionally, and not with any feeling of condescension; we may only make the offer in the spirit of privileged help.

One of the deeply rooted ideas, held consciously or

unconsciously in the mind of Western Christianity when contrasting itself with Eastern Christianity, is that the latter wholly lacks the missionary ideal, and that this missionary ideal is the monopoly of the Christian West. Though this is patently true of the present, some acquaintance with the history of the Oriental Churches quickly convinces us that this was not always the case. So long as the Eastern Churches retained any semblance of freedom of action they manifested a missionary enterprise, zeal, and initiative, and a spirit of personal sacrifice in the missionary cause of Christianity, such as have never been equalled, let alone surpassed, by the efforts of the comparatively recent missionary work of the Churches of the West. For fourteen centuries the missionary ideal was pursued by one or other of the Eastern Churches; not until they were all but exterminated and their activities heavily fettered by political oppression and social degradation, applied sometimes crushingly and always severely by their Moslem rulers, did their missionary powers droop and wither.[1]

Long before the evangelization of England from Rome, and while the Celtic Church was still grappling with the heathenism of Ireland, the west of Scotland, and parts of England, Oriental Christians, with their base successively at Antioch, Edessa, and Seleucia-Ctesiphon, were fighting, and fighting with magnificent success, their Lord's cause away in the Far East. From Mazdeism the Edessene Church made innumerable conquests, and the first "National Church," in the modern sense of the term, was set up in Persia. This Church was wholly cut off by political boundaries from the Roman Empire.

[1] The precise nature of the obstacles placed by Islam in the path of the growth of Christianity we shall touch upon elsewhere in the chapter.

Its bishops could take no direct part on the Œcumenical Councils, and its language, Syriac, was such as did not enable it easily to follow the subtleties of Byzantine doctrinal interpretation and definition. This political isolation and this unadaptability in language were largely to blame for the Nestorianism on the one extreme, and the Monophysitism on the other, which finally separated the Churches east of Antioch and south of Alexandria from Byzantine orthodoxy, and branded them as heretical in the eyes of the West. But of all this the rank and file of the Edessene and Persian Churches knew, and could know, little. They preserved the faith, and took every means of teaching the faith, as it was known to them.

The Persian Church in the reign of Shapur II, in the middle of the fourth century, endured the heaviest and bitterest martyrdoms known in the whole history of the Church. The historian Sozomen gives the total of 16,000 martyrs who died in Shapur's reign. Undaunted by such persecution, they pressed on with their missionary work and penetrated the wildest parts of the world's surface—through Tibet into China, and southwards to India. Buddhist ritual, to this day, preserves traces of early Christian ritual; the present Mongolian alphabets are plainly relics of the Syriac Christian culture introduced centuries ago by the Persian Christian missionaries; and the old Syriac language and liturgy are still to be heard on the Malabar coast in the south of India. Before the final catastrophe of the Tamerlane invasion the Nestorians had created an enormous Asiatic Church, consisting of no less than twenty-five metropolitan sees, missionary centres throughout Khurasan, Turkistan, India, and China.

Again, from the Eastern Christians of Edessa the Gospel was taken to Armenia as early as the third century, and it was the Coptic monks of Egypt who, in the fifth and sixth centuries, revived, reorganized, and preserved Christianity in Abyssinia; while the greatest national conversion in history, that of the Russian nation, was the fruit of Byzantine Christianity at the end of the tenth century.

Farther East, where Islam had not yet gained its ascendancy, the Church of Persia persisted in its missionary work for centuries after the Hijra. Its Patriarch and metropolitans were honoured in the courts of the Mongol Ilkhan rulers of Persia in the thirteenth century, and converts were made within the reigning family itself. It was long confidently supposed in the West that the Mongol rulers and their followers were Christians, or on the point of embracing Christianity; it was a long-cherished idea that, though the Crusaders were driven out of the Holy Land, a united effort of Christian princes of the West and Mongol allies from the farther East would yet again eject the Moslems from Palestine.[1]

History, therefore, leaves us in no uncertainty as to the inherent missionary enterprise of our Christian brethren of the ancient Oriental Churches, such time as the least semblance of freedom and growth has been permitted them. Whenever our thoughts turn to questioning what they are doing, or what they can do or ought to do towards furthering the faith among non-Christians, we have no right to overlook what they have done in the past.

The fact, however, to be faced is that during the centuries of Islam's existence the ancient Oriental

[1] In 1287 we find a Nestorian Christian, a Mongol, the "archdeacon" of the Patriarch Yaballaha III (also a Mongol) presenting himself at the court of the English king, Edward I, with the object of negotiating such an alliance.

Churches have not advanced the Christian cause against Islam, but have, to a greater or less extent, retreated before it. There is an old rabbinical saying: "Judge not thy brother till thou art in his place." We may not pass judgment on the supineness of Christianity under Islam until we know better the position in which these Oriental Christians found themselves once the flood of Islam had overwhelmed them. It is a hard saying, but, humanly speaking, missionary endeavour becomes possible only when there is an acknowledged or unacknowledged moral, and even material, ascendancy in the would-be missionary or missionary body. Such an ascendancy the Eastern Churches failed to preserve before the wave of Islam. It was no inherent superiority in Islam which crushed them, but the combination of internal dissension, political subservience, and failure to retain their old spiritual life and vigour.

What, then, was the lot of those Christian bodies which still survived under Moslem political rule? Some would have us believe that they, as "people of the Book," enjoyed the amplest toleration.[1] Our attention is called to the decree[2] said to have been issued by the Caliph Omar after the capture of Jerusalem:

"In the name of God, the Merciful, the Compassionate! This is the security which Omar, the servant of God, the commander of the faithful, grants to the people of Aelia [Jerusalem]. He grants to all, whether sick or sound, security for their lives, their possessions, their churches and their crosses, and for all that concerns their religion. Their churches shall not be changed into dwelling-places, nor destroyed, neither shall they nor their appurtenances

[1] Sir T. W. Arnold, *The Preaching of Islam*, London, 1896, *passim*.
[2] Abū Tabarī, *Annales* (Leiden, 1885–93), vol. 1, p. 2405.

be in any way diminished, nor the crosses of the inhabitants nor aught of their possessions, nor shall any constraint be put upon them in the matter of their faith, nor shall any one of them be harmed."

This document may be genuine, and this policy may have been pursued for a brief space; but the history of Christianity under the Moslems tells a very different story of the treatment consistently meted out in later centuries to those who still clung to the faith of the Church in Moslem lands. "Toleration" was certainly extended in return for the payment of *jizyah* (the capitation tax imposed on *dhimmîs*, non-Mohammedans living under Mohammedan rule); but what a "toleration"![1] A more accurate picture of the conditions is given in another ordinance[2] likewise attributed to the Caliph Omar, but obviously belonging to a later age which sought primitive sanction for what had become established usage:

"In the name of God, the Merciful, the Compassionate! This is a writing to Omar b. al-Khattab from the Christians of such and such a city. When you marched against us, we asked of you protection for ourselves, our posterity, our possessions and our co-religionists; and we made this stipulation with you, that we will not erect in our city or the suburbs any new monastery, church, cell, or hermitage; that we will not repair any of such buildings that may fall into ruins, or renew those that may be situated in the Moslem quarters of the town; that we will not refuse the Moslems entry into our churches either by night or by day; that we will open the gates wide to passengers and travellers; that we will receive

[1] de Goeje, M. J., *Mémoire sur la conquête de la Syrie*, Leide, 1900, pp. 143 ff.; Leone Caetani, *Annali dell' Islam*, Milano, 1910, vol. 3, p. 957.

[2] Gottheil, Richard J. H., *Dhimmis and Moslems in Egypt* (Old Testament and Semitic Studies in Memory of William Rainey Harper), Chicago, 1908, vol. 2, pp. 382–4.

any Moslem traveller into our houses and give him food and lodging for three nights; that we will not harbour any spy in our churches or houses, or conceal any enemy of the Moslems; that we will not teach our children the Koran; that we will not make a show of the Christian religion nor invite any one to embrace it; that we will not prevent any of our kinsmen from embracing Islam, if they so desire. That we will honour the Moslems and rise up in our assemblies when they wish to take their seats; that we will not imitate them in our dress, either in the cap, turban, sandals, or parting of the hair; that we will not make use of their expressions of speech, nor adopt their surnames; that we will not ride on saddles, or gird on swords, or take to ourselves arms or wear them, or engrave Arabic inscriptions on our rings; that we will not sell wine; that we will shave the front of our heads; that we will keep to our own style of dress, wherever we may be; that we will wear girdles round our waists; that we will not display the cross upon our churches or display our crosses or our sacred books in the streets of the Moslems, or in their market-places; that we will strike the bells in our churches lightly; that we will not recite our services in a loud voice when a Moslem is present; that we will not carry palm-branches or our images in procession in the streets; that at the burial of our dead we will not chant loudly or carry lighted candles in the streets of the Moslems or their market-places; that we will not take any slaves that have already been in the possession of Moslems, nor spy into their houses; and that we will not strike any Moslem. All this we promise to observe, on behalf of ourselves and our co-religionists, and receive protection from you in exchange; and, if we violate any of the conditions of this agreement, then we forfeit your protection and you are at liberty to treat us as enemies and rebels."

Thus no ingenuity was spared in harassing the Christians, in impressing upon them, and demonstrating to their Moslem neighbours, the degraded social status of all who persisted in their adherence to Christianity, and in suppressing any possibility of healthy internal development or of propagating the Christian Faith among those that were without. Add to this the fact that real or supposed prosperity among non-Moslem sections of the community marked them down as obvious victims of extra fiscal oppression whenever the State was in need of revenue—and we shall see how effectively Christianity was hedged in and held under, not only by the outside world's assumption of the degradation then synonymous with Christianity, but also by the lowering of moral standards thereby induced among the Christians themselves. The wonder is, not that Christianity failed to make any headway in such circumstances, but that it survived at all under the imposed burdens of restrictions and enforced sense of social inferiority.

It is true that the last century has seen a change. The stigma of social degradation had largely been removed long before the war, and political changes since have tended, or are tending, to place the adherents of all religions on a basis of complete equality; outside oppression may no longer be brought forward as an excuse for loss of spiritual life. But it requires more than a decade or two to wipe out the effects of centuries. Modern psychological jargon speaks of an "inferiority complex"; and such a thing it is, to a very great extent, which centuries of Moslem rule have endeavoured to instil into the moral being of the ancient Oriental Churches. In the nature of things the attempt could never have achieved complete success, yet some results of the treatment, both in the ruling and in the victimized races, were bound to endure for a time. These results cannot be eliminated at once; they will be eliminated still more slowly if members of the free, untrammelled Churches of the West thoughtlessly perpetuate the process of centuries of Islam, by adopting a similar pose of supercilious contempt.

In these ancient Churches we may hope to find allies in the advancing of Christ's cause—but they are allies who have already fought and suffered ; they have suffered wounds and sickness the like of which we, in the providence of God, have been spared. These points we must never forget ; they should guide our thoughts in all our relations, actual and possible, with them. God has not suffered them to perish. He still has work for them to do. It is our part not to pass judgment on what they are doing or ought to do, but to discover how it may be in our power to help them to recover the health and vigour of their youth. We know that they are endowed with special gifts which make them eminently suitable and well equipped in the struggle against the ranks of Islam—in the very nature of things they must possess an intimate personal knowledge of Mohammedanism's popular forms, its particular weaknesses and its particular strength ; they already have, what the Western Christian can never wholly acquire, an intimate acquaintance with followers of Islam ; they have many things in common with their opponents—language, traditions, environment, history, and social usages. These strong points in their armour are too obvious to need stressing. But it would be foolish to blind our eyes to the other side of things, the positive weaknesses in these ancient Churches. Not merely have they lost their old missionary zeal, but they regard the notion of the conversion of the Moslems with actual abhorrence. Too often any reference to the call to missionary effort and to our responsibility to try to win the Moslems arouses in them obvious astonishment; they would argue that such people are beyond the pale, that we may not degrade our holy things by giving them to the dogs! Thus a colporteur on the Cairo station platform once offered a Bible for sale to a Moslem; a native Christian standing by indignantly struck the Bible out of the man's hand on to the ground, and rebuked the colporteur most sternly for "casting pearls before swine." And this, unhappily, is the attitude of mind of a very large proportion of the native Christians of the East to-day.

Rightly, therefore, can we believe that we have much to contribute to the well-being and effectiveness of the Christian East—the conviction that the Christian must strive to maintain a standard of life worthy of his Master, and that Christianity, by its very nature, must needs be aggressive; that the Christian believer must needs offer the glad tidings to those who have never heard. Also we have educational resources and institutions, we have an accumulation of knowledge in missionary work throughout the world, we have organized bodies of devoted workers, all of which we can gladly place at the disposal of our fellow-workers of the Eastern Churches. In other words, our part is to work and pray that God will use us as a means to strengthen the hands of the remnants of these ancient armies of Christendom, to strengthen the *moral* of these veterans—a *moral* which has been so sorely tried by centuries of oppression and solitude.

The process of working side by side has already begun, yet results have been very slow to show themselves. In more than one of these Oriental Christian communities a younger generation has arisen whose members have come into close contact with the ideals of the Western

Churches and have learned to re-examine their own Church and fellow Christians in the light of this contact. They begin to see how it may be in their power to put aside much that, while it made for security and preservation, clogged the forward action of their Church. Generally speaking, and of course not forgetting a very few individual and isolated examples to the contrary, there is amongst the laity some desire for wider education and reform; but this is not altogether a longing for more spiritual life, but is mixed up with the desire of acquiring national independence. The majority of missionaries who work amongst Moslems would emphatically say that there are not yet any indications of a real desire among Eastern Christians to evangelize the Moslems. But a real step forward has been taken in that a generation is arising which has learned to see in the Western Churches allies in Christ and not, as they have long feared, sometimes with reason, merely rival claimants to the allegiance of the native Christians. How such mutual confidence can, in practice, be called forth may be illustrated by the fact that the period of closest contact with the Coptic Church in Egypt was when the Church Missionary Society developed its most definite evangelistic work amongst the Moslems—when both Moslems and Copts became convinced of our sincerity.

. . . . .

The ancient Oriental Churches can never be more than a blunted weapon in the campaign of Christianity against Islam until, by aid from without and by spiritual revival within, they shall, by life and conduct, again win that respect from the Islamic races which they have lost so long. Centuries of oppression have not failed to leave their mark on both oppressor and oppressed. Travellers in the East have not been slow to say hard things of native Christians who have come under their notice—that they are backboneless creatures, Christians only because their fathers were Christians before them, that their religion is only an external armour of inherited habit and belief, that they are, so to speak, crustaceous rather than vertebrate in their spiritual construction. Christians of the West who contemptuously sit in judgment on Christians of the East should realize that this is not the way to help them. We shall only confirm them in that loss of respect if we ourselves treat them with contempt; we shall then be continuing, with deplorable results, that same work which Islam began and carried on for 1,300 years—of deliberately striving to make Christianity something despicable! Islam all but succeeded in its attempt; must it be left to fellow Christians to complete that work?

Beginning with sympathy, we must, on our part, learn to respect and honour these Churches and create, so far as lies in our power, conditions which shall justify such respect and honour. Oriental Christianity, the spiritual mother of all Christianity, will then the better hold high its head before Islam and, freed from the bondage of contempt, not wholly earned but largely imposed from without, be at liberty to play a real and full part in the evangelization of the East. We may leave the rest to God and His guidance.

ORIENTAL CHRISTIAN COMMUNITIES AND THE EVANGELIZATION OF THE MOSLEMS

BY THE REV.

W. H. T. GAIRDNER, B.A.,

Secretary, Church Missionary Society, Cairo

CHAPTER XVIII

ORIENTAL CHRISTIAN COMMUNITIES AND THE EVANGELIZATION OF THE MOSLEMS

Is it not now universally recognized in every mission country that the problem of problems and the hope of hopes is the evangelization of that country by its own Christian community? The following thought-sequence, which occurs in a paper recently read before Oriental and missionary leaders in Cairo, would probably be accepted by all as possessing almost mathematical cogency. We cannot do better than to begin with it, and immediately thereafter consider why it is ten times harder to turn the theoretical syllogism into a practical one in the Moslem East than in any other part of the mission-field. For this procedure will take us straight to the heart of our subject.

"We are all agreed that when Jesus Christ founded His Church He purposed to spread His message of salvation everywhere by means of that Church.

"We are all agreed that this work is the main duty of the Church as a whole; that Christ's congregation in this world is not intended to live to itself, not even to build up itself in holiness, but to live for its evangelizing task. The community whose entire energies are spent in maintaining itself will ultimately lack the energy to do even that.

"We are all agreed, then, that if this task and this ideal are universal, it must be made the conscious aim, the enthusiasm of the lesser communities included within the Church Universal—that is to say, of each denomination and of each local congregation of each denomination; and that this, again, should mean that all the families and individual members of those congregations have the same conscious aim, the same enthusiasm. It is only by particularizing, in ever-narrowing circles of application, that any campaign is won: as was discovered, for example, in the Great War or in the spiritual warfare of the Early Church.

"We are all agreed that the responsibility for the evangelization of each whole country is and must be mainly, indeed almost entirely, upon the local Christian community, denominations, congregations, families, and church-members in that country.

"We are all agreed, again, that the ultimate aim of all missionary work initiated in every country from the outside is the evangelization of the non-Christians of that country.

"We are all agreed that the missionary societies entered the Mohammedan lands of the East for just this purpose, and that this is the immediate or ultimate aim of every society and of every missionary in those lands.

"So, then, the abiding test of the success of missionary work in these lands will be, how far the Christian Church which has been influenced or raised up by missionary effort does take up and prosecute the evangelization of the non-Christians of these lands: for assuredly only thus, and not by the performances of foreigners, however devoted, can the task be accomplished or even carried on in a healthy way.

"If these things be true, we are then agreed that the abiding test of the success of missionary work in Mohammedan lands will be how far the Christian community in these lands, and especially that community which has been influenced or raised up through missionary effort, takes up and prosecutes the evangelization of Islam."

If these things are so, why is it that the old Oriental Churches are more causes of despair than of hope in this regard? Nay, why is it that the Reformed communities, whether Anglican, Presbyterian, or Congregational, which have been raised up in Near Eastern lands during the last eighty years, numerous, powerful, well-educated though they be, are an almost complete disappointment in the very matter which, as we have seen, touches their actual *raison d'être*? This fact is too unquestionable to be denied, too serious not to be faced, and, let us at once say, too simply intelligible not to be treated with sympathy. Indeed, it is only when the causes of the disappointment are frankly faced that they can be clearly understood, only when clearly understood that they can be appreciated with sympathy, and only when they are appreciated with sympathy that they can be changed. And changed they must be if the syllogism remains so inexorably true, and if the mission Churches continue, nevertheless, to be such a disappointment in the one thing for which they were founded by their great pioneers.

In the first place, the old Oriental Churches, such as the Greek-Orthodox, Coptic, Gregorian, and Uniate communities, have a long non-evangelistic and non-"proselytizing" tradition behind them reaching back to before Islam. And they are also, taken broadly, inert, timorous, and destitute of evangelistic fire. The Reformed communities mentioned above are composed of ex-members of those Oriental communities and their descendants, not of converts from Islam, who are either non-existent or form (except in Persia) an infinitesimal and unassimilated element in these communities of hereditary Christians.

There seem to be three main difficulties. The first

and fundamental one is the age-long pressure of a conquering, a domineering, and an unsparing state-religion: a religion which has made "proselytism" and even preaching criminal offences; a religion which has barely conceded to the depressed members of other faiths the right to exist, and then only on the express condition that they kept themselves to themselves, i.e., did not fulfil what we have seen above is the law of their being; a religion which has caused its adherents to accept acts of kindness, friendliness, and Christian service as the due of a lordly from a menial people; which has attributed even such acts and services to cowardice, to ulterior motives, to the mean currying of favour; and which thus has discounted, neutralized, and spoiled the very conduct in which Christ most reveals Himself, and by which men are impressed and won.

With all the centuries of this treatment, and the deep, inherited thought-attitudes created by it, has come fear, distrust, disbelief in the possibility of the Christianizing of such people. And, with the attitude and power of the governing class largely unchanged to-day, how can we expect the Christian community in the East to clear at one leap the 1,400 years that separate it from the days when Christianizing and conversion of non-Christians were part of normal Christian life?

The second difficulty is that the historic development of religious communities in the East has tended to turn them all into something resembling nations, the governing bodies of which are charged with a multitude of duties concerning the personal and social and political status of their members: the direct result is the disinclination to admit outsiders, and the denial of the desirability or even possibility of conversion, along with a strong development of those feelings of antipathy and antagonism which are associated with national community-feeling. We are thus faced with another colossal historic difficulty with a standing of a millennium and a half.

The third difficulty is the fact that too often the Christian communities have been disappointed in converts from Islam, some of whom should never have been admitted, others of whom ran well and then turned traitor. The fact that some of these failures were directly due to soil and atmosphere uncongenial to the new plants, does not weaken the point, while it strengthens another one, namely, that until there exists in the East a Christian Church in which converts from Islam can be at home, missionaries will continue to work almost in vain.

These enormous and baffling difficulties must be bravely, truthfully, sympathetically recognized, without the slightest assertion or feeling of moral or spiritual superiority in any quarter. Only so can we begin to face and to attack these Anakim which, while the Christian Church was in bondage, have occupied these lands of promise.

Moreover, what makes these difficulties acute, and the failure which they spell so serious, is the fact that the small number of Christians who have come out from Islam have remained, on the whole, an unwelcome, unwanted, and unassimilated element in Oriental Christian communities, in the "Reformed" no less than in the "Orthodox." We here come to the core of that which is to-day the problem and for the solution of which we must look to to-morrow. The reasons—if you will, the excuses—for this strange, disconcerting, baffling fact have already been sufficiently analysed. But we simply cannot accept the fact as necessary or as permanent. For if the ultimate success of the evangelistic enterprise depends upon the way in which it is taken up and finally taken over by the Oriental Christian community, this is only to say that it depends upon the extent to which that community becomes a home for those who turn from Islam to Christ. For the Church or congregation which desires to be, sets out to be, and succeeds in becoming, a home for those converted to Christ from Islam is in itself a gospel—the best, highest, and most Christlike gospel of all: the gospel that will be most easily loved by those without, and will most powerfully attract them to enter. Precisely such a Church will certainly be the one most forward in preaching to non-Christians in the ordinary sense of the word.

Therefore, to see these congregations and communities as homes for those who are not yet Christ's but for whom Christ is seeking, is the supreme task, the highest ideal, the fairest dream. Only in such nurseries can new-born souls thrive. Only when the soil of Christ's garden-plots is thus congenial to these new plants will they survive the shock of transference from their native soil and thrive and grow and flower and yield fruit.

There is a special reason why this holds true in Moslem mission lands. Whatever we may think of Islam, it has markedly stood for a brotherhood, a universal brotherhood of a sort. It may be that many of the manifestations of this brotherhood are imperfect, unspiritual, even most injurious to those without. But, from the point of view of those within, it does stand for something—with many for much, with some for everything. If this is so, it is obvious that unless we can show them a brotherhood that is higher, better, more spiritual, warmer, tenderer—in one word, truer—they will marvel how we have the face to preach to them at all. And contrariwise, a people so familiar with the idea of brotherhood will specially appreciate the real thing when they see it.

How, then, shall the three baffling difficulties mentioned above be faced and then wrestled with and overthrown ?

To the first must be opposed once more the ideal of Christian courage and hope. In spite of all, the mentality is not just the same to-day as it was in 1725 or in 1825. The ideas of civil and religious freedom, at least, have been given a start. So the moment is favourable for the Church to re-learn hope. But in any case it needs to re-learn courage. And why should not those races which withstood 1,300 years of persecution and dying for being Christians, be equally willing to withstand persecution—aye, and even death—for being evangelists ? And the missionaries must be willing to suffer both persecution and death with them.

To the second difficulty must be opposed the original conception of the Christian Church, whose specially warm fraternal love within the spiritual brotherhood did not in the least spell chilliness, much less hostility, to those without ; but rather guaranteed a universal friendliness and an all-embracing benevolence, the very qualities which most of all attracted souls to join the fellowship, so that they might share the more intense warmth within.

To the third difficulty missionaries must oppose a revised procedure and make a candid confession of many mistakes in the past, such as unwisdom, hastiness, inefficient pastoral care, insufficient co-operation with one another and with their Oriental fellow-Christians.

But are these suggestions practical ? In order to change a situation which has been wrong for 1,500 years, and which is still to-day difficult and complicated to the last degree, the most practical thing is to analyse it as clearly, as fearlessly, and as lovingly as possible, and then to concentrate attention on changing the thoughts which for historical reasons have been warped so long. For thoughts are practical things, because they lead to actions. While missionaries, in their haste to act, perhaps call thoughts unpractical things, Oriental mothers are busy instilling the old thoughts into another generation of children, which will inevitably produce the old actions and attitudes and will continue to thwart the glorious plans of the Divine Son of Man.

If, then, it is almost a new philosophy of Christianity and its history that is involved, this can be taught only by leaders of Oriental Christianity, by the clergy, ministers, evangelists, elders, school-teachers, and church-members, who are fathers and mothers. It is to them the appeal must be made, thus to learn and thus to teach: to let this beautiful idea be known and loved, the idea of their Church as a home for the souls shivering in the cold without, or as a garden-plot for the wild plant transplanted thither. Let these folk get the right attitude, the attitude of welcome, of friendliness, of sympathy for the cruel difficulties of the newly baptized. This demands clear thinking, clear teaching, and clear leading from those responsible for planning, for instruction, and for guidance.

From history and experience we know that similar thought-campaigns have been waged in the West and have prevailed to change minds to action—but not without time and travail. One sees here a truly vast enterprise, an enterprise as definite and as great as that of the Student Volunteer Missionary Movement in the West, although the emphasis will be on education rather than on life-service, education that will begin at the very centre—in the synods, the clerical and ministerial assemblies, and will radiate to the very circumference, to the general membership of every local congregation; education which shall be definitely planned and controlled, and carefully watched and regulated by those who shall be responsible for oversight ; education behind which shall be the dynamic of continual prayer, and which shall work itself out by sermon and address, study-circle, textbooks, and example ; education to be applied to congregation, schools, and home, to the end that public opinion and social consciousness may be changed —nay, that change may be wrought in something even deeper and more dynamic than consciousness, namely, the sub-conscious life that is the deposit of the inherited and accumulated thought and feeling of the centuries.

Who is sufficient for these things? Surely no one. They call for the impossible. Nevertheless, there come to mind fragments of words, old yet ever new: "And nothing shall be impossible to you"; "only have faith! all things are possible to the man who has faith"; and, "I have found all things possible—in my dynamic, Christ."

THE MYSTICAL LIFE IN MODERN ISLAM

BY

GEORGE SWAN,

Secretary, Egypt General Mission

CHAPTER XIX

THE MYSTICAL LIFE IN MODERN ISLAM

"With a measure of light and a measure of shade
The world of old by the Word was made;
By the shade and light was the Word conceal'd,
And the Word in flesh to the world reveal'd
Is by outward sense and its forms obscured;
The spirit within is the long-lost Word,
Besought by the world of the soul in pain
Through a world of words which are void and vain.
O never while shadow and light are blended
Shall the world's Word-quest or its woe be ended,
And never the world of its wounds made whole
Till the Word made flesh be the Word made soul!"

ARTHUR EDWARD WAITE.

Is it not true that at the back of all religions there is the quest of the knowledge of God? In the words of St. Paul, "God . . . hath made of one blood all nations of men . . . that they should seek the Lord, if haply they might feel after Him, and find Him."[1] Some seek Him, *ab initio*, by the deductive or inductive processes of philosophy; others, taking as their basis a revelation which they accept, seek by defining and systematizing this revelation to come to a clearer conception of the Deity; while still others seek in various ways a personal experience of God. It is these last who are generally termed the mystics of any given religion. Against this

[1] Acts 17: 26, 27.

we must always bear in mind that great mystics, like al-Ghazālī in Islam, were often philosophers and systematic theologians as well as seekers after a personal and inward experience of God.

For every individual, however, who truly seeks after God there are multitudes who are satisfied with the results of others' search, who adopt a philosophy, a dogma, a creed, a ritual with more or less credulity or imitate the processes which some revered saint found helpful as he "practised the presence of God," or sought to reproduce the ecstatic condition which he believed to be communion with the Infinite. When we come to study the mysticism of the masses of Moslem lands we find it, with very few exceptions, thus imitative and traditional.

For the first six centuries of Moslem history mysticism was largely individualistic, except for occasional schools that gathered round those who had become famous for their mystical attainments, and who had also the gift of passing on to others the acquisitions of their contemplative life and their intuitively gained knowledge of God. As we approach the close of this period we begin to find less strict individualism. The number of really great mystical teachers has so increased as to have become an important factor in the life of every Moslem country. They have become eclectic, recognizing, criticizing, and adopting much of the learning and experience of other mystic teachers, now generally known as Sufis. In their eclecticism they do not confine themselves to Islam, and so we find, taking one example only, a very strong Neo-Platonist influence derived from the great work of the Pseudo-Dionysius, the Areopagite of Alexandria, a work which, through the translation of Johannes Scotus Erigena, profoundly affected the mysticism of Europe, and which accounts for many of the similarities between mediæval Catholic and Arab mysticism. This systematizing of mystic lore became concrete and generally available by the writing of certain famous books, such as *Qūtu 'l-Qulūb*, by Abu Tālib al-Makki (d. A.D. 996); the *Risālatu'l-Qushayriyya*, by Abu'l-Qāsim al-Qushayrī (d. A.D. 1074); and, greatest of all, the *Ihyā'u 'Ulūm ad-Dīn*, by al-Ghazālī (d. A.D. 1111). It was this book that dispelled the fears of the Moslem world as to the orthodoxy of Sufism, and therefore did much to facilitate the popular movement which led to the formation of the dervish orders, a movement which very probably commenced under the influence of Abd al-Qādir al-Jilāni, who died only fifty-five years later.

The transitional period is quite admirably portrayed in the life of Abu'l Hasan ash-Shādhilī. As those who know Arabic literature will acknowledge, that which we in the West recognize as biographical material is generally wanting in it; but, fortunately, in a small book issued by the Shādhilī Order, we have a real picture of Mohammedan life in North Africa in the beginning of the twelfth century A.D., which bears internal evidence that it was compiled from contemporary sources.

Ash-Shādhilī was brought up in the ordinary Koranic school of his village, Ghamara, in Morocco, possibly also in Fez, but moved when yet quite young to Tunis. He early became interested in Sufi teaching, his interest deepening into a veritable quest. He heard that the saint of saints, the Qutb-al-Ghawth (Axis of Aid), was to be found in Iraq; he therefore set out right across North Africa, through Arabia, to Mesopotamia in search of the Qutb, hoping through him to be initiated more fully into the *gnosis*, the esoteric knowledge of God. We read of encounters with wild beasts and evil men, we read of the jealousy and persecution of scholastic theologians, we read of miracles that God performed on behalf of His servant, and of wonderful mystical experiences which he encountered on the way. On arrival in Iraq, the reputed Qutb told him that he was mistaken ; the one whom he sought was in Morocco, living a hermit life in a cave near Ras-al-Jabal. Ash-Shādhilī made his way back the three thousand odd miles, and found it even so. Both journeys were full of incident. They comprised quite long stays in some of the towns, just how long we cannot learn ; pupils attached themselves to him in each town ; he had considerable influence on the rulers of the countries, confirming what we gather from other sources of the power the saints wielded in affairs of government at that period. The more enthusiastic pupils left all to follow him when he moved off on his quest ; as we read we are strongly reminded of the schools of the prophets and of that lower form of prophetism, hints of which are to be found throughout the whole history of Israel after the entry into Canaan.

Having met the Qutb and stayed with him some days, he professed to have received great inward knowledge of God and of the things of God and the assurance that he himself was to be the future Qutb, God's pivot of the universe. After this we read of several more pilgrimages to Mecca and a growing reputation as a saint, especially in Egypt. We get glimpses of popular interest in his movements, his teachings, and his miracles. Incidentally we get a new conception of the unity of the Moslem world, with its constant pilgrim caravans moving to and from Mecca, generally counting in their numbers one or more notable Sufi saints, their protection to the caravan more greatly prized than that of a band of soldiers.

Their words and works form the main topic of conversation through the weary months of travel, and, as the pilgrims return once more to their homes, they bring with them many wonderful tales of the saints that accompanied them, and of others they have met, and the still greater number of those of whom they have heard. One often is astonished at the remarkable unity of the Moslem world, even its uniformity in so many respects; perhaps these great and leisurely pilgrim caravans during all the centuries prior to the advent of the locomotive and steamboat may supply us with the reason.

Abd al-Qādir al-Jilāni died about thirty years before ash-Shādhilī was born, but Ahmad al-Bedawi, who is generally looked upon as the founder of dervish orders in Egypt, died some nineteen years only after ash-Shādhilī, and it is doubtful whether the full organization of their orders took place in their life-time. In the lives of both al-Jilāni and ash-Shādhilī we get the picture of the whole world going after the more notable of the saints, from the Sultan on his throne to the poorest vendor in the streets. That the movement towards definite organization began under Abd al-Qādir al-Jilāni is maintained by the orders themselves. He was a great teacher at Baghdad, and became so popular that no building in the city was found large enough to hold his audiences. He seems to have been pre-eminently a preacher, and several collections of his sermons are still procurable in the ordinary Arab bookshops; but the remarkable thing is that, though admirable as sermons, probably quite the best in Islamic literature, they are singularly devoid of mystic lore or of principles that could have moulded the customs and practices of the orders. This is also true of most of the standard works of the dervish orders; one looks for mysticism and finds orthodoxy. It is puzzling why this should be. Is it that they fear their esoteric teaching may by the printed page become available for the uninitiated, or is it their eagerness to convince the schoolmen that they are orthodox? A suggestion for the development of the Qadirîya Order, which is worth serious consideration, is based on the fact that Abd al-Qādir had forty-nine children, and that at least eleven of his sons followed him as teachers in his school of mysticism, and several travelled and became heads of Qadirī orders in other countries, notably Spain. It may be to the organizing ability of one of them that we must look for the system which is practically the basis of all dervish orders.

The organization is so good, and the dervishes can be so readily marshalled and a fanatical fighting force so quickly mobilized from peaceful peasants and pedlars, that all foreign governments desiring to maintain their power in Mohammedan countries have had to invent some secret method of controlling the orders. Even at the present time in Egypt, when dervishism has tremendously dwindled from the effect of the impact of Western civilization, one's first impression, on seeing a great dervish procession, as on the Prophet's birthday, is that of its disreputability; but, as one continues to see order after order pass with its banners, the impression grows of an immense latent and possibly sinister power.

At the head of each order there is a Sheikh al-Sajāda. He is either an hereditary descendant of the founder of the order or one who owes his position to what might be termed a species of "apostolic succession," each head of such an order appointing his successor and investing him with the official cloak, or turban. The *sajāda* is generally the traditional prayer-carpet, or sheep-skin of the founder of the order, who, though dead perhaps for almost six centuries, has a very effective place in all its functions. This is specially true of Abd al-Qādir al-Jilāni, who is a very living and beloved personality to every Qadirîya dervish, and a little knowledge of whose life and most famous sayings will be found to be an "open sesame" to the heart of many a dervish, even to those who belong to other orders.

The Sheikh al-Sajāda generally has four young henchmen, or *nuqabā*. These form his innermost circle of pupils, and usually it is one of these who follows him in office in those orders where the headship is by appointment.

The next official is the Wakīl Sheikh al-Sajāda, the agent or substitute of the head of the order. It is he who is usually the active, organizing head, the Sheikh al-Sajāda sometimes being an infant in the hereditary orders and in the others being more noted for the contemplative ecstatic life than for the administrative. The orders very often have considerable material effects that need careful administration, besides the natural duty the Wakīl has of holding together a widely scattered order with a host of minor officials responsible to him.

Next in order comes the Khalīfa, who is the local representative or vicar of the Sheikh al-Sajāda. In large cities there may be many *Khulāfa* of the same order, in which case one bears the name of *Khalīfat al-Khulāfa*, vicar of vicars, and is the responsible local head.

Then come the great mass of *Ikhwān*, or brothers. These comprise both fully initiated dervishes who are wholly given over to the contemplative life and earn a bare subsistence in a very humble walk in life, and those whose connexion with the order is more or less loose and who are engaged in the ordinary pursuits of life, like the tertiaries of the old monastic orders. To this latter class belong the great masses of the people, mostly quite illiterate, or having only the education of the Koranic schools. It is rarely that those who have had even a simple Western education join the orders; by such the orders are despised.

In addition to these heads and sub-heads there are teaching and initiating sheikhs who may or may not hold other office. They are generally called by the name of *Am*, a word which in ordinary language means a paternal uncle, but in the idiom of the orders is equivalent to the spiritual director of the monastic orders. The word possibly may have reference to the distinctive turban which he wears, and which in pre-Islamic times was given by the Arabs as a sign of acknowledged lordship. His apostolic succession of the *gnosis* is always given in terms of having been invested with this turban through an unbroken chain of sheikhs, often going back to the immediate entourage of the Prophet Mohammed.

All small manuals of the orders have reference to the implicit obedience that must be paid by the novice to his *Am*. R. A. Nicholson, in his valuable book entitled *The Mystics of Islam*,[1] to which the reader who desires to pursue this subject might well turn for his first studies, does not exaggerate in speaking of the obedience expected from the novice as "grovelling submission to the authority of an ecstatic class of men, dependence on their favour, pilgrimage to their shrines, adoration of their relics, devotion of every mental and spiritual faculty to their service," and as being deplorable in its practical results. But there still remains a worse feature, and that is that the novice must accept the saintliness of his teacher in spite of every evidence to the contrary. This

[1] London, 1914.

most demoralizing position has for its foundation the encounter of Moses with the ever-living saint al-Khidr, recorded in the Koran, Sura, 18 : 64–81, and highly and grossly developed in dervish books to cover every form of open and flagrant vice.

We have looked at the hierarchy of the orders, but to account fully for all the phenomena we meet we must seek to comprehend the extraordinary reality of the unseen to the Eastern mind. Dr. Duncan B. Macdonald has brought this out well in his book entitled *The Religious Attitude and Life in Islam*.[1] To the Mohammedans the unseen world all around is peopled with the saints of Islam. The true governors of the world are the members of the parliament of saints, which meets every night in the more immediate heavens; living saints take part in this with the departed ones; the chief of all the saints, the Qutb who presides, is always a living saint. No wonder, then, that the cult of saints is the outstanding feature of the Moslem masses, and that it has restored to Islam all the features of a gross animistic idolatry which had almost disappeared on the first impact of the original militant monotheism.

We are confining ourselves, in this article, to things as they are and not dealing with the idealistic system that has been conceived and developed by some of Islam's best thinkers and has been the stimulus to much of its best poetry. One does, on rare occasions, meet individuals who really seek to use these systems in their quest of the knowledge of God; one does occasionally meet men who have some claim to saintliness. But these are so rare that the student wishing to obtain first-hand information of the orders is often tempted to think that he has been misled in believing that the

[1] Chicago, 1909.

religion of the dervishes is the real religion of the Moslem masses. On every hand he finds complete ignorance of the system, even of the simplest technical terms of the orders; he finds the teaching sheikhs to be gross impostors, vile parasites of the Moslem community; he finds the officers using their office to make a living by cheap magic. But if he goes further in his studies, and especially if he lives with an open and observant mind amongst the people in towns and villages least affected by Western influences, he will come to see how far-reaching are the influences of Islamic mysticism.

The ultimate proof of the falsity of any philosophy lies in its outworking in following generations. This is especially true of the pantheistic and mystical philosophies that underlie the religion of the dervishes. In their beginnings often very attractive, they produced some noble lives and they inspired much of the very best of Islamic poetry; but undoubtedly their full fruit is to be found in the debasing ideas of the Moslem masses of to-day. They may use the dervish prayers, some of which are beautiful, and also the *zikr*, or repetition of special phrases designed for the purification of the soul's diseases, wholly with the idea of piling up merit; they may attend the public performance of *zikrs* only because of the pleasurable emotions there stimulated; their minds may be wholly uneducated and densely ignorant; yet it will be found that the really formative influences that mould their lives are to be found in the mysticism which has degenerated into dervishism.

Missionaries going to Moslem lands are apt to take for granted that the religion of the land is the religion of the Koran and the Traditions; they may become skilful in dialectics, and remove every ground for further belief in Islam, and yet never touch the true heart religion of the people. The whole vast problem of a sympathetic approach to the masses of Islam remains as yet practically unsolved, and it will remain so as long as there exists the tendency to leave the subject as a specialized study for the few. Every missionary to Moslems must get to work at it, and must supply his information to the missionary body as a whole. It is not so much the information of Orientalists and experts that we desire as the practical advice of missionaries who can tell us how to convince these people that they are being beguiled of their " reward in a voluntary humility and worshipping of angels " by men who are " vainly puffed up " by their fleshly minds, " which things have indeed a show of wisdom in will-worship, and humility, and neglecting of the body ; not in any honour to the satisfying of the flesh," and who can tell us how to present to them in an acceptable way " the riches of the glory of this mystery . . . which is Christ in you, the hope of glory."

NEW TRENDS IN MOSLEM APOLOGETIC

BY THE REV.

ARTHUR JEFFERY, M.A., M.R.A.S.,

Professor, School of Oriental Studies, American University, Cairo

CHAPTER XX

NEW TRENDS IN MOSLEM APOLOGETIC

THE contacts with Western life and thought have not been without their influence on the apologetic literature of Islam which rises out of the perennial religious controversy between Islam and Christianity. On the one hand, there has been a stirring of new life in the old orthodox apologetic; and, on the other hand, the new intellectualism which has come about as a result of Western education, and which has brought to birth the reform movements of India and Egypt, and the heretical sects, such as the Bahais and the Ahmadiyas, has resulted in an entirely new type of apologetic written from these new points of view.

The apologetic literature of the old orthodoxy at the present day is little more than a rehash of the old work of Ali Tabari, Ibn Hazm, and Ibn Taymiyya, who all wrote before the fifteenth century; but there is a new note of "awakeness" to modern conditions in many of the pamphlets and tractates called forth by the successful work of Christian missionaries in Egypt, Syria, Turkey, or India. Some are urgent warnings to Moslems against Christian hospitals and schools, and against the circulation of Christian books. And some are replies to Christian books whose effective attack has roused Moslems to counter-attack. One such pamphlet, very well known in Cairo, is called *Poisoned Arrows: A Reply to those who Disturbed the Thoughts, Pretending they were Enlightening the Minds : Arrows Aimed at the Breasts of the Rascal Preachers.*

Both in the attacks on Christianity and in the defence of Islam there is a valiant attempt to adapt the new arguments to modern circumstances. Two very interesting instances of this are : (*a*) the curious attempts being made to defend polygamy and hold it up as a solution of the social evil ; and (*b*) the endeavours to defend Mohammed. The unorthodox, of course, can throw tradition overboard, and thus get rid of uncomfortable facts handed down about the Prophet. The orthodox writer, however, is bound to acknowledge these facts. So they have evolved the theory of the all-round man. Every prophet, they say, came with a special message to his own age. The age of Jesus was given up to debauchery and needed an example of asceticism ; so Jesus was an ascetic. But Mohammed was the seal of the prophets, the culmination of the prophetic line ; so it was necessary that he should give men an all-round example. He was married to give men an example of married relations ; he went to war to give men an example of courage in the fight ; and so on. In answer to the question why Mohammed needed so many wives, they say that marriage is the most important of human relationships, and men need more detailed example there than in other things ; so, as men marry different types of women, it was necessary for the Prophet to give in his own life an example of how life should be lived with each kind of woman. Thus, with Khadija, he gave an example of how to live with a wife older than oneself ; with 'Aisha, how to live with one younger than oneself ; and so on, with all his wives according to their several types.

Turning to the unorthodox and reforming apologetic, we find that it turns round much the same problems as the older, orthodox polemic, but is characterized by a new attitude.

In the first place, it is better instructed. When the Shulamite maiden in Canticles 5 : 16 tells the daughters of Jerusalem that her beloved is "altogether lovely," the older apologetic found in the Hebrew word *Mahmadim* a prophecy of the coming of Mohammed. The new controversialist is sensitive to the crushing weight of philological argument, and makes no such blunder. The older apologetic, again, made great collections of the so-called miracles of Mohammed, and was content to record such incidents as the following, set forth in the *Izhar al Haqq*.

"It is said that Jabar one day killed a sheep, and, after he had prepared it and cooked it, he served it to the Prophet at table. Everyone ate of it, but the Prophet said, 'Eat, but do not break the bones.' When they had finished, the Prophet put the bones together, placed his hands over them, and muttered a few words, and lo! the sheep became whole again, got up, and wagged its tail."

The modern apologetic has faced up in some measure to the facts of modern knowledge and the demands of modern scholarship, and tries to write its new apologetic in terms of this.

Secondly, it is freer. It is not bound by tradition, as is orthodox Islam. The Bahais get out of this difficulty by teaching that with the Bab there came a new revelation which superseded that of orthodox Islam. A new start was again made in Baha'ullah, who superseded the Bab, and so all the authority of the earlier dispensation has come to an end, and they are free to write their new apologetic in the light of the new revelation. The Ahmadiya Movement, also, to some extent found the same freedom through teaching the Messiahship of its founder, Mirza Ghulam Ahmad of Qadian. The rationalistic reformers, both those of the Aligarh School in India and their confrères in Egypt, free themselves by making onslaught on the validity of tradition. Goldziher, in his epoch-making *Muhammedanische Studien*,[1] has brought to a head for European Orientalists the attack on Moslem Tradition, and has shown its utter worthlessness; but even earlier than Goldziher, the exigencies of the controversy with Christianity had forced Moslem writers in the East to seek to be freed from it. Sir Syed Ahmad Khan, the founder of the Aligarh Movement, led the way, and his disciples followed.

Moulaví Cherágh Ali, in his *Critical Exposition of the Popular "Jihád,"*[2] and his *Proposed Political, Legal, and Social Reforms under Moslem Rule*,[3] for example, characterizes various Traditions as "spurious and fictitious," "not based on any critical, historical, or rational principles," "unblushing and fabulous," "one-sided and imperfect." Ameer Ali also pays scant respect to tradition, and Sir Abdur Rahim, in his *Muhammadan Jurisprudence*,[4] states that "zeal gave rise to many a false and inaccurate Tradition." So Muhammad Badr of Egypt, in his little book, *The Truth about Islam*,[5] tells us that in his school "the Traditions as a whole are becoming more and more neglected, and the Qur'an is regarded in the light of pure reason and modern science."

[1] Ignacz Goldziher, *Muhammedanische Studien*, Halle, 1899.

[2] Calcutta, 1885.

[3] Bombay, 1883.

[4] Abdur Rahim, *The Principles of Muhammadan Jurisprudence*, London.

[5] Cairo, 1910.

Some of the Ahmadiya writers also have taken this way out.

And not only is it tradition from which they seek to free themselves, but from the whole body of law which has grown up through the centuries around the primitive kernel of legislation contained in the Koran.

> "It was only from some oversight," writes Cherágh Ali, "that in the first place, the civil precepts of a transitory nature, and as a mediate step leading to a higher reform, were taken as final; and in the second place, the civil precepts adapted for the dwellers of the Arabian desert were pressed upon the neck of all ages and countries. A social system for barbarism ought not to be imposed on a people already possessing higher forms of civilization."[1]

This freedom, of course, gives them the right of private interpretation, and makes it possible for them to make a new face to the attacks of Christianity.

Thirdly, it has newer and better weapons, using Christianity's own methods and availing itself of weapons provided by modern rationalism and other movements in the West. At its feeblest this is seen in the readiness of the Moslems of the new movements to adopt Christian methods of propaganda. For example, there is a Muslim Book and Tract Depot, at Lahore; and Hamid Snow, an English convert to Islam, has produced a Moslem Prayer Book and Catechism. Sheikh Rashid Ridha has made great plans in Cairo for a Missionary Training School to equip missionaries of Islam to proceed to Christian countries. Sheikh Shawish's ill-fated magazine, *Al-Hidayah*, was an effort to copy Christian religious magazines. The Ahmadiya Movement par-

[1] Moulaví Cherágh Ali, *A Critical Exposition of the Popular "Jihád,"* p. xcii, Calcutta, 1885.

ticularly, both in its organization and in its publications, follows closely the Christian model, and the Bahai propaganda is shot through and through with Christian ideas.

At its keenest, this third characteristic is seen in the diligent way in which the anti-Christian material produced in the West is used to attack the work of the Christian missionaries in the East. Sometimes this is used in rather an insincere way, as by the Syrian writer Salim at-Tannir, who has exploited many of the ultra-critical theories of European writers in order to make it seem to the Moslems of the East that what is being preached by the missionaries is no longer believed by the intellectuals of the West. Usually, however, it is used quite sincerely as a new weapon of offence. Examples of this are Sheikh Rashid Ridha's use of the "Pagan Christs" theory of Drews and J. M. Robertson, in order to prove that the great doctrines of Christianity are little more than a working over of old pagan theology; or Sheikh Hifnawi's attempt in his *Kafayat at-Talibin* to work up evidence that modern Christianity is based, not on the Scriptures, but on the traditions of the Fathers.

A very interesting illustration of this point is found in a curious volume that would appear to be unique in the annals of Moslem polemic. It is called *Al-Madhhab ar-Ruhani* (The Spiritual Sect) by Abdallah Abahi, and gives a long account of the origin and growth of Spiritualism, and its rapid spread among the Western nations, expounds and defends the main teachings of Spiritualism, and then, from this ground, proceeds to show that, while Islam can agree with the results of such teaching, Christianity cannot and thus is self-condemned.

Full advantage has also been taken of all favourable references to Islam in the works of European writers.

The Muslim Tract Depot of Lahore, for instance, publishes typographically attractive pamphlets giving the favourable judgments of Carlyle, Bosworth Smith, and others. In Cairo there has been published in Arabic a translation of Tolstoi's favourable account of Mohammed and Islam. The Woking group have been even more ambitious, and have published by private subscription such considerable works as John Davenport's *Apology for Muhammad and the Qur'an,* and the seventeenth-century lucubration of one Henry Stubbe, or Stubs, *An Account of the Rise and Progress of Mahometanism, with the Life of Mahomet and a Vindication of him and his Religion from the Calumnies of the Christians.*

This newer apologetic, of course, is addressed in the main to a new public, the Western-educated classes, and much of it is intended for European consumption rather than for use in the East. Both in India and in Egypt we find considerable use made of the English language. Anti-Christian pamphlets are published in North Africa in French, and the compendious *Izhar al Haqq* has been issued in that language. The Ahmadiya community has works in English, French, and German, and we hear occasionally of the prospects of a magazine in Japanese.

The apologetic is naturally two-sided—an attack on Christianity, and a defence of Islam. The attack on Christianity mainly concerns the validity of the Scriptures and the great Christian doctrines of the Trinity, the Person of Christ, and Redemption. The defence of Islam in turn is mostly as relates to the Koran as the Word of God, the Prophetship of Mohammed, and such questions as holy war, the position of women, etc.

In its attacks on Christianity, the older apologetic was largely contented to make long collections of supposed contradictions and variations in the historical accounts of Chronicles as compared with Samuel and Kings, or among the four Evangelists. For example, 2 Samuel xxiv: 1, states that God moved David to number the children of Israel, while 1 Chronicles xxi: 1, says that the instigator was Satan. Or, again, Matthew, in chapter viii, tells of the cleansing of the leper after the Sermon on the Mount, then the curing of the centurion's servant after Jesus entered Capernaum, and lastly the cure of Peter's wife's mother. In Luke, however, the cure of Peter's mother-in-law came first (chapter iv), then that of the leper (chapter v), and later the centurion's servant (chapter vii). And so on, as is drawn out in great detail in such works as the *Izhar al Haqq*, *Al-Ajwiba as-Saniya*, *Lisan as-Sidq*, and many other of the old polemical masterpieces. The new school, however, is much more subtle. Dr. Tawfiq Sidqi, a disciple of Sheikh Rashid Ridha, is a good example of their method. In his *Nazra fi Kutub al Ahad al Jadid*, he utilizes such works as Cassel's *Supernatural Religion*,[1] to work out an argument against the authenticity of the New Testament. First, the uncertainties of patristic testimony are worked up to demonstrate the weakness of the external evidence for the Gospels' being the work of their traditional authors. Then internal evidence is examined in detail, and John's Gospel, for example, is disposed of by the author's supposed ignorance of the topography of Palestine. Attempts are also made to find origins of New Testament incidents and logia in Talmudic and other sources. Thus, Matthew's story of the Temptations is asserted to have its origin in a Buddhist source claimed to be much older than Christianity; and so on.

Missionaries on the field no more see eye to eye on questions of Biblical criticism than their brethren at

[1] Walter R. Cassel, *Supernatural Religion*, New York, 1912.

home, and these writers have been quick to take advantage of this fact by entrenching themselves in positions from which they know quite well the liberal scholar can drive them, but dare not for fear of betraying the position of his more conservative brethren.

It is noticeable, also, that the theory of the Abrogation of the Christian Scriptures has dwindled to quite insignificant proportions in the works of the newer school. In the Woking version of the Ahmadiya *Commentary on the Koran*,[1] for instance, we find that in the interests of the new apologetic for the Koran the orthodox doctrine of Abrogation in the Koran is denied *in toto*, and consequently the claim of the abrogation of previous Scriptures has to be toned down to a statement that a new and universal law like Islam of course supersedes a national and limited legislation like that of Moses.

The old orthodox argument was to accuse Christianity of polytheism, and to prove that it was contrary to reason to believe in a metaphysical puzzle like the Trinity or to believe that God was capable of generation. Sheikh Rashid Ridha and his followers here again draw on Drews, Kalthoff, and J. M. Robertson to prove that the Christian ideas are but a rehash of paganism. More effective, however, is a recent writer, Mr. Muhammad Amir Alam, in an interesting little book, *Islam and Christianity*,[2] in which he maintains that Jesus may be called the Son of God in a moral and spiritual sense, yet in that same sense we are all in some measure equally sons of God. He quotes very effectively in this connexion from Dr. Rashdall's speech at the Conference at Cambridge in the summer of 1921, on the real humanity of

[1] Maulvi Muhammad Ali, *The Holy Qur'an*, containing the Arabic Text with English translation and Commentary, Woking, 1917.

[2] Calcutta, 1923.

Jesus, though apparently he has not grasped the full significance of all that scholar's words.

The Bahais have taken over into their system the concept of Incarnation, and their attitude on the question is that, while Jesus was certainly the Incarnate Word, God manifest in the flesh, yet He was a manifestation only for His own day. Incarnation did not stop with Him, and in our day Baha'ullah was the Divine Essence manifested in human form.

One might have expected a similar claim to have been made by Mirza Ghulam Ahmad of Qadian, who founded the Ahmadiya community; but, while he claimed to be the Messiah and to come in the spirit and power of Jesus, he has only ridicule for the divine Sonship and the Trinity. On the latter, indeed, he could stoop to write in the *Review of Religions*, vol. 1, p. 280:

> "The manner is very amusing in which the three Persons of the Trinity shifted the responsibility of the reformation of mankind from one to the other. There was the Father, who, having a certain superiority, in name if not in reality, thought of restoring man to his original state—one should think it means the savage state, for the human progress has been gradual from a lower to a higher stage—but he found his hands tied by the strong manacles of justice. Out of filial reverence the Son offered himself, but when he came into the world he went away with the empty consolation that the third partner shall come and teach them all truths and guide them into all truth. The third Person, being only a pigeon, found himself unable to undertake the teaching of truths, but thought he had done his duty by teaching the Apostles a few dialects, which they were thus able to speak stammeringly."

The very core of the matter, of course, is redemption, and curiously enough it is the modern writers who are mostly concerned with it. Muhammad Din, the head of the Ahmadiya community in Chicago, goes to the heart of the difficulty when he writes: "A Moslem has to reject crucifixion, because otherwise he has to believe in the supreme value of sacrifice."[1]

Some writers argue against the "barbarous nature" of the doctrine, maintaining that "evolution" has led us beyond such conceptions as lie behind the Christian theory. This very modern attitude of the Western-educated, evolution-indoctrinated Moslem, is taken by Amir Alam in the work above mentioned. Thus he writes (p. 27):

"This doctrine is worse than unnatural. It is barbarous. The notions of vicarious atonement may be traced to the savage custom of sacrificing an animal for the expiation of sins. Its roots lie deep down in the prehistoric idea of primitive heathenism, or in the undeveloped brain of a fetish worshipper of the Dark Continent. It establishes to the hilt the fetish worshipper's notion of animal sacrifice to appease his angry spirits. This is horrible—too horrible for a modern man. To think of the innocent Lamb of Nazareth as having been sacrificed on the cross for the redemption of the sins of mankind by the Just and Merciful God, is too great a contradiction. God is just."

Sheikh Rashid Ridha has devoted a special brochure, *Aqidat as-Salb wa'l-Fida* (Belief in Crucifixion and Redemption) to giving an exposition of his "Pagan Christs" theory. He works along his usual lines, showing that some early Christian heretical sects did not believe that Christ had died; that some modern European writers have evolved a "swoon theory" to explain the Resurrection; that the conception of a God who dies

[1] *The Moslem World*, 1924, p. 23.

and rises again was associated with various heathen salvation cults; that originally there was nothing mystic about the death of Christ, but that later it was turned into a mystery by theologians who were acquainted with the old pagan mystery-religions.

The founder of the Ahmadiyas was so impressed with the necessity of explaining away the Sacrificial Death, that he also revived the "swoon theory," and then added to it a garbled version of Nikolai Notovitch's weird story that Christ had journeyed to India and studied the wisdom of its wise men. Notovitch made the journey take place before the baptism by John, but the Mirza apparently had forgotten the details of the story, so he makes the visit take place after Jesus had recovered from the swoon on the cross, and links this story to his theory that the Afghans are the "lost tribes" of Israel, the "lost sheep of the House of Israel" to whom Jesus came to preach. He even asserted that he had found the tomb of Jesus in Srinagar in Kashmir, where he was buried after reaching the age of one hundred and twenty.

As regards the defence of Islam, the old orthodoxy has written a whole library of books on the miraculous eloquence of the Koran and its sublime beauties. Rahmatu'llah says that its divine nature is proved by the fact that one never grows tired of reading it. Ibn Taymiyya says that, since the smallest verse of the Koran is a miracle of eloquence and elegance, the whole book contains thousands of miracles. Al-Jili says that all that is contained in all religious books is contained in the Koran, that all the Koran is contained in the opening sura, that all the sura is contained in the *Bismillah* (the conventional phrase which heads each sura but one), that all the Bismillah is contained in the B, and all that is in the B is contained in the point that is beneath it in the Arabic script. This attitude has naturally been reflected in the older apologetic, which devotes considerable space to elaborating the proof of the divine qualities of the Koran.

In the modernist books this type of argument is conspicuous mostly by its absence. Certainly they argue that the Koran is a divine book and the final revelation from God, but they are keenly alive to the results and methods of Biblical criticism, and will make no claim that may entangle them in an impossible position. In fact, the modern school works almost exclusively at attempts to reinterpret the Koran in the light of modern knowledge. Its vivid realism is taken as symbolical, the sensual joys of Paradise being symbols of spiritual delights (a theory as old, however, as the Muʿtazilites); its limited morality and historical blunders are carefully explained away; and a book is produced which would hardly be recognized by the old orthodoxy. Muhammad Badr, for example, writes [1]:

> "The ultra-figurative language of the Qur'an lent itself to such misconstruction to a peculiar degree. The stories told in many cases, when regarded in their true light of rhetoric device, are allegories of most poetic fashion. Read literally, they are incredible."

The result is the rise of a new type of commentaries. In Cairo these are appearing in Arabic. There is Tantawi's *Tafsir*, of which only the first part has yet appeared, which claims to be able to find aeroplanes, electricity, etc., all foretold in the Koran, and which performs wondrous acrobatic feats of exegesis. There is Mohammed ʿAbdu's *Tafsir* being edited by Sheikh Rashid Ridha, of which Parts 2–7 are on the market, Part 1 having

[1] *The Truth about Islam*, p. 25.

been apparently suppressed. This commentary is characterized by all Mohammed 'Abdu's careful scholarship, and is a noble attempt at a rationalistic interpretation of the Koran, not too far removed from orthodoxy. The most outstanding examples of this tendency, however, are the English commentaries produced by the Ahmadiya Movement. Each of the rival parties within this community has made this attempt, but only that of the Woking group is complete. The old original party at Qadian have published the preliminary sections of their commentary and promise its speedy completion; but their method, so far as one can judge from the parts issued already, does not seem to differ much from that of *The Holy Qur'an; Containing the Arabic Text with English Translation and Commentary*, by Maulvi Muhammad Ali, of Lahore. Here we find the Koran dressed up in Biblical garb, carefully doctored for English consumption. Let us take just one illustration of its method from the Sura of Joseph.

First, the translation is doctored. Take, for example, the passage which tells of Jacob's sight being restored. The story runs that Jacob had become blind through weeping for his lost Joseph; so, when Joseph revealed himself to his brethren in Egypt, and learned of his father's condition, he sent his shirt to be cast in his father's face, whereat he would recover his sight. Let us place the two versions side by side (italics are ours):

Ordinary Version	*Ahmadiya Version*[1]
"Go with this shirt of mine and *cast it on my father's face*, (and) he will *recover his sight*: then come to me with all your	"Take this my shirt and *cast it before my father*; he will *come to know* and come to me with all your families." And

[1] Maulvi Muhammad Ali, *The Holy Qur'an*, chapter xii: 93–6, p. 493, Woking, 1917.

Ordinary Version (continued)

family." Now when the caravan set out their father said, "Verily I perceive *the smell* of Joseph, unless you are making mock of me." They said, "By God, you are in your old error." Then, when the bearer of good tidings came, he *cast it on his face* and he *was restored to sight.*

Ahmadiya Version (continued)

when the caravan had departed, their father said, "Most surely I perceive the *greatness* of Joseph, unless you *pronounce me weak of* judgment." They said, "By Allah, you are most surely in your old error." So, when the bearer of good news came, he *cast it before him;* so he became certain.

Secondly, the commentary is made to match. All the old commentators take the passage in its natural sense, and have various reasons to give for the healing properties of the shirt. But this is not to modernist taste, and a way out is found by giving forced meanings to certain words. He makes "smell" become "power" or "predominance," interprets "seeing" as "mental perception," and says that "when Jacob saw Joseph's shirt he would possess certain knowledge of Joseph's abiding place." To get over the difficulty of a blind man's seeing the shirt, he contends that the word in the previous sentence does not mean blindness of the eyes, but only "the filling of the eyes with tears." The references to the Arabic authorities, whether lexicographers or commentators, are throughout quite misleading.

Thirdly, there is continual suppression of fact. For instance, in this story wherever there is the possibility of suggesting that the Koranic story is an improvement on that of Genesis, the Biblical story is quoted and commented upon; but there is nothing said about the fragmentariness of the Koranic story which really assumes the Biblical record as its background, nor is there a word about the fact, perfectly well known to the author, that many of the Koran's numerous embellishments on the story of Genesis are merely reproductions of Jewish apocryphal tales from the Talmud and Midrashim.

Much the same method of reinterpretation is followed in depicting the character of the Prophet. The new apologists take but little account of the old argument from the wondrous miracles of the Prophet, or of hunting for Old Testament prophecies which he may be claimed to have fulfilled. They seek rather to explain away what to Western eyes are the very obvious defects of his character, and present before us a highly idealized picture of—

> "His complete trust in God, his refraining from showing the slightest impatience, his calm and severe manner, his noble and dignified manners, his unshaken activity and zeal in the performance of duties entrusted to him, his perseverance, his fearlessness of his enemies, his forgiveness of injuries, charity, courage,"

etc., which, of course, is just taking over the picture of Jesus and applying it to Mohammed, as Tor Andrae in his brilliant study [1] showed was done in the work of the early theologians. It is curious to note that some Moslems have felt so strongly the contrast, when Mohammed has been compared with Jesus, that they have attempted to besmirch the character of the latter. Mirza Ghulam Ahmad, of Qadian, for instance, accused Jesus of having committed the sins of drunkenness, lying, cowardice, gross disrespect to his mother, blasphemy, rudeness, and fondness for the company of loose women. A little Syrian tract goes further in this direction, making charges so foul that they cannot even be recorded here.

The modern attempts to explain away *jihad*, or the Holy War, follow the same lines. Words have to be

[1] Tor Andrae, *Die Person Muhammeds in Lehre und Glauben seiner Gemeinde*, Stockholm, 1918.

given unusual meanings, traditions cast aside, and history interpreted to show that all Mohammed's wars were defensive, and fighting for the faith save by spiritual weapons has never been part of Islam. So with regard to the position of women. Syed Ameer Ali's essay on the *Legal Position of Women in Islam* is a masterpiece in the setting forth of half-truths in order to convey a false impression, and is sad reading when compared with a frank, sincere investigation such as Mansur Fahmy's excellent monograph, *La Condition de la Femme dans l'Islamisme.*

The conclusion one comes to, from the study of these works of modern Moslem apologetic, is that perhaps the greatest contribution Christianity can make toward the solution of the present problems of Islam is education. It is Western education that has caused the already enormous advances from the old position, and it seems very clear that larger doses of that same thing will reveal how untenable the present positions are. Christianity has nothing to fear from the fullest exposure to the light of modern knowledge. Islam has everything to fear, and, let it be said, everything to gain.

CHRIST'S CONTRIBUTION TO THE MOSLEM

BY

PAUL W. HARRISON, D.Sc., M.D.,

*Medical Missionary of the Reformed Church in America,
Kuwait, Arabia*

CHAPTER XXI

CHRIST'S CONTRIBUTION TO THE MOSLEM

1. His Valuation of Men

"Why don't we allow you to come and set up a missionary hospital here on the Pirate Coast?" The speaker was a Sharja merchant. "Because, if we admit you, just behind you will come the English with a telegraph office and a consulate. And we, after that? Nothing but vassals!" Nor was the man, in the bitterness of his hostility, a fool or blind, and the justification for his attitude has been given, not by alien rulers, but by the missionaries themselves. Do they not associate with these rulers and cultivate their friendship at every possible opportunity? Do they not reckon a decoration by the alien power that rules the country as the achievement of a lifetime? A traveller returns home to announce that the greatest political asset of the colonial administrators in a certain province is the reputation of the resident medical missionary. Thus it is that the Gospel, in its appeal to the hearts of the Moslems, must carry on its back the whole evil weight of Western imperialism.

The trouble is that, deep down in his heart, the missionary too often believes that the only hope of the Gospel lies in its support by Western bayonets. Unless the protection of Western Governments, with their military power, is given to the missionaries, their lives will not be safe, and they cannot proclaim the Christian message. Unless that same worldly and un-Christian power is prepared to protect the lives of converts from Islam to Christianity, we shall never have any. To expose the converts to the rigours of persecution with no protection except that of God in heaven would be hopeless. To expect missionaries to live thus unguarded, outrageous.

The Moslem understands this sort of thing. In his mind, too, religion and political imperialism are tied up in the same bundle. Every Moslem missionary is the advance agent for Moslem imperialism—an imperialism that is satisfied with nothing short of world dominion—and in this conflict of political imperialism he will fight to his last breath.

But sometimes it is possible to escape from this reputation. " I am not an Engleezee. I am an Americanee," and among the Arabs America enjoys a reputation for international unselfishness which I am afraid is undeserved. So it seems possible that this missionary is not the advance agent of Western imperialism, in spite of his white skin. " What is your name ?"—this by the doctor to a venerable patriarch of the desert who had come to the Bahrein hospital for treatment. The man leaned over and whispered confidentially into the doctor's ear: " My name is Mohammed. I told the man who writes our names in the book at the door that my name was Khalid, for no doubt he is sending all our names back to America as converts to Christianity." The book at the door had been started so that discharged dispensary patients could be followed up, but we had to drop the plan. How foolish! One of the medical missionaries whom I used to know treated free those who would come early and listen to an earnest Christian talk which preceded the clinic. Those who failed to listen to the talk were compelled to pay for their treatment. The Moslem understands this too. Determined, unresting propaganda in favour of a religious system he believes in. He is probably more or less of such a propagandist himself.

The missionary, as a keen and enthusiastic lieutenant of Western imperialism, offers nothing new to the Moslem. Such things he finds in his own faith. This is equally true of the missionary who is simply a propagandist for a Western religious system. Extremes meet on this platform. The extreme liberal regards a redeemed social order as the Kingdom of God. It constitutes his whole religious system. In comparison individual redemption is contemptible, if indeed it is not a pure myth. The extreme conservative names his system God's will and glory. In that he sees something so inexpressibly great that the eternal destiny of men is that of insects in comparison. There is nothing in these ideas that puzzles the Moslem. He has beds for them both in the caravanserai of his own theology.

But, when He talked with the woman at the well, Christ evidently believed that He was facing the supreme value of all eternity. He was not concerned about any religious system, and still less about any political imperialism. He was eager to save this woman. Here is something that the Moslem knows nothing about. That individual men are mere insects as compared with a religious creed or system he understands. That all the religious systems in the world, all the creeds, all the rituals, all the world's ecclesiastical pronouncements, and all its political organizations are insects compared with individual men, the only real eternal value in God's universe—this he does not understand. That we seek men because of their supreme incomparable value, because they are the only thing on the earth beneath or in heaven above that God cares anything about—for the Moslem such an idea is treason to God and religion when seen from the outside, and a dazzling new truth, with divine power in it, when seen from the inside.

This is a vision of truth that makes heavy demands upon the missionary. It means that an attitude of comradeship with these men must run deeper, if that be possible, than even the supreme objective of missionary work, which is giving men eternal life. Standing by itself, the desire to give men eternal life opens the door to very subtle and dangerous temptations. The Moslem recognizes this, even if the missionary does not. Every Pharisee was eager to give men eternal life, or would have been had his system been built on Christian theology. Zeal for men's souls while we care not at all for them personally, detest their company, and prefer to keep away from all intimate acquaintance with them, is a very hideous form of hypocrisy. Christ loved men, loved to be with them, loved them for their own sake, and found pure joy in association with them whether or not there was an opportunity to preach. He was like a jeweller who loves to handle and study and admire pearls even though he makes no profit in the process; like an artist who loves to sit before fine paintings with no thought at all regarding their effect on his ability or wealth. The way to bring Christ's message to the Moslem is to imitate His attitude.

2. His Faith in the Truth

A boy from inland Arabia brought his friend to the Bahrein hospital for treatment. Both of them were members of the great Wahhabi fraternity, the most fanatical of the orthodox Sunni Moslem sects. During their stay the Shias of Bahrein celebrated the Muharram festival. The Shias are the great heretical sect of Islam, and the Muharram celebrations embody in a condensed form all their heresies. The boy went with me to see the celebration. He was overcome with horror. "Do you have such things in Nejd?" I asked, not for information, but to draw him out. His reply came with difficulty because of the intensity of his repulsion. "Such things in Nejd? In the domain of Abdul Aziz? They would be killed if they tried it." The words seemed to stick in the boy's throat. He did not even call down God's curse upon them. A little later we were visiting a Shia district in Mesopotamia. It was a medical visit, and we were in high favour. One of my hospital assistants questioned the sheikh's attendant accompanying us. "Are there any Sunnis here?" "Sunnis?" repeated the man in great contempt. "Praise the Lord, there is not an infidel in all these parts."

This clash of rival coercive religious systems the Moslem understands. Nothing is more agreeable to his unregenerate nature. His history is made up of little else. Therefore he understands, unfortunately, a large amount of our missionary work. For coercion is of many kinds. Physical coercion, with death as the final penalty for resistance, is now, we hope, decades and centuries in the past, so far as we are concerned. But the milder forms of coercion, rewards for listening to the Gospel, and such punishment as we are in a position to inflict for refusing to listen—coercion of that sort is still with us. Intellectual coercion, hammering down old religious conceptions, and hammering in our new ones by sheer force of a superior intellect and training, is only now ceasing to be fashionable. How many books can be collected designed expressly to train missionaries for just that sort of work? The Moslem understands this sort of thing perfectly. He glories in it.

"The trouble with your religion," I told a leader of the Wahhabi brotherhood, "is that its foundation is coercion."

"Coercion," he replied, "is not its foundation. Coercion is its crown."

Missionaries of that kind belong in the Moslem camp. A very different atmosphere surrounded Christ. He had such faith in the hostile crowds that He addressed and who eventually crucified Him, such a faith in them and in the truth, that He desired His message to receive no help whatever from any source. Naked and unadorned, unexplained and undefended, in its divine power Christ knew that it would draw men by virtue of its own inherent attractiveness, and save them once they accepted it. The clash of rival coercive systems the Moslem understands. Faith in a divine message and in men such as Christ showed, and such as He expects us to show, leaves the Moslem either utterly puzzled or divinely charmed.

And this, too, makes profound demands upon the missionary. We have the same message to carry that Christ had. We have every reason for the same faith in it that He showed. But no man can have the faith that Christ showed in His message unless he has, to some extent, the same comprehension of it that Christ had. Until something of the divine height and depth and breadth of that message is visible, its divine power will be as a fairy-tale. There never was, perhaps, a more unfortunate fad in missionary work than the present one which lays the major emphasis upon understanding the religious system of the people we work with. Ninety-nine out of every hundred missionaries would be far better advised to devote every hour sacrificed to an understanding of some non-Christian faith to a profounder study of their own message, and a deeper acquaintance with their own Christ.

3. His Universality

In the opinion of the Moslem true religion is inseparable from its Arab attire. His dream of the universal triumph of Islam is simply the hope that the world will put on these Arab clothes, just as the Christian, and too often the missionary, hopes to see the day when the whole world will put on the political and social and religious clothes of the Anglo-Saxon.

Christ was not concerned with these traits that are so dear to our Western hearts. He had never a word to say about cleanliness, or order, or thrift, nor even education or representative government. He sent forth His message in the superb confidence that it was suited to men who were hospitable but not clean, mystical instead of orderly, generous and not thrifty. This undisturbed confidence that the divine message will work out in all sorts of races diverse results in life and practice and creed, all according to the will of God, who is the source of the message and the power residing in it—such faith is the basis of the missionary's universality, as it was of Christ's. The Moslem finds it staggering and impossible, but none the less supremely beautiful.

4. His Conception of God

But the evaluation of religious systems is as the dust of the balance in comparison with the supreme value of men, faith in the divine message as capable of winning men, not by means of coercion, but by virtue of the power of God which it contains, and confidence in its universality based upon its divine character. All of these, new and outstanding contributions to the Moslem mind as they may be, are only scattered rays of the great incandescent divine truth which stands at the centre of Christ's teachings, a truth not merely heretical but highly offensive to orthodox Islam, namely, that God, the omnipotent Creator, is not a distant judge, but an affectionate Father. "Sahib," said an old man to me as he took me from the Sunday morning service to see his sick boy, "I have listened to many sermons in the mosques, and I never heard anything like that before. Is it really true that God, the Creator of all things, the Almighty, looks down upon us with the eyes of a father upon his children? None of our mullahs ever told me anything as beautiful as that." I have watched many audiences, large and small, listen to this good news, and, obnoxious as it is to orthodox Islam, I think I have never seen it presented without obviously captivating the listeners. This conception is not merely a new contribution to the spiritual furniture of a Moslem. It is not simply a useful addition to his comprehension of the universe. It revolutionizes the whole world in which he moves.

I have never seen this truth fail to captivate those who listened, but that does not mean that those who listened became Christians. It is one thing to recognize the beauty of a conception, and quite another to be convinced of its truth. This idea, as simple as it appears, once it is accepted to be true simply turns the world upside down for the Moslem. Scarcely anything in the whole realm of family relationships is more fundamental than the fact that the father has individual relations with each of his children. The last thing wanted is for one child to coerce another and to dictate to him his relationships with their common father. Each child comes to his father himself, and the father takes personal and individual interest in him. But, if God is really our Father, this means that there is absolutely no place in religion for coercion and intolerance, and none for the conceit and self-satisfied superiority which is the backbone of Islam's strength. It seems remarkable that this splendid conception of God, which stands at the centre of Christ's revelation to us, has not been stressed more in dealing with Moslems. Possibly because too many Christians have not been dominated by it, as is indicated by the present epidemic of vituperative and even coercive intolerance in the Christian Church itself. For no man can be intolerant and coercive toward other Christians without rejecting the picture of God that Christ brought us and erecting in its place an idol of his own manufacture.

This conception of God gives us also a conception of salvation that goes beyond anything that the Moslem even understands. The Moslem feels the need for the forgiveness of sins, but he rejects all idea of Christ's sacrifice as making that forgiveness possible. To the Western mind, the price which was paid for our forgiveness in the sacrifice of Christ has been the most appealing element in the whole divine work of redemption. Perhaps because the point has been the subject of much controversy, perhaps because the Arab mind differs from ours, the presentation of this seems to repel rather than attract him. To his realization of the need for forgiveness the Moslem adds a somewhat washed-out repentance as a necessary preliminary to forgiveness; but that is all. The price of forgiveness he does not at all realize, and the climax and crown of the Christian view he knows nothing about, that forgiveness has for its object restoring the prodigal to his place in the family of God.

5. His Definition of Discipleship

Christ's definition of discipleship has also a strong attraction for the Moslem, an appeal as powerful perhaps as the great central vision of God's Fatherhood itself. Not only is God our Father. Christ is our Good Shepherd. Some years ago, in an effort to determine what aspect of Christianity makes the greatest appeal to the Moslem, we tried various presentations, all by means of intimate personal talks. The different reactions that the message produced were carefully written down, and at the end of the year we had some interesting records to study. The greatest appeal was made to these men by what might be called the mystical aspect of the Gospel, and of the material available we found the parable of the Good Shepherd the most useful of all.

We learned another thing, the necessity for repeated presentation of the same material if the message is to be understood and appreciated. It is hard for us to realize the strangeness of the religious ideas that we bring to the Moslems, trained as they are in an entirely different atmosphere. The parable of the Good Shepherd, repeated every day for perhaps two weeks, leads to a comprehension of the truth that is very beautiful. "Sit down here, sahib, and I will tell you the story to-day," said a Kuttar Bedouin to me once after he had been with us about ten days. The Arabs are wonderful story-tellers, and I am sure that he told it much more graphically than I had ever done. He explained how Christ wants to be a shepherd to those who are willing to follow; how, just as the shepherd leads his sheep out in the morning and finds them nice clean water to drink, and fresh green grass to eat, so the Good Shepherd leads us to those experiences, and that knowledge that will nourish our spirits, and give us strength of soul. He explained how, just as the shepherd protects the sheep from the wolves of the desert and from the thieves of the town, so Christ protects His sheep from the temptations that rise within their own hearts, and those that Satan sends against them from without. And, finally, the shepherd leads the sheep home as the sun is setting, and so Christ wants to lead us home to our Father's house when our sun sets. The truth had penetrated far deeper than mere comprehension in that man's mind: it was easy to see that it had gone down far enough to grip powerfully his very soul.

The missionary working among Moslems becomes more and more convinced that the kernel of the Gospel comes to them as an entirely new contribution. They have little or nothing of its essential elements in the entire landscape of their minds. But the theory of the Gospel is a small contribution, if indeed it is any. The essential contribution of Christ to the Moslem lies in that real contact with God and that participation in the divine life which He offers. If the missionary can bring the Moslem to accept Christ, and so enter into eternal life, he has succeeded. Failing there, we have failed. The humanitarian aspects of missionary work have caught the public eye, and as a result the foreign missionary enterprise now enjoys an abnormal, indeed a very harmful degree of popularity. One of the reflex results of this popularity in essentially unChristian circles has been an increased emphasis upon the humanitarian by-products of the enterprise and their elevation to a false position as perhaps the real reason for carrying on missionary work at all.

This is a complete reversal of Christ's programme. The introduction of education and civilization first, and the redemption of individuals afterwards, is not the way He told us to do it. Moreover, experiments have been made, and they teach the same lesson. In Mesopotamia a full-fledged Anglo-Saxon political system has been set up. Western education has been introduced, a sanitary and health service has been organized. It has been done by men of great ability and of unquestioned integrity and good intentions. The result of that splendid experiment is that never have the Arabs of Mesopotamia been so dominated by greed as to-day. Their hearts have never been devoured by such acute unrest and discontent. Immorality and drunkenness have never been so common. Christ undoubtedly has a large contribution to make to the social order in Mesopotamia, but He has nothing to do with the present experiment. The contribution that Christ wants to make to Mesopotamia now is the redemption of individual Arabs. The social order that He will one day create will grow out of their minds, not out of ours.

Moreover, it is not by attention to creeds that we shall accomplish the results that Christ wants. A very attractive young Arab in Bahrein became interested in the Gospel. He studied it earnestly for two years, and finally became thoroughly convinced of the fact that Christianity is the true religion. He was baptized, and in six months had made shipwreck not of his faith only, but of his old morality and diligence as well, ending with a more deteriorated character than before.

It is possible to change the professed creeds of some men by physical force, and those of others by intellectual arguments, but coercion of any sort is utterly unable to introduce the divine life into a man's heart. What we need for that is missionaries who can spread it by contagion. Men of excellent ability and training are wanted, of course, but ability and training do not spell success in this enterprise. The missionary from within whom flow rivers of living waters, who is a radiant centre of divine life, is the man the situation demands. The man whose soul is dry had better work somewhere else. Our main business is to reflect Christ as a mirror, and the missionary who does that, however imperfectly, will not only be a magnet to attract the unreached Moslem: he will also be a guide and a helper to the recent convert. There are few greater pleasures for me than to sit on the floor of my Arab reception-room with two very splendid Christians drawn from Islam by a missionary of this type. It is not a meeting for formal instruction in doctrines or Biblical history. Each of us reads a passage from the Bible which has been a real transmitter of life to his own soul, and explains what he has found in the passage. We discuss the messages and pray together, and find that a meeting of this sort really helps to bring the divine life into our souls.

Christ, then, comes to the Moslem with a new vision of God and of man and of spiritual freedom. He offers a salvation which consists of a new relationship to God, and a participation in His divine life. The missionary's task consists in showing men the vision, and in helping them afterwards to participate in the divine life.

THE ISSUE BETWEEN ISLAM AND CHRISTIANITY

BY

ROBERT E. SPEER, M.A., D.D.,

Secretary, Board of Foreign Missions of the Presbyterian Church in the United States of America

CHAPTER XXII

THE ISSUE BETWEEN ISLAM AND CHRISTIANITY

THERE is an issue between Islam and Christianity. Historically it was Islam that raised it. Christianity was already in the world with its message and claim. Islam arose to dispute and supersede these. But this bare statement needs various qualifications.

In the first place, it appears to have been only corrupt or inadequate representations of Christianity with which Mohammed came into contact. We cannot be sure how widely he travelled or what his opportunities were for really knowing Christianity, but it would appear that he met it in forms far removed from spiritual truth and simplicity. Tradition records that he led a successful trade caravan for Khadija into Syria, where he encountered Christianity of the type which had survived there with its almost polytheistic caricature of the doctrine of the Trinity and its exaltation of Mary into the place at least of the consort of the Deity.[1]

In the second place, the Koran and the Traditions adequately show that Mohammed had no true conception of Christianity at all. Both in the Koran and in the Traditions many of the references to the Bible or to Christian doctrine are grotesquely confused. "Having heard a Mary mentioned in the story of Moses and

[1] William Muir, *The Life of Mahomet*, London, 1861, vol. ii, p. 19.

another in the story of Jesus, it did not occur to him to distinguish between them."[1] And Mohammed's knowledge of Jesus and of His teaching was of the slightest, while the whole world of Paul's thought was stranger to him. In reality, then, the issue of Mohammed with Christianity was with a Christianity with which pure Christianity would have an issue almost as deep.

In the third place, Islam's attitude, at the very first at least, was not one of clear hostility to Christianity. Mohammed's view was that it simply preceded and prepared for him. "Remember," said he in the Koran, "when Jesus the Son of Mary said, 'O children of Israel! of a truth I am God's apostle to you to confirm the law which was given before me and to announce an apostle that shall come after me, whose name shall be Ahmad.'"[2]

And there are various friendly references in the Koran to Christians. "Thou shalt certainly find those to be nearest in affection to them [i.e. to Moslems] who say, 'We are Christians.' This, because some of them are priests and monks, and because they are free from pride."[3] This kindly feeling did not last long, but the change was due, in the Moslem view, to the perversity of Christians, who ought to have recognized in their own Bible the prediction of Mohammed as a prophet to excel Jesus[4] and who must have done so but for the corruptions and alterations in the Bible.[5] Something of the earliest attitude of Mohammed has returned into modern Islam. A strong spirit of conciliation can now be found.

[1] D. S. Margoliouth, *Mahommed and the Rise of Islam*, New York, 1905, p. 6.

[2] Koran: 61: 6. [3] Koran: 5: 85.

[4] W. Goldsack, *Mohammed and the Bible*, Madras, 1915.

[5] Sir Syed Ahmad, *The Mohammedan Commentary on the Holy Bible*, "The Seventh Discourse."

Some hold that, after all, the various religions, Islam and Christianity among them, are only many different doors into the same house.

"Standing opposite Fort William, a missionary heard the Mussulmans and Chinamen saying, 'There are very many gates into Fort William—there is an hospital gate, a water gate, and others. Now, sahib, it is just the same in regard to heaven. Chinamen get in at one gate, Mussulmans in at another, and Hindus in at another.'"[1]

Others hold that Islam is only a richer extension of the partial and preparatory revelation of Christianity, that both are expressions of the one true religion existing from the time of Adam to Mohammed, and propagated by all the great succession of 124,000 prophets, containing the same fundamental truths and moral precepts, but differing in outward and ceremonial observances. Still other Moslem reformers of to-day are ready to make many concessions regarding historical Islam in the interest of a broad and synthetic religious view. As Mr. Theodore Morison, the Principal of the Aligarh Muslim University, wrote, these reformers—

"... Believe that in their faith are enshrined the great truths of religion and morality, but that in the past they have misread the Word of God, and that narrow-minded mollahs have expounded it amiss."[2]

Christians should be foremost to feel and to express the spirit of kindness and consideration. In our relations to Islam it is Raymond Lull, and not the Crusaders, that must furnish our model of approach:

[1] W. A. Rice, *Crusaders of the Twentieth Century*, London, 1910, pp. 322–3.
[2] *The Spectator*, December 29, 1900.

"I see many knights going to the Holy Land beyond the seas and thinking that they can acquire it by force of arms; but in the end all are destroyed before they attain that which they think to have. Whence it seems to me that the conquest of the Holy Land ought not to be attempted except in the way in which Thou and Thine apostles acquired it, namely, by love and prayers, and the pouring out of tears and of blood." [1]

But, while we are bound to welcome and to exceed any mood of conciliation which we may find in Islam to-day, we must not deceive ourselves on either of two points. In the first place, while Islam, as may be shown, is not the rigid and impregnably convinced power it has been deemed, there is still deep conviction there on the part of five groups: (*a*) sincere and thoughtful Moslem scholars, (*b*) men of reformed and tolerant views who believe that Islam has a place among the forms of ethnic religions, (*c*) mystics of deep emotional experience,[2] (*d*) simple-hearted people to whom the prayers and religious life of Islam are a habit of reality, and (*e*) the men to whom Islam is a social and political fanaticism. In the second place, Islam and Christianity are not the same religion, nor are they alike in either their primary or their secondary principles. Thoughtful Moslems are as clear on this point as we are. Our issue with Islam is not superficial. It is fundamental. I am sure that a thoughtful Englishman is right on this matter when he writes in a unique little book, *Five Years in a Persian Town*:

"In the case of Islam there are really not many [points in common] to note, and in support of this statement I

[1] S. M. Zwemer, *Raymond Lull*, New York, 1902, pp. 52–3.

[2] D. B. Macdonald, *Aspects of Islam*, New York, 1911, pp. 145–209.

may relate a story told by an officer of Indian troops. One day a Mohammedan, in the course of a conversation, said to him: 'Of course, sahib, your religion and ours are very near together. Your Christ is one of our prophets.' My friend replied: 'What do you mean? Of course Christ is one of your prophets, but to us He is more than a prophet; He is the Son of God, and the pattern of our lives. Besides, there is hardly a single practical point where Mohammedans and Christians are not entirely at issue.' The man looked up and said: 'Sahib, you have read the Quran, and you have read your Bible. I always make that remark to Christians: I made it to a padre the other day: and they almost always say, "Very true; Mohammedanism has a great deal in common with Christianity." Well, Sahib, when they say that, I know that they have not read the Quran and they have not read their Bibles.'"

And Mr. Malcolm sets down his own deliberate judgment:

"In Mohammedanism, in spite of its greater pretensions, almost every apparent truth crumbles into mere truism or actual falsity the moment that you try to make it the basis of anything practical. Also, the more I read of the life of Mohammed, the more convinced I am that the radical rottenness of the system is due to his original teaching. I firmly believe that the difficulties in the Islam of to-day are due rather to the essential wrongness of the system than to its corruption by the masses." [1]

Of all the religions in the world, there is none as to which Christian missions are more justified and by which Christian missions are more demanded than Islam. The fundamental issue between Islam and Christianity is

[1] Napier Malcolm, *Five Years in a Persian Town*, New York, 1905, pp. vii, viii, 64, 65.

found just where too often they are supposed to resemble each other, namely, in their idea of God. Each is monotheistic. As over against idolatry and polytheism and pantheism, Christians feel a strong sense of agreement with Islam and they seem to themselves to breathe a purer air when they pass out of a Hindu temple, with its idols, and often its obscenity, into the austerity and simplicity of a Mohammedan mosque. And also there can be no doubt that Mohammed thought he was setting forth the true conception of God, which in some measure the Jews and Christians whom he knew had corrupted. Even so, however, he believed that it was the same God. "Our God and your God is one," says the Koran. But they are not the same God at all. In the prevalent Moslem view there are seven attributes of God, and ninety-nine names. The attributes are life or unity, knowledge, power, will, hearing, seeing, and speech. The early Moslems, the companions of Mohammed and their followers, held, however, that inquiries into the nature of God and His attributes were not lawful. It was sufficient, as Mohammed had taught them, to—

> "Say: He is God alone:
> God the eternal!
> He begetteth not, and He is not begotten;
> And there is none like unto Him."[1]

Moslem apologists for Islam have sought to Christianize the God of Islam. Syed Ameer Ali first describes the Christian doctrine, and especially the historic view of Jesus and His revelation of God as Father, and then transfers the whole Christian conception to the Allah of Mohammed.[2] But the facts of history cannot be so

[1] Koran: 112.
[2] Syed Ameer Ali, *The Spirit of Islam*, London, Revised Edition, 1922, pp. 143–52.

easily dissipated. The Moslem view of God has been seen both in itself and in its effects to be defective in its unmoral autocracy, its irresponsible fatalism, its implication in human sin, the mere verbalism of its compassion, its inadequacy in holiness and love, the capriciousness of its justice, its repudiation of the conception of fatherhood, and its denial of the possibility of incarnation and of the immanence and indwelling of God.[1]

Two testimonies from outside the missionary ranks will suffice:

Johannes Hauri, in his study of Islam, says:

> "What Mohammed tells of God's omnipotence, omniscience, justice, goodness, and mercy sounds, for the most part, very well indeed and might easily awaken the idea that there is no real difference between his God and the God of Christianity. But Mohammed's monotheism was just as much a departure from true monotheism as the polytheistic ideas prevalent in the corrupt Oriental Churches. Mohammed's idea of God is out-and-out deistic. God and the world are in exclusive, external, and eternal opposition."[2]

And James Freeman Clarke calls it the "worst form of monotheism," and says:

> "Islam saw God, but not man; saw the claims of deity, but not the rights of humanity; saw authority, failed to see freedom—therefore hardened into despotism, stiffened into formalism, and sank into death. . . . Mohammed teaches a God above us; Moses teaches a God

[1] W. A. Rice, *Crusaders of the Twentieth Century*, London, 1910, pp. 231–43; S. M. Zwemer, *The Moslem Doctrine of God*, New York, 1905; W. H. T. Gairdner, *The Muslim Idea of God*, London, 1909; W. R. W. Gardner, *The Qur'ánic Doctrine of God*, Madras, 1916; W. Goldsack, *God in Islam*, London, 1908.

[2] Johannes Hauri, *Der Islam*, Leiden, 1881, p. 44.

above us, and yet with us; Jesus teaches—God above us, God with us, and God in us."[1]

It is the business of Christians, in love and joy, to make known the God of Jesus Christ to Moslems.

Bound up in this fundamental issue between Islam and Christianity is their difference with regard to Jesus Christ Himself, with regard to sin from which Christ is the only Saviour, and with regard to the life of salvation in Christ, its ideals and its power. It is true that our Lord is assigned a place among the tens of thousands of recognized prophets. He is even ranked among the first six: Adam, Noah, Abraham, Moses, Jesus, and Mohammed. He is recognized to have worked miracles. "And we gave unto Jesus, the son of Mary, manifest signs and strengthened him by the Holy Spirit."[2] But—

"There is no one cardinal fact concerning the Life, Person, and Work of the Lord Jesus Christ which is not either denied, perverted, misrepresented, or at least ignored in Mohammedan theology."[3]

And the Koran is explicit. The office of Jesus was temporary and local. He was only the prophet to the children of Israel, and even as such was superseded by Mohammed.

"Jesus is no more than a servant, whom we favoured with the gift of prophecy; and we appointed him for an example unto the children of Israel."[4]

And again:

"Christ the son of Mary is no more than an apostle; other apostles have preceded him; and his mother was

[1] James Freeman Clarke, *Ten Great Religions*, Boston, 1895, Part II, p. 68, and Part I, p. 483.

[2] Koran: 2: 81.

[3] W. A. Rice, *Crusaders of the Twentieth Century*, London, 1910, p. 244.

[4] Koran: 43: 59.

a woman of veracity: they both ate food [i.e. were human, not divine beings]."[1]

In the view of Syed Ameer Ali Jesus was only a human teacher deified by his subsequent worshippers.[2] The Christian conception of Him as the Incarnate Son of God, Redeemer and Saviour of men, Revealer of the Father, Supreme and Living Lord, is a conception so totally different from anything in Islam that so long as Christians hold it they are bound to seek in love to persuade Moslems of its truth and to share with them its joy.

The Moslem and Christian conceptions of sin are necessarily as widely variant as their ideas of God. Sin, in the Moslem view, is "a conscious act of a responsible being against known law."[3] Some hold that there are seven great sins: idolatry, murder, false charge of adultery, wasting the substance of orphans, taking interest on money, desertion from *jihad*, and disobedience to parents. Others add wine-drinking, witchcraft, perjury, and other sins. Mohammed's declaration was:

"'The greatest of sins before God is that you call another like unto the God who created you, or that you murder your child from an idea that it will eat your victuals, or that you commit adultery with your neighbour's wife.' All sins except 'great' ones are easily forgiven, as God is merciful and clement."[3]

The Moslem ideas of sin and righteousness are legalistic.

"Nothing is right or wrong by nature, but becomes such by the fiat of the Almighty. What Allah or his Prophet forbids is sin, even should he forbid what

[1] Koran: 5: 79.
[2] Syed Ameer Ali, *The Spirit of Islam*, London, 1922, p. xxxviii.
[3] Samuel M. Zwemer, *Islam: a Challenge to Faith*, New York, 1907, p. 121.

seems right to the conscience. What Allah allows is not sin and cannot be sin at the time he allows it, though it may have been before or after." [1]

In Islam—

"There is an absolute denial of the statement, upon which most Christians more or less consciously base their belief in the perpetuity and absolute nature of the law of human morals, that 'in the image of God created He man.' Consequently we shall afterwards find that in Islam there is no belief in the permanency of the moral law, for nothing is thought by the Mussulman to be necessarily permanent except things connected with the nature of God; and, as our nature differs entirely from that of the Creator, the law given for it cannot be necessarily permanent." [2]

Sin is infraction of imposed law, not bias of nature, nor flaw of character, nor a fundamental congenital taint in humanity.

And, even as to deliberate infractions of known law, some of the Moslem teachers have found a method of safe sin, through the attribute of mercy in God. In a paper on the Mohammedan question in *Missions*, the late Henry O. Dwight of Constantinople told this incident:

"In travelling in Turkey, I once fell in with a Pasha, governor of one of the provinces of Asia Minor. He was a most agreeable and even attractive man, and during the voyage, which lasted several days, we talked on almost every conceivable subject of interest to plain and decent men.

"This sensible and well-meaning man showed me the corner-stone of his character one evening at table in the cabin. He asked me to take a glass of wine with

[1] Samuel M. Zwemer, *Islam: a Challenge to Faith*, New York, 1907, pp. 121-2.

[2] Napier Malcolm, *Five Years in a Persian Town*, New York, 1905, p. 82.

him. I declined. Then the Pasha said: 'You may think it strange that I, a Mohammedan, should ask you, a Christian, to drink with me when wine-drinking is forbidden by our religion. I will tell you how I dare do this thing.' He filled his glass, and held it up, looking at the beautiful colour of it, and said: 'Now, if I say that it is right to drink this wine, I deny God's commands to men, and He would punish me in hell for the blasphemy. But I take up this glass, admitting that God has commanded me not to drink it, and that I sin in drinking it. Then I drink it off, so casting myself on the mercy of God. For our religion lets me know that God is too merciful to punish me for doing a thing which I wish to do, when I humbly admit that to do it breaks His commandments.'"

And Dr. Dwight added:

"Let it not be supposed that there is no recognition of sin in Islam. It is everywhere denounced. But it is everywhere regarded as wrong by the decree of God. God's decree can make vice virtue. Sin calls for retribution, not reform. Repentance is simply regret for the punishment of sin. Mohammed put his seal upon this materialistic view of repentance when one of his companions asked him what should be done with the body of a man stoned to death for adultery: 'Bury him,' said the Prophet, 'as a good Mussulman, for he has repented with such a repentance that, if it were divided among the whole human race, it would suffice for all.' In fact, it seems to be thoroughly wrought into the intellect of the Mohammedan that character is an endowment of God which cannot be changed. The very idea of a change of character is omitted from the Koran."

Those who hold to the Christian doctrine of sin and wrong cannot refrain from making it known to Moslems in order that they may share the salvation of Christ.

If there were space it could be shown fully that Islam's statutory conception of moral and social principles is fundamentally different from Christ's living principle of spiritual freedom and loyalty, and that the oft-praised Moslem idea and practice of brotherhood are partial and illusory and radically inferior in theory and in fact to the fellowship of Christianity.

In spite of all that has been said and written of late years to defend Islam against the charge that its teaching and influence degraded woman's position, fostered slavery and war, and retarded social progress, the Mohammedan people know that historically these charges are true, and the present-day efforts of the apologists and the earnest struggles of the Moslem peoples are evidence of the new life that is moving through the whole world of Islam. Turkey has already dealt remorselessly with the theory of the unity of Church and State and the supremacy of the Caliph. The Wahhabis are awake again and reasserting ideas, some good, some bad, which contradict much of the new apologia. The women are discarding the veil, perhaps too hastily, and seeking education and freedom. Reformers are speaking out, some boldly, some timidly. *Kaveh*, a monthly magazine published by young Persians in Berlin, recently printed a series of articles on famous men. In the article on Martin Luther in the issue of October 2, 1921, the writer praises the deliverance which Luther wrought for the human mind from ecclesiastical control and calls for similar reforms in Mohammedan laws, as regards:

1. Considering others than Moslems unclean.
2. The imprisonment of women by the purdah system.
3. The legalizing of polygamy.
4. The ease of divorce.
5. Deeming those of religions other than "ahl-i-kitab"[1] infidels and worthy of death.

[1] *Ahl-i-kitab* (people of a book), e.g., Christians, Jews, Sabians.

6. The restriction of religious teaching to the Arabic language.

In *Azad* (Freedom), a paper published in Tabriz, Persia, but later suppressed, appeared an article on January 1, 1922, entitled "A Medicine for Those Tied to Moslem Ecclesiastics," declaring:

"In every point all Moslems over the world are low, poor, unclean, without civilization, foolish, ignorant, and in general they are two hundred years behind American and European Christians and even behind the Zoroastrians. If it were only in some places that we found Islam in this condition we might attribute the results to some other reason, but where we find Islam everywhere in the same condition we can see no other reason but Islam itself."

One of the most highly educated men in Persia has written picturing the low ideals and attainments of life in Moslem lands, and declaring:

"The fountain-head or source of all these evils which bid fair to swamp and disrupt the whole country is the present religious system of Islam."

These testimonies could be multiplied indefinitely, and they are reinforced by the judgments of quite impartial observers. "The great intolerance of Mohammedanism," says Professor Sir Flinders Petrie, "and the lower position accorded in law and practice to women will always be a bar to its surpassing in civilization the races of other creeds."

Both in Persia and in Turkey the women are already beginning to cast off the old shackles. As recently we came out of the mosque of St. Sophia in Constantinople, we met a company of seventy or eighty Moslem schoolgirls coming in in a body. They wore their black tcharscheffs but not over their faces. As they went by with their laughing eyes and ruddy cheeks unconcealed, they vividly illustrated the change that is taking place. The old ideas still hold with such a tenacious grip, however, that many Moslem women have no hope. One of the ablest apologists for the old order in Tabriz is a Mohammedan woman who was educated in Europe and who returned with bold ideas which she has come to despair of realizing, and who is now preaching the doctrine of resignation to the inevitable. The subjugation of woman to the ownership of man is not inevitable, however. It is inevitable that human society will ultimately rebel against any estimate of woman which prevents her rendering her full service towards social progress. It is a tribute to the durability of the fine elements in womanhood that they have not been crushed out under the influences of Islam, and no small part of Persia's hope is to be found in the undestroyed capacities of Persian women.

The forces which are struggling throughout the Moslem world for freedom and life are the results in large part of the contacts of Islam with Christianity. Christians owe it both to their Gospel and to the Moslem people to share with these sturdy, loyal folk the Light that is the True Light and the Power of the Risen Christ. Let there be no hesitation. There is in Christianity what Islam lacks and what the Moslem people need and have a right to have. Mohammed and Mohammedanism have never had a more efficient defender in the West than Mr. R. Bosworth Smith, the biographer of John Lawrence. But, knowing Islam, Mr. Smith knows, too, the missionary duty which is owed to it by Christians. In an address before the Fellows of Zion's College on February 21, 1888, he said:

"The resemblances between the two creeds are indeed many and striking, as I have implied throughout; but, if I may, once more, quote a few words which I have used elsewhere in dealing with this question, the contrasts are even more striking than the resemblances. The religion of Christ contains whole fields of morality and whole realms of thought which are all but outside the religion of Mohammed. It opens humility, purity of heart, forgiveness of injuries, sacrifice of self, to man's moral nature; it gives scope for toleration, development, boundless progress to his mind; its motive power is stronger even as a friend is better than a king, and love higher than obedience. Its realized ideals in the various paths of human greatness have been more commanding, more many-sided, more holy, as Averroes is below Newton, Harun below Alfred, and Ali below St. Paul. Finally, the ideal life of all is far more elevating, far more majestic, far more inspiring, even as the life of the founder of Mohammedanism is below the life of the founder of Christianity.

"If, then, we believe Christianity to be truer and purer in itself than Islam, and than any other religion, we must needs wish others to be partakers of it; and the effort to propagate it is thrice blessed—it blesses him that offers, no less than him who accepts it; nay, it often blesses him who accepts it not." [1]

But it is felt by some that the real virtues of the Moslem peoples and the solid tenacity of Islam are perhaps better for these peoples than any Christian efforts to unsettle them, or if not so that at any rate our efforts are hopeless and small. In a recent illuminating book entitled *India, a Bird's-Eye View*, the Earl of Ronaldshay speaks of the insistent strength of the call of Islam. Surely this strength is there. No one can go among

[1] Frank F. Ellinwood, *Oriental Religions and Christianity*, 2nd Edition, New York, 1896, pp. 218, 219.

the Moslem peoples without feeling it, and without a deep and friendly regard for all the good qualities of courage and loyalty and democracy and vigour found among them. But also no one can know them without realizing how great is their need of Christianity and how much Christianity would do to lift them into greater things. The Moslem world is backward in education, in morality, in hope, in resolution, and in brotherhood. Burton's *Pilgrimage to Al-Medinah and Meccah* is only one of many inside views of the real weakness and hollowness of Islam. Vambéry, in *Western Culture in Eastern Lands*, makes clear enough the need and the doom of the old Mohammedanism. The Young Turk has taken the new and old road of secularism. The old religion is gone for him, and he thinks no new religion is necessary in its place, unless it be the religion of nationalism elsewhere already antiquated. The simple truth is that the old Islam drew its strength from some of the good basic elements in the human material it worked on, from some partial truths about God, and from the acceptance or even the consecration of human forces which were sure sooner or later to work out social ruin. There is only one remedy. It is not primarily political or educational. It is religious. The Moslem peoples need to know and love and obey God as revealed in Christ. The issue for the Mohammedan world is not Mohammed and Christ. It is not Mohammed or Christ. It is Christ. It is Christ or decay and death. The only true Islam [1] is surrender to Christ. Then life and freedom.

There is, then, this deep issue between Islam and Christianity. But there are many Moslems to-day who do not hold to the Moslem ideas which are at variance

1 "*Islam*, an Arabic word, implying submission to God" (Irving, *Mahomet*, vol. i, p. 72).

with the Christian conceptions. Just as Buddhists have departed from the teaching of original Buddhism in the direction of Christian ideas of God and immortality and the soul and its relation to the world, so Moslems are prepared to assent to many Christian doctrines. Syed Ameer Ali seeks to Christianize all the great teachings of Islam. As time goes on this attitude of mind among Moslems will extend more and more. Our attitude toward them must be one of entire good-will and friendship, of patient appreciation of their problem and of humble penitence for our own shortcomings and our failure to understand and to present persuasively the Gospel of Jesus Christ, the Son of God, the only Saviour of Jew or Gentile, of Moslem or Christian.

THE OUTLOOK IN THE MOSLEM WORLD

BY

JOHN R. MOTT, M.A., LL.D.,

Chairman, International Missionary Council; Chairman, World's Student Christian Federation

CHAPTER XXIII

THE OUTLOOK IN THE MOSLEM WORLD

THE chain of conferences of workers among Moslems, held February, March, and April, 1924, in different parts of Northern Africa and Western Asia, and culminating in the General Conference in Jerusalem, were most timely. Several considerations accentuate their timeliness. The recent extensive and profound changes in nearly all parts of the Moslem world called for a fresh orientation of the work of Christian missions to this important part of the missionary task. The remarkable developments within Islam rendered a fresh, united study imperatively necessary. It was recognized that experiences of recent years in other parts of the world-wide missionary movement should be made available to those engaged in mission work among Moslems. The need felt in the home base countries of knowing the mind and wish of the workers throughout the Mohammedan lands, as well as the desire of the missionaries and native leaders in these lands for opportunity to speak with united voice to the Churches in the West, made these gatherings peculiarly opportune. It is difficult to see how they could have been held even six months earlier, and the Christian movement would have suffered loss had they been deferred another year.

These assemblies of missionaries and leaders of native Churches were held at the initiative and under the auspices of the International Missionary Council. Three Regional Conferences were followed by a General Conference in Jerusalem, April 3–7, which was attended by delegations from each of the preceding gatherings and also by deputations from other areas of the Mohammedan world, including Arabia, Iraq, Persia, Turkistan, China, British India, and the Dutch East Indies. Although the conference was limited to eighty persons, this number included outstanding missionary administrators, educators, medical and social workers, and other recognized leaders of the Christian forces of all parts of the Mohammedan world, reaching from North-West Africa to the Dutch Indies, and from Central Asia to the heart of Africa, as well as workers from the mission boards of Europe and America engaged in work for Moslems. There were present not only missionaries, but also leaders of native Churches, including distinguished converts from Mohammedanism. In the annals of Christian missions there has never been brought together such a representative and influential company of the leading minds at work on the problems of Christian missions to Moslems.

The entire membership of the conference was divided into ten Committees of Findings on the following subjects: Accessibility and Occupation, Evangelization, the Christian Church, Christian Education, Christian Leadership, Christian Literature, Women's Work, Medical and Social Needs, Co-operation, and Spiritual Dynamic. Each Committee of Findings based its work on surveys and papers prepared and circulated in advance, on the findings of the various Regional Conferences, on the discussions of the General Conference, and upon the constructive, corporate thinking of the committee itself. The last long day of the conference was devoted to receiving, discussing, amending, and adopting the reports of the ten committees. The findings, which have been printed and made available for Christian workers among Moslems and for missionary societies related to work in Moslem lands, have served to co-ordinate the experience, thinking, and vision of workers among Moslems throughout the world. They constitute an up-to-date, prophetic view of work among Moslems.

The conferences were in no sense legislative bodies. Their findings have no more weight or worth than the weight of the truth and insight which they embody. This, however, should be great indeed as we think of the personnel and their exceptional background, rich experience, and wide outlook.

Particular attention is called to the following among many points brought out in the discussions and findings, as reflecting the common mind of the delegates and as being of special concern to all who have at heart the extension of the Kingdom of Christ.

1. The conferences revealed unmistakable evidences of the weakening or disintegration of Islam. This is true politically. Generally speaking nationalism is taking the place of Pan-Islamism. The Turkish Moslem, for example, is becoming more Turk than Moslem. The abolition of the Caliphate has had a profoundly disturbing effect not only in Turkey but also throughout the Mohammedan world. There are signs on every hand of the weakening of the social hold of Islam. This is illustrated in the changing position of women, especially in the cities: for example, in the postponement of marriage and the greater freedom of choice on the woman's part, in attendance of women at lectures and entertainments, in the formation of women's clubs, in the larger liberty in the use of the veil, and in the ever-growing

demand for education. The spread of Western industrialism and the startling development of the material aspects of modern civilization have had a marked disintegrating influence. I asked one of the most eminent professors of Al Azhar in Cairo what gave him greatest hope for Islam. He replied, " I see no hope ; materialism is overwhelming us."

Intellectually great changes are observable. On every hand one encounters a hunger for knowledge. A new mentality is being developed as a result of contact with Western science and civilization during the war. Above all, one is impressed with the religious unsettling among Moslems. Many are sorely perplexed, and do not know where they are going. There are multiplying evidences of rebellion against tradition and external authority. Much of the old bigotry and fanaticism have gone. There is a spirit of inquiry abroad, combined with a determination to make the most of themselves and of the new day. Many workers bear testimony that no longer do they encounter the proud, self-satisfied Islam which they knew before.

2. The marvellous accessibility of the Mohammedan world to the friendly and constructive ministry of the Christian religion was also revealed. The discussions of the conferences led to the conclusion that perhaps four-fifths of the 235,000,000 who constitute the population of the Moslem world are now increasingly accessible to every method of missionary approach. This may be said of all British India, the Dutch East Indies, Persia, Mesopotamia, China, the Balkans, the whole of North Africa, and likewise Central, East, and West Africa, with the possible exception of Northern Nigeria. Whole regions and entire classes of people who never before were reached by the message of Christ have now become

physically accessible. There have been rapid and fascinating developments in ease of communication throughout North Africa and the Near East by the construction of thousands of miles of railways and modern highways, the use of automobile transport, and the air post. Even the Sahara has within a few months been crossed repeatedly by automobiles, and a railroad is now under construction. The trip from Baghdad to Damascus, which formerly required weeks, has, within a year, been reduced to nineteen hours.

Political conditions have become much more favourable in nearly every field unless it be Turkey. Many governmental restrictions have been removed. Colonial governments once hostile to missions among Moslems have become more and more friendly and in some cases are even supporting medical and social missionary programmes. The new mandates for the Near East, and the new Constitution promulgated in Egypt, contain definite promises of religious freedom. The war brought vast numbers of Moslems into direct contact with Western civilization and opened their eyes to a new world. Moslem men and women of wealth and social position are visiting Christian lands in increasing numbers, and literally thousands of Moslem students have gone from Asia and Africa to European student centres. A multitude of labourers from North Africa are streaming into France. It was stated at the Jerusalem Conference that more Moslems annually visit Paris than Mecca. Contacts between Moslems and European Christians are unparallelled in extent and influence.

Attention should also be called to intellectual accessibility. In almost every Moslem land education is being actively promoted by the Government as well as by Christian missions, and the rate of literacy is rapidly increasing. The rising generation is gaining an entirely new outlook because of the newspaper, books, the cinema, and the theatre, while modern pictorial advertising has created a hundred points of contact with Western civilization. A far larger proportion than formerly of pupils and students in the mission schools and colleges of the Near East and Southern Asia are Moslems. The same is true of parts of Africa. A missionary stated at the conference in Egypt that formerly in Abyssinia parents forbade their children to look in the direction of the mission schools; now they bring them to these schools. He added that the parents may not wish to change their own religion, but allow their children to do so. This suggests the new religious hospitality or accessibility. Workers from every field testified to the new willingness to hear the gospel message as well as to the larger response. Certainly a remarkable change has taken place in the attitude of Moslem men and women to the Gospel. They are attending meetings more largely; they gladly accept literature; they are buying and reading the Bible more and more. Religious prejudice is being broken down in every conceivable way. Professor Levonian at the Jerusalem Conference reported that a daily paper in Constantinople had for seven months been conducting a discussion on the Personality of Christ. The problem in the Moslem world to-day, therefore, is not that of accessibility, but one of adequate multiplication of workers, of a better distribution of the forces available, and of augmenting the spiritual forces.

3. Relatively there has been a neglect of Moslems on the part of the Protestant Christian forces. We are not comparing the Protestant forces on the one hand and those of the Roman Catholic or Eastern Church Com-

munions on the other, for these other great bodies have likewise overlooked work for Moslems. But in proportion to their importance and extent Protestant missions to Moslems have received vastly less attention, fewer missionaries, and less adequate financial backing than those to any other great non-Christian religion. Notwithstanding that the Lucknow Conference in 1911 laid the facts before Protestant Christendom, the following areas or countries in which the population is wholly or predominantly Moslem are still practically unoccupied: Afghanistan, the provinces of Hejaz, Asir, Nejd, and Hadhramaut in Arabia, Russian Turkistan, parts of Siberia, Bukhara, the eastern part of the Malay peninsula, and Socotra; also the Moslem populations of Madagascar, Albania, Bulgaria, Jugoslavia, the Crimea, Georgia, and Russia in Europe, Tripoli in North Africa, the French Sudan, the great Aurès Mountains, Saharan Atlas ranges, the central populous mountain region of Morocco, and the vast Sahara itself—fields having in them a total population of nearly 40,000,000. The Mohammedans of China, numbering over 8,000,000, have scarcely a missionary devoting himself entirely to them. The 69,000,000 Moslems in India also present a field largely unoccupied, for very little special work is carried on among them. It was pointed out in the Jerusalem Conference that in large cities like Bombay, Lucknow, Delhi, and Lahore, where formerly there was special effort to win Moslems, to-day there are no missionaries wholly devoted to the task. Even taking into account all the missionaries who are giving portions of time to Moslems, it must be admitted that, in proportion to the total number of more than 5,000 missionaries in India, the aggregate amount of time bestowed upon the Moslem task is almost negligible. Even in the Near East and the Nile Valley only a very small number are wholly engaged in Christian work among Moslems.

In the Moslem world there are probably 100,000,000 women and girls still unreached. Miss Trotter, the pioneer and spiritual leader of an heroic band of women workers in North Africa, said, "Each of these Moslem women needs a human soul lashed alongside in sympathy and prayer. If we could place a hundred thousand who had their hearts on fire we could touch the problem." Facts like these brought to the attention of Churches in the West and students in the universities and seminaries, should correct a widespread misconception that the demand for missionaries is less urgent than formerly and likely to diminish rapidly in the future. This certainly is not the case in by far the larger part of the Moslem world. The dearth of Moslem converts is to be explained largely on the ground of the extreme shortage of workers equipped and set apart especially for this undertaking.

The surveys conducted in certain Moslem fields show an excessive concentration of forces in a few main centres, resulting in a corresponding neglect of vast areas. Moreover, the preoccupation of a majority of missionaries with appointed tasks in institutions, or in the work of general supervision, leaves the number definitely devoting their whole time to work for Moslems very small indeed. In certain fields, such as Syria and Palestine, the present number of workers might prove to be sufficient were they more advantageously distributed. It seemed to be the opinion of the delegates at the different conferences that the mission boards should re-examine the assignment of workers in the light of greatly changed conditions. Certain missions and Churches need to catch a new perspective and to bring about an entire readjustment of emphasis and effort. In some fields, chiefly in the Near East, the time has come when the native evangelical Churches should be led to constitute themselves the chief agency for the evangelization of Moslems by shifting the emphasis of their work from missionary activity among the Eastern Churches to direct effort for Moslems. As a Greek priest said to one of the delegates, "We should not work in each other's nets, but launch into the deep."

4. Moslems can be converted, Moslems have been converted, Moslems are being converted. In each area one of the most rewarding inquiries was the following, "Do you know of definite cases of the conversion of Moslems? If so, give the circumstances and indicate the influences which were brought to bear." The delegates were requested to speak from personal knowledge only. The answers constitute a most remarkable record of the vital and conquering power of the Christian faith. Representatives from all parts of the vast Moslem world recounted with particularity and with thrilling effect incidents among the most interesting and impressive to which the writer has ever listened. Some workers confined themselves to describing single cases of conversion, others told of whole groups brought to Christ. A few were able to bring in reports of scores or of hundreds of converts of whom they had first-hand knowledge. Missionaries from Abyssinia and from the Dutch Indies told of even thousands of baptized Moslems.

There are also, in the judgment of some missionaries, what in the aggregate amounts to a multitude of secret inquirers and disciples of Christ. In one conference a prominent missionary said, "I believe there are so many secret seekers and inquirers at present that if ten people in this room would throw their weight toward the winning of these men and women we could soon tell, not of tens but of hundreds turning to the leadership of Christ.' The cumulative evidence of these witnesses reminded one vividly of the corresponding stage in missionary work for Hindus and for the ancient literati of China. The impression is too widely prevalent in the Churches at the home base that work for Moslems is comparatively fruitless and hopeless. The truth of the matter is that the time has come to reap. Whereas formerly indirect methods of approach were necessary on account of government restrictions and Moslem opposition and fanaticism, yet in many Moslem lands to-day the way is open to widespread and direct evangelization. The minds of the Moslems are now in a plastic and impressionable state, and must be given the Christian message.

5. The positive, constructive, irenic, and sympathetic approach, method, and spirit now largely prevail in Christian work among Moslems, as contrasted with the negative, destructive, polemic, and unappreciative. Only along the pathway of heroic and sacrificial experience on the part of workers who have devoted all their powers to the task, and who deserve all praise for their prophetic, pioneering ministry, have the deeper lessons been learned and has the way been prepared for the larger fruitage of to-morrow. The following excerpts reflect the virtually unanimous attitude and practice of the representative companies of missionaries and native leaders who attended the conferences. "Avoid all negative and unfruitful controversy and rely on the positive preaching of Christ crucified and the implications of His Cross, supporting one's appeal to the Moslem heart by the testimony of one's own personal experience." "Winning men by winsome truth is the true basis of approaching Moslems." "The controversial method is to be avoided and the

Christian worker should seek, through the spirit of love, to find points of contact in the Moslem's own faith and experience through which he can lead him to Christ." " Seek the highest and best in the Moslem peoples and lay hold of that and build upon it." Our message has been too much occupied with the weakness of Islam rather than with the power of Christianity. The present is a time for working quietly. The Moslems are pulling down their own house, but they do not want foreigners to do it. Let us continue to present the all-sufficiency of Christ rather than to make polemical attacks upon Islam. When a new and a true conception of Jesus Christ is created in the Moslem mind, they will be drawn unto Him.

6. Is there need of a shifting of emphasis in the methods employed to reach Moslems ? It is difficult and probably impossible to reflect adequately the mind of the different conferences, but there are some outstanding impressions from the many debates on the subject.

In every field work among and for the very young should be emphasized. While this may seem like a truism, there is every reason for giving priority to such work in Moslem lands. The blighting influence of Islam begins very early. The little children, therefore, should be brought to Christ before mentality and character have set in Moslem moulds. On this point the experience of the missions in Algeria, as set forth in the findings of the North Africa Conference, is fresh and convincing. Without shadow of doubt the method most likely to produce permanent results is that of work among children.

Educational missionary work in the past has been one of the most effective means of ensuring the entrance into new Moslem territory, the holding of ground already occupied, and the gaining of a hearing for the Christian message. It has also been indispensable as a means for raising up and training an adequate leadership for the Christian forces. Christian education still constitutes one of the best methods of approach to Moslems. The demand for the expansion of such work is increasing in every field. Even where government systems of education have been established there is still recognized need for the character-building processes of Christian education. It should be up-to-date and second to none in point of educational efficiency.

As was strongly emphasized in Jerusalem, there is clear and universal testimony that the present situation in the Moslem world creates a need for literature as a dynamic and penetrating instrument of Christian educational evangelism altogether without parallel in range and urgency in the literary history of Moslem peoples. Literacy is rapidly increasing in most Moslem areas. This is developing an ever-expanding demand for literature. In these days every printing press in Islamic lands should be working up to its capacity. The conferences brought out even more, however, the importance of emphasizing the qualitative aspect of the subject. The discussions were based on the splendid piece of survey work set forth in the volume, *Christian Literature in Moslem Lands*, which had been placed in the hands of every delegate. The General Conference acted unanimously on the recommendation which came up from each of the regional meetings, as well as from North America and Great Britain, and set up a Co-ordinating Committee on Christian Literature for Moslems, with Bishop MacInnes as chairman. The prompt and generous backing of this new policy by the mission boards will satisfy the demand of discerning workers in the entire Moslem field.

Medical work is still one of the most valuable and efficacious means employed in work among Moslems. It not only relieves human suffering, but manifests powerfully the spirit of Christ, obtains a hearing for the Christian message where other means fail, and is a fruitful agency for widespread evangelization.

Social work is especially needed because Islam constitutes a close society, social as well as religious, and makes provision for the whole life. New converts should be received into an equally organized community to satisfy that need for brotherhood which the Moslem always craves. If we recognize and deal with religious feelings and theology only we shall fail, because of the enormous weight of social conditions binding the Moslem in every detail of practical life. Social activities cannot replace but should accompany, aid, illustrate, and complete the direct teaching of the Gospel. The Jerusalem Conference placed special emphasis also upon social reform, including infant welfare, child marriage, child labour, general conditions under which industry is carried on as to hours of labour, living wage and sanitary condition of factories, temperance reform, elimination of opium, hashish, and coca-leaf and their derivatives, traffic in women and children, and prevention of cruelty to animals.

7. More thorough and more highly specialized training for missionaries and native leaders is absolutely essential. Christian work among Moslems to-day is such as to require workers who not only possess the largest native ability but also have acquired the most complete preparation. In addition to general culture and professional training for special types of activity which are necessary for work in any field, there are two lines of preparation so vital that they are regarded as indispensable.

a. Training in linguistics which will develop facility in mastering the languages, both colloquial and classical, used by the people.

b. Thorough training in Islamics which will impart real understanding of the mind and heart of the Moslem to-day. The scheme of training should include historical Islam and also contemporary mystical and other movements within Islam. A limited number of carefully selected workers should be set apart by the missions to specialize on Islam with a view to their directing the studies of other workers on this subject. The programme of preparation exhaustively outlined in the booklet entitled *The Presentation of Christianity to Moslems,* and issued by the Board of Missionary Preparation of the Foreign Missions Conference of North America, was strongly endorsed by the Jerusalem Conference. The Cairo School of Oriental Studies was also commended, and it was advised that similar schools be established in large areas which cannot be adequately served by this institution.

8. If we depend largely on the Oriental Churches to meet the situation as it exists to-day in the Moslem world, we shall miss the present opportunity; nevertheless, faithful and persevering efforts should be put forth to enlist their full co-operation. The question recurs from time to time, In view of the fact that the Oriental or Eastern Churches are located directly in front of large sections of the Moslem world, why not let them at least divide the responsibility of evangelizing the Moslems? With this in mind the writer had extended interviews with the Patriarchs, Metropolitans, Archbishops, and other ecclesiastical leaders, as well as educators, of the various Eastern Churches. This included the Greek Church proper, the Armenian Church, the

Syrian Church, the Coptic Church, the Abyssinian Church, the autonomous Churches of Roumania, Bulgaria, and Jugoslavia, as well as representatives of the Russian Church who are at present so widely scattered in lands outside Russia. Few, if any, of the outstanding present-day leaders in the realm of thought and action of any of these great Communions were overlooked. Each one was asked this question: "What is the present policy or programme of your Communion with reference to the evangelization of Moslems?" In every case the answer indicated that they had no such plan or programme. This, then, led to another question: "Why has your Church no such programme?" Various reasons were given, but the serious fact in every instance was that they were not ready at the present time to co-operate in this vast and urgent undertaking.

One came to the clear conclusion, therefore, that we could not in the near future depend upon these religious bodies for any large reinforcements. Nevertheless, a careful study of the impact of these Churches on the Moslem world will convince one of the great desirability and necessity of leading them to undertake a missionary programme. It was encouraging to meet here and there, especially among the younger clergy and teachers, an intelligent and sympathetic response to the appeal for co-operation. Moreover, the work of the Student Christian Movement in the Near East in recent years has revealed the large possibilities in the direction of enlisting among the students who are members of the Eastern Churches volunteers for aggressive Christian work on behalf of Moslems. This is one of the largest unworked leads. Moreover, one cannot speak too highly of the sympathetic attitude of not a few of the present-day leaders of these Churches. The Committee on the Church at the Brumana Conference well expressed the thought of the various conferences in the following finding:

"The missionary societies and native Churches should use every practicable means, especially through friendship, to reinspire the Oriental Churches with the apostolic and missionary spirit which characterized them in the days of the early Church, and to encourage both individuals and the Churches as a whole, now that recent changes have made it possible, to take their full share in the evangelization of the Moslem world." [1]

A deeper note was struck at the Jerusalem Conference by the Committee on Christian Leadership:

"As the sufferings of Christ win human hearts, so the loving service of those who have suffered most at Moslem hands will most powerfully attract those who are now opposed to Him. Native leaders, therefore, have a peculiar opportunity to give irresistible evidence of the power of Christ." [2]

9. The time has come for bringing about closer cooperation among the leaders of the Christian forces at work among Moslems. For several years the need has been recognized of a closer co-operation among the missionaries and other Christian workers in the Moslem fields. The Cairo and Lucknow Conferences and their related activities revealed the advantages to the missionary cause resulting from more intimate fellowship and collaboration in planning and in effort. While these benefits are now being realized by the workers of India and China through their well-planned and efficient National Christian Councils, and in more limited areas such as Egypt, Syria, and Palestine through inter-mission

[1] *Conferences of Christian Workers among Moslems, 1924*, New York, 1924, p. 109. [2] Ibid., p. 29.

councils, there has been no arrangement which has made possible united action on the part of the workers throughout Northern Africa and the Near and Middle East. The following finding unanimously adopted at the Jerusalem Conference is, therefore, highly significant, and it is believed that its fulfilment now in progress will do much to ensure the carrying out of the many other important resolutions of the recent series of conferences and the realization of the high hopes entertained by the delegates and by all others who have at heart the highest welfare of the work of Christ among Moslems :

"The conference has reviewed with interest the development of the National Christian Councils in China, Japan, and India, enabling the Christian forces in those areas not only to increase opportunities for co-operation on the field, but to speak with a united voice to the home Church.

"The Conference is convinced that the time has come for the formation of a Council representing the various Christian agencies and conferences in North Africa; Egypt, Northern Sudan, and Abyssinia; Syria and Palestine; Turkey and the Balkans; Arabia and Mesopotamia; and Persia. We, therefore, recommend that a Preliminary Committee be appointed at this time to formulate a plan for a Council for Western Asia and Northern Africa, to present it to the various agencies concerned, and to confer with the International Missionary Council concerning affiliation to that body. Pending the adoption of the permanent plan of organization the Preliminary Committee shall seek to conserve and promote the realization of the findings of this and of other committees of the Conference."[1]

10. Our Christian faith is involved and, in fact, is at stake in the way in which we at this time deal with the

[1] *Conferences of Christian Workers among Moslems, 1924*, New York, 1924, p. 41.

need and opportunity presented by the Moslem world. To prove the validity of our faith we must bring Christ to the entire Moslem world. Archbishop Whately has said, " If my faith be false, I ought to change it; whereas if it be true, I am bound to propagate it." There is no middle ground. We must either modify or abandon our faith or be logical, consistent, and apostolic and expand our plans and practice so as to give all Moslems opportunity to know Christ. The fact that there are still difficulties apparently insurmountable and that the conquering of them inevitably calls for great sacrifice, and, perchance, martyrdom, does not break the force of our obligation.

To preserve our faith, or to maintain its purity, vitality, and conquering power, we must give ourselves more largely to its propagation by persuasive message, and, above all, by contagious character, throughout the vast areas of the Moslem world. We need to remind ourselves in all solemnity of those early Christian Churches which existed in thousands across the breadth of North Africa, not to mention parts of Western Asia, and which have disappeared leaving no living trace, and to ask ourselves what was the reason that for over a thousand years Islam reigned supreme where once these Churches witnessed for Christ. Moreover, the state of certain of the Oriental Churches to-day, and even of sections of the Roman Catholic Church, and of the Protestant Communion here and there which have neglected their missionary responsibility, and thus lost their world-conquering power, are present-day evidences and warnings of the danger.

The essential victory or ultimate triumph of our Christian faith is involved as well as its validity and vitality. A Gospel which cannot, after being adequately brought to bear upon Moslems, win their minds and hearts and command the allegiance of their wills, must fail to satisfy the deepest longings and the highest expectations of the followers of other religions and of those without any religious faith. Ultimately, therefore, the triumph of the Christian cause in other foreign fields and at the home base is involved in what takes place in the heart of the Mohammedan world. The most searching experience and possibly the most creative hour in each of the conferences was the consideration of the topic, "What has Christ to bring to Moslems which they cannot under any circumstances obtain from their own religion or from any other source?" The corporate thinking and intercession of those memorable hours confirmed the faith of everyone as to the absolute uniqueness, supremacy, and sufficiency of Jesus Christ the Living Lord.

APPENDIX

LIST OF MOSLEM NEWSPAPERS IN INDIA

LIST OF MOSLEM NEWSPAPERS IN INDIA [1]

1. Madras Presidency

Name of Paper.	Language.	Where published.
Azad Hind	Urdu	Triplicane
Dar-ul-Islam	Tamil	Madras
Gnana Suriyan	Tamil	Vijiapuram
Hakeem and Vythian	English	Madras
Hythayath	Malayalam	Calicut
Islam Dootan	Malayalam	Kayamkulam
Kerala Chandrika	Anglo-Malayalam	Travancore
Malabar-Islam	Anglo-Malayalam	Cochin State
Mukhbir-i-Deccan	Urdu	Madras
Muneerul Islam	Malayalam	Kayamkulam
Muslim Akhiam	Malayalam	Travancore
Muslim Sahakari	Malayalam	Calicut
Nilgir Times	English	Ootacamund
Qasim-ul-Akhbar	Urdu, Tamil, and English	Madras
Quami Report	Urdu	Madras
Rahbari-Deccan	Urdu	Hyderabad
Risala-i-al-Maalij	Urdu	Afzalgang
Risala-i-Ataliq	Urdu	Hyderabad
Risala-i-Mahbub-un-Nazair	Urdu	Hyderabad
Risala-i-Now-Nihal	Urdu	Hyderabad
Risala-i-Wais	Urdu	Hyderabad
Risala-un-Nisa	Urdu	Hyderabad

1 This was secured from the Indian Government through the Rev. William Paton, Secretary of the National Christian Council.

Name of Paper.	Language.	Where published.
Sahifa	Urdu	Hyderabad
Saiful Islam	Tamil	Madras
Shamsul Islam	Malayalam	Karunagapalli
Sugathara Bodhini	Tamil	Madras

2. Bombay Presidency

Aftab-e-Islam	Gujarati	Rajkot Para
Akhbar	Gujarati	Bombay
Akhbar-e-Islam	Gujarati	Bombay
Al-Aziz	Gujarati	Jodiya
Al-Haqiqat	Gujarati	Larkana
Al-Haq	Anglo-Sindhi	Sukkur
Al-Islam and Momin Mitra	Gujarati	Bombay
Al-Kamal	Gujarati	Bombay
Al-Khashif	Arabic-Sindhi	Larkana
Al-Wahid	Arabic-Sindhi	Karachi
Bag-e-Momin	Gujarati and Urdu	Amreli
Bahai News	English and Persian	Karachi
Bahare Majlis	Gujarati	Bombay
Fayze Am	Gujarati	Ahmedabad
Gulzari Sukhan	Urdu	Poona Cantonment
Insaf	Gujarati	Bombay
Irfan	Urdu	Bombay
Ishaat-e-Islam	Gujarati	Bombay
Ismaili	Anglo-Gujarati	Bombay
Kathiawad	Gujarati	Upleta
Khilafat	Gujarati	Bombay
Khilafat Bulletin	English	Bombay
Manhar	Gujarati	Bombay
Memon Mitra	Gujarati	Bombay
Memon Samachar	Gujarati	Karachi
Merchants Advertiser	Gujarati	Bombay
Mohib	Gujarati	Limbdi
Muslim Herald	Urdu	Bombay

Name of Paper.	Language.	Where published.
Political Bhomiyo	Anglo-Gujarati	Ahmedabad
Rahe Najat	Gujarati	Bhavanagar
Roznama-e-Khilafat	Urdu	Bombay
Sat Panth Prakash	Gujarati	Ahmedabad
Sind Zamindar	Anglo-Sindhi	Sukkur
Sultan-ul-Akhbar	Urdu	Bombay
Talim	Sindhi	Hyderabad
Tohid	Sindhi-Arabic	Karachi
Vafadar	English, Gujarati, and Urdu	Navsari (Baroda)

3. The United Provinces

Agra Akhbar	Urdu	Agra
Al Bashir	Urdu	Etawah
Al Bureed	Urdu	Cawnpore
Aligarh Gazette	Urdu	Aligarh
Al Imdad	Urdu	Muzaffarnagar
Al Khalil	Urdu	Bijnor
Allahabad Advertiser	English	Allahabad
An Nazir	Urdu	Lucknow
Dabdaba-i-Sikandari	Urdu	Rampur State
Darbar	Urdu	Agra
Dilchasp Akhbar	Urdu	Fatehpur
Haqiqat	Urdu	Lucknow
Hamdam	Urdu	Lucknow
Hamdard	Urdu	Cawnpore
Indian World	English	Cawnpore
Inqilab	Urdu	Lucknow
Iqdam	Urdu	Moradabad
Ittihad	Urdu	Amroha
Jadu	Urdu	Jaunpur
Mansur	Urdu	Bijnor
Mashahir	Urdu	Budaun
Mashriq	Urdu	Gorakhpur
Mecca Medina	Urdu	Moradabad
Medina	Urdu	Bijnor

Name of Paper.	Language.	Where published.
Millat	Urdu	Meerut
Maarif	Urdu	Azamgarh
Mukhbir-i-Alam	Urdu	Moradabad
Naiyar-i-Azam	Urdu	Moradabad
Najat	Urdu	Bijnor
Naqib	Urdu	Budaun
Nawad	Urdu	Bulandshahr
Nizam Alam	Urdu	Cawnpore
Oudh Punch	Urdu	Lucknow
Paigam	Urdu	Fyzabad
Pardah Mashin	Urdu	Agra
Rahouma	Urdu	Moradabad
Rohilkhand Gazette	Urdu	Bareilly
Rozana Akhbar	Urdu	Bareilly
Sayyarah	Urdu	Lucknow
Shia College News	Urdu	Lucknow
Surmani-i-Rozgar	Urdu	Agra
Tabligh	Urdu	Agra
Zarif	Urdu	Saharanpur
Zul Qarnain	Urdu	Budaun

4. The Central Provinces and Berar

Adib	Urdu	Nagpur
Al Burhan	Urdu	Burhanpur
Gulzar-i-Hakimi	Gujarati	Khamagaon
Sasimi-i-Saha	Urdu and Gujarati	Narsinghpur
Taj	Urdu	Jubbulpore

5. Burma

Arakan News	English	Akyab

6. Bihar and Orissa

Islah	Urdu	Raghunathpur

7. Bengal

Name of Paper.	Language.	Where published.
Ahale Hadis	Bengali	Calcutta
Ainul Islam	Bengali	Dacca
Al Jamaya	Arabic	Calcutta
Al Kamal	Urdu	Calcutta
Al Rafique	Urdu	Calcutta
Bahadur	Bengali	Calcutta
Bangiya Moslem Sahitya Patrika	Bengali	Calcutta
Bengal Presidency Gazette	English-Bengali	Nator
Dhumketu	Bengali	Calcutta
Hanter Phatker[1]	Urdu	Calcutta
Inqilab Zamana	Urdu	Calcutta
Islam Darshan	Bengali	Calcutta
Jadu	Urdu	Dacca
Mohammadi	Bengali	Calcutta
Mussalman	English	Calcutta
Noakhali Hitaishi	Bengali	Noakhali Town
Noakhali Sammilani	Bengali	Noakhali Town
Peace	English	Dacca
Ratnakar	Bengali	Asansol Town
Rayat Bandhu	Bengali	Calcutta
Sonar Bharat	Bengali-English	Calcutta
Sultan	Bengali	Calcutta

8. The Punjab

Ahl-i-Hadis	Urdu	Amritsar
Akhtar	Urdu	Lahore
Al-Aziz	Urdu	Batala
Al-Burhan	Urdu	Lahore
Al-Bushra	English	Qadian
Al-Falah	Urdu	Jullundur
Al-Faqih	Urdu	Amritsar
Al-Fazl	Urdu	Qadian

[1] Or *Hunter Phathār*.

Name of Paper.	Language.	Where published.
Al-Hakam	Urdu	Qadian
Al-Hakim	Urdu	Lahore
Al-Islam	Urdu	Lahore
Al-Kamal	Urdu	Lahore
Al-Mailij	Urdu	Amritsar
Al-Munir	Urdu	Lahore
Al-Quaaish	Urdu	Amritsar
Angora	Urdu	Amritsar
Anwar-us-Sufia	Urdu	Lahore
Doctor	Urdu	Lahore
Dur-i-Najaf	Urdu	Sialkot
Faruq	Urdu	Qadian
Hamdard	Urdu	Lahore
Hazar Dastan	Urdu	Lahore
Hubb-i-Watan	Urdu	Miani
Humayun	Urdu	Lahore
Hurriyyat	Urdu	Lahore
Indian Architect	Urdu	Lahore
Indian Cases and Statutes	English	Lahore
Intikhad-i-Lajawab	Urdu	Lahore
Inqilab	Urdu	Lahore
Ishatat-i-Islam	Urdu	Lahore
Isha'atul-Quran	Urdu	Lahore
Islah	Urdu	Ludhiana
Islamic World	English	Lahore
Ismaili Sadaqat	Urdu	Rawalpindi
Istiqlal	Urdu	Panipat
Ittihad-ul-Islam	Urdu	Amritsar
Kakkezai National Magazine	Urdu	Lahore
Kashmiri	Urdu	Lahore
Manzar	Urdu	Lahore
Mashir-ul-Attibba	Urdu	Lahore
Mister Gazette	Urdu	Lahore
Muhabbat	Urdu	Lahore

Name of Paper.	Language.	Where published.
Mussalman	Urdu	Sodhra
Muslim Outlook	English	Lahore
Muslim Rajput	Urdu	Amritsar
Muzarah	Urdu	Jullundur
Naqshband	Urdu	Sialkot
Nur	Urdu	Qadian
Nusrat	Urdu	Lahore
Paisa Akhbar	Urdu	Lahore
Payam-i-Muhabbat	Urdu	Lahore
Phul	Urdu	Lahore
Political Rahnuma	Urdu	Lahore
Political Rahnuma	Urdu	Amritsar
Punjabi Khiyalat	Urdu	Batala
Rafiq-i-Sadiq	Urdu	Batala
Rafiq-ul-Talim	Urdu	Lahore
Rahnuma-i-Sehat	Urdu	Lahore
Railway Union	Urdu	Lahore
Riaz-i-Hind	Urdu	Amritsar
Risala-i-Anjuman-i-Himayat-i-Islam	Urdu	Lahore
Rissala Sutlej	Urdu	Ludhiana
Rissala Sheikh Qanungoyan	Urdu	Lyallpur
Sanaat	Urdu	Lahore
Shahab-i-Urdu	Urdu	Lahore
Silk-i-Marwarid	Urdu	Batala
Siyasat	Urdu	Lahore
Sufi	Urdu	Pindi-Bahauddin
Tabib	Urdu	Lahore
Tabligh	Urdu	Lahore
Tabsirat-ul-Atibba	Urdu	Shahdara
Tafrih	Urdu	Lahore
Tadib-un-Nisa	Urdu	Qadian
Tahrik	Urdu	Lahore
Tahzib-ul-Niswan	Urdu	Lahore
Tauhid	Urdu	Amritsar

Name of Paper.	Language.	Where published.
Ustani	Urdu	Batala
Watan	Urdu	Lahore
Zamindar	Urdu	Lahore
Zamzama	Urdu	Lahore
Zaraat	Urdu	Lahore
Ziafat. Panch.	Urdu	Lahore
Zulifiqar	Urdu	Lahore

INDEX

Published by

Facsimile Publisher
Ashok Vihar, Delhi-110052 (India)
Website: www.facsimilepublisher.com

Distributed by

Gyan Books Pvt. Ltd.
5, Ansari Road, Daryaganj, New Delhi-110002 (India)
E-mail: books@gyanbooks.com, Website: www.gyanbooks.com

2 222000 015961